AIDAN OF LINDISFARNE

Aidan of Lindisfarne

Irish Flame Warms a New World

To Rosemary
Pass on the Flame

RAY SIMPSON

RESOURCE *Publications* · Eugene, Oregon

AIDAN OF LINDISFARNE
Irish Flame Warms a New World

Resource Publiations
An Imprint of Wipf and Stock Publishers
199 W. 8th Ave., Suite 3
Eugene, OR 97401

www.wipfandstock.com

ISBN 13: 978-1-62564-762-7

Manufactured in the U.S.A.   05/30/2014

To Aodhna Rua, Cara, Caoimhín, Dara, Donnacha, Fiachra,
Fionnula, Micah, Oisin, and Rian.

Moses taught us something . . . the world we build tomorrow is born in the stories we tell our children today.

RABBI JONATHAN SACKS

To make you hear, to make you feel—it is, before all, to make you see.

JOSEPH CONRAD ON THE WRITER'S TASK.

This story weaves fact with supposition, adds some imaginary characters and ventures such as Aidan's pilgrimage to Alexandria, grounded in a realistic picture of the time. I have "lived" with Aidan for twenty years on his Holy Island of Lindisfarne, and have trodden in his imagined steps in Ireland and Iona. This is the story of the spiritual formation of first, a person and then of a people: it is a parable for our time

Historical fiction is an honoured tradition that encompasses works such as Louis de Wohl's *Citadel of God: A Novel about Saint Benedict* and Melvyn Bragg's *Credo,* a novel about Saint Cuthbert. It is a tradition that incorporates what we know about the subject, and imagines what might have been that is consistent with what we know of the subject's life and times.

RAY SIMPSON, WHITE HOUSE, HOLY ISLAND OF LINDISFARNE.

CONTENTS

PART ONE

KINDLING FIRES
Ireland and the Early Years

chapter 1

THE BOY

597 BIRTH AND NAMING

It was 9 June 597. Cara gazed into a tributary of the mighty river Shannon that nourished half of Ireland. She was heavy with child, heavy, too lest her progeny be edged aside by the Ui Neills from the north. Her people once proudly strutted across Connaught's stage. They defeated Columba's clan at the battle of Cum Druine, but ever since the Ui Neills had pushed her clan to the margins. This was hard for a mother who dreamed great things for her offspring. She and her husband Lugar knew what they would name the child. Finn if it was a boy; if it was a girl, Fiona would be her name.

Shortly after darkness fell her eyes bulged in astonishment. The water had turned bright red. Looking up she saw a pillar of fire stab awake the night. Never before, nor ever again, would she see its like. The fiery cloud divided into two. The larger part zoomed off towards the coast, taking what seemed like some awesome presence with it. The smaller part became the shape of a finger. The finger moved towards her, pointing, she swore it, at the very babe in her womb. A bird flew overhead.

Cara cried out. Birth pangs seized her. The nurse came running from the house. There was painful struggle. A boy's head popped out. The nurse carried him away. Lugar came, but to their surprise cries still came from the womb. There was another struggle. A finger popped out. It did not clutch. It pointed upward.

They had no name for a child they did not expect. Next day, as they discussed what to call him, a relative arrived, breathless, with solemn news. Blessed Columba was dead. He had died across the sea on Iona Isle in the early hours of dark. "The whole sky of Alba and Ireland was lit up with fire" said he, "as his holy soul was escorted to the other world." Then it was that Cara knew the meaning of that flaming sky. Then, too, she knew what they must name their second twin—Little Flame—Aidan in their tongue.

* * *

THE PROPHECY

I baptize you "Little Flame," the priest said, "in the name of the Father, the Son and the Holy Spirit. A flame goes where it wills. At times it burns low or peters out. Maybe this child will at times wish to die away. But a flame can blaze up, race, crackle; it can ignite and spread far. A flame takes many colors, many forms. It is never still, it dances, and others catch fire wherever it goes. You will be hidden at first, little one, as others flare up, but you are a spark from heaven. From you fires will be lit that one day will circle the world."

Aidan's mother told her child what that prophetic priest had spoken over him. The significance of his name impinged upon him noiselessly, seamlessly. Throughout his childhood flames danced before his eyes—but in such different ways. There was the flame that flickered, there were the legendary fires lit by Patrick and Brigid, there were flames of passion and battlefield, and there was another flame.

* * *

His parents owned a farmstead at the foot of Crag Liath, near to the great Shannon crossing at Killaloe. Here the fields were lush. They grew barley, and kept hens, sheep and goats. They had serfs to help the family maintain the farm, and a man who made barrels and buckets from wood. On Sundays they gathered everyone into the cart. Their two biggest work horses would pant and pull them up to the top of the crag, where the chief had his fort. An aged priest gave them Holy Communion, and a blacksmith made knives and shoes for the horses. The serfs wore woolen cloaks over linen tunics. Aidan's family did, too, but theirs were brightly colored. When Aidan was six he felt uncomfortable wearing these clothes. He stopped wearing these when he was with the serfs. Finn put his hand to the practical things that made up farm life. He learned to milk cows, make things out of wood and dig the soil. He grew freckles and had the gift of the gab.

The twins had an elder sister, Fionnula. She was tall and fair-haired, useful to her mother and attractive to boys, but very much her own person. Once she was led round their paddock on the horse. "I want a ride too," Aidan piped up. "You are too young, little one, but your time will come," his father assured him. A tear dropped from Aidan's cheek. "Why don't you give the horse a treat?" said his father, feeling pity for him. They fetched a chunk of honeycomb from the kitchen, Aidan held out a flat hand, and the horse swept it into its mouth with relish. A fiery tingle swept through Aidan as the horse licked his hand. That began a life-long love of horses. However, being the second twin, and the youngest, Aidan felt he was a Number Two person. He assumed it was natural for others to take the lead, and so he held back.

Aidan's father was lithe and caring. He worked hard on the farm and loved to row his boat on the river. When Aidan was seven Lugar paid for an excellent woman to become his foster mother. It was normal in Ireland, and according to the law, that parents of good standing made such a contract. The foster parent often came from a family with royal connections, and could introduce the child to the knowledge and social skills of a wider world. Some children lived with the foster parent, but most, like Aidan, made regular visits. As the Christian Faith had spread, holy and wise women who had made vows to Christ were prized as foster mothers. Such was Wise Dara, a widow. She was quite short, with swept back gray hair, a large wrinkle in her forehead. She had a bright smile, knowing eyes and wore a shawl intertwined with purples, greens and browns. She knew about many things. That first year she helped Aidan to think about what he did, and about his name, Little Flame.

One day Aidan rushed through her room, not noticing what was in it. He trod on the eggs Dara had carefully placed there. Dara did not scold him, but asked him gently if he would clear up the mess. "I have a suggestion," she then said. "Would you bring me one egg from your home each time you visit me, until the number of eggs we have lost is made up?" She taught him one of the sayings about three things that the Irish loved to learn: Three things will get you into trouble—stealing, violence and lying; three things will bring you life—eggs, child-birth and prayer. She taught Aidan to think before he fell asleep about things he had spoiled because he had rushed. She wanted him to become mindful.

Dara understood that Aidan was insecure. That is why she talked to him about the meaning of his name. She told him of the fire lit by holy Patrick, who first brought the news of Christ to their tribes north of the Shannon. The pagan High King of all Ireland had gathered his people on the Great Hill of Tara to celebrate the Spring Equinox. Opposite, on the Hill of Slane, Patrick lit a fire to celebrate the resurrection of Christ. "If you do not put this fire out today," the king's Druid declared, "the fire of this new religion will burn for ever in our land." The king sent his warriors to arrest Patrick and his fellow Christians, but all they could see were deer running down the hill. Patrick did not scorn the sun. He called Christ the True, Uncreated Sun; the sun He had created was His precious gift. Dara suggested that Aidan was a ray of light from the sun. She wanted him to grow in confidence as a child of Light.

"I've noticed you spend your time with people who are nice to you," Dara said one day. "Isn't that natural?" Aidan said. "It depends what you mean by 'natural' ," Dara replied. "Suppose one day you find yourself in a place where no one welcomes you?" "What could I do about it?" Aidan asked. "Well, for a start, you could look out for someone who looks un-happy and chat with them. To make a friend, be a friend." Dara taught him a triad: "The three elements of friendship: respect, understanding and a loving heart." "Why don't you look out for someone tomorrow who looks unhappy" she suggested. Dara planted a seed that day that turned into a life-long practice of Aidan—taking the first step in befriending another.

* * *

Aidan's father was a descendant of the famous saint Brigid of Kildare. People spoke of her as the midwife who brought Christ to birth in Ireland and they imagined her as the midwife of Mary, mother of God's Son. Of-ten in the kitchen they told stories about her just as, before Ireland became Christian, people told stories about their great goddess Brigid. Sometimes they mixed the two together. They imagined that Brigid took fire from God's sun, and this danced inside her heart. From the fire of her hearth she wrought healing medicines, from the fire in her head she created poetry and writing, and from the fire of her heart compassion spread throughout Ireland in acts of mercy and hospitality to the poor. One thing was for sure, her large monastery for men and women at Kildare, in the central plain of Ireland, still drew many people, and night and day its sisters replenished its ever-burning fire.

604

In 604 it was decided that the twins were old enough to make their first big journey, and they would visit their relatives in Kildare for the Beltane festival. The family piled their satchels of clothes and food on to their carriage, and the horse cantered its way eastwards across the esker ridge. At last they were welcomed by their cousins. Their boy Cormac and his sister Dacey played with the twins. In Kildare the best horses in Ireland race on the curragh. The elders had declared the curragh would for ever be land where horses and people were free to roam. They did this out of respect for Brigid. As soon as possible the children sped to the curragh's vast expanse of green. Horses raced such as Aidan had never seen before. His heart raced inside him:

> When the horses race on the great Curragh
> I want to shout Hurrah! Hurrah!

he bellowed, reveling in his first outburst of poetry. They chanted his little poem over and over again, marching round the edge of the curragh, causing heads to turn.

Cormac and Dacey told stories about Brigid when she was their age. She used to help her mother in the kitchen. She always laid a spare place at the meal table in case Christ came in the guise of a needy person. The next day they, too, laid a table with a spare place. Aidan would commend this custom throughout his life. Before they went to sleep Cormac and Dacey told Aidan and Finn that Brigid, when she heard Jesus' words that we should always pray, asked herself how she could do this, even if it was night. As she lay down to sleep she stretched out her arms in the shape of a cross, so that even as she slept her arms would be in prayer. They tried to copy her, but their arms became tangled up!

The following day they took their seats early at the court of the king of Kildare. Various people spoke, animals and acrobats performed their tricks, and Tewdric the bard spoke thus:

> Brigid, Virgin most fair
> Brigid, Queen of Eire.
> Where once warring rulers had their forts
> Now your servants of Christ hold heavenly courts.
> The glittering river Liffey—all this is your domain
> The light-filled Curragh stretches to the plain.
> Here love replaced hatred, blessings multiplied
> Here you enthroned Christ, in valley and hillside.

The people made sure the poor were fed
There was mead of welcome in every homestead.
Strains of song pierced the air
Instead of boasting, now there was prayer.

The renown of your King sped like a star
To Britain and Gaul and lands afar
Ships bearing goods became a familiar sight
A land that was dark now filled up with light.

You reign for ever with the Great King
On your finger the royal bride's ring.
Easy it is to grow proud and set
But we your children will not forget.

On and on the bard sang in the mead hall that night and Aidan's wonderment at Brigid grew. The next evening they again took their seats early, since Gododdin, the Britons' most famous bard was due to appear. His words would for ever be etched in Aidan's memory:

I tell you a tale of Christ and pagan darkness,
Of great warriors and men of treachery.

Urien of Rheged, generous was he,
And has been since Adam.
He, wise ruler, Christ's king
Had the most wide-ranging sword of the kings of the north.

Into our land poured hordes of Saxons
Like a pack of wolves chasing sheep.

Yet, if there's an enemy on the hill
Urien will make him shudder.
If there's an enemy in the hollow
Urien will pierce him through.
If there's an enemy in the mountain
Urien will bruise him.
If there's an enemy in the dyke
Urien will strike him down.

Aidan, son of Gabran, and all the thirteen kings joined Urien.
They goaded the Saxons to the Isle of Medcaut

Near to Bamburgh's fort.
There they circled the enemy—poised for great victory.

But Tragedy! Tragedy!
Urien, king of the baptized world
Was struck down, not by the Saxon foe,
But by Morcant, one of the thirteen kings.
That Judas, thinking to take Urien's place,
Forfeited the trust of defending troops
They fled in disarray.
The Saxons stayed, and now rule all Northumbria.

Yet Aidan's throne at Dunadd still remains secure.
The Irish in the Britons' land are still "the land of the baptized."
And Arthur, Aidan's son, fights battles for another day.
This Arthur, about him prophecies will come
And tales will be told hard to imagine.
Arthur, bearing on his shield the mother of our Lord,
Leading the legions of Christ —
A man whose pact halts the foes of Christ.

That night Aidan could not sleep for thinking about the king who had the same name as himself, and about Medcaut, an island of such promise and such tragedy. For a reason that would only become clear to him years later, that island touched a chord deep within him.

On the Sunday Aidan's father took them to the monastery founded by Brigid. Never had he seen such huge buildings: large timber posts supported a church, dormitories, and work places made of mud and wattle. Recently the bodies of Brigid and Conleath, the holy hermit she appointed as bishop, had been transferred to each side of the altar. Nuns were making linen hangings that would be draped over their tombs. On the altar, they saw the most wonderful book he had ever seen. It was The Kildare Gospels, in Latin. Each letter seemed to shine. The words were like sparks from a burning bush that fell into his lap. Outside, in a little walled enclosure, was the flame that never went out. This had been Brigid's wish. Twenty sisters took it in turn to keep the fire burning as a sign of the ancient prophecy of the High King's Druid. Throughout their return to Crag Liath, the image of that eternal flame danced before Aidan's mind.

* * *

Those days at Kildare were the happiest memories of Aidan's life. They only served to highlight, however, his unsettled spirit at home. He was not happy. He oscillated between wanting to hit out at people, to prove that he deserved to be noticed, and to run away. Sometimes he tried to prove himself by showing off, but if he thought he would be out-done by others, he avoided their company. Life was difficult: why bother with it? One day he did half run away. A boy named Micha was bullied by others and was a dreamer. He told Aidan that the previous month he had run away and had found something special that he had kept a secret. He asked Aidan to accompany him to this secret thing, or place. "Why did you run away?" Aidan asked Micha. "Because my father shouts and scowls, and I can't be myself in my own home" Micha told him. "Where did you go when you ran away?" "I took food, went out to the mountain and hid in a cave. I wanted my parents to become anxious and search for me, then I would know that they took notice of me" Micha said. "And did they? "Oh, yes, but they did not find me that night. I have to admit that what made me go back home was hunger, and the cold—and I felt lonely." "Did you say sorry?" "No, why should I? I said that my father should say sorry for the way he treated me before I would say sorry to him. He is older than me. That is only fair." "And did he say sorry to you?" "Well, he said that he had lots of problems that I knew nothing about. One day he would tell me about them." "Did that make you feel better?" Aidan asked Micha. "A bit," said Micha, "but I still won't tell him about my secret—so will you come with me please?"

That is how Aidan spent a day trekking to Micha's secret place. It took longer than he had thought. Eventually they crawled through scree into a series of caves. Water came out of a rock. On a ledge above them was a stone that looked like a pillow. "This is Jacob's pillow," said Micha. "Which Jacob do you mean?" Aidan asked him. "The Jacob in the story the Christian priests tell," said Micha, "you know, Jacob lay his head on it and as he slept he saw a ladder go from the earth to heaven, and angels went up and down on it." "But that was in a far country, long ages ago" Aidan reminded him. Then Micha told him the story that his cousin had heard from a bard.

Jacob had anointed that stone pillow with oil in that place in the desert of Luz that he called "God's house." Years later God told Jacob to return to that sacred place. There he gave him prophecies. "From this place will come the living stone of Israel who will be a shepherd to my people in far places" said the divine oracle. Jacob's name was changed into Israel, meaning the one who struggles with God and overcomes. Jacob told his children and they told their descendants about the stone pillow. Some of them returned to that sacred place to see the stone.

Centuries later King David had this stone brought into the tabernacle he built. The builders of Solomon's great temple, however, rejected this stone. But the stone that the builders rejected did in fact become the main stone in the spiritual foundations of great kings. Thus, the bard had said, the young King Joash stood on the stone pillar at his coronation. Tragedy came when the Assyrians took Israel captive. The stone disappeared from the story of the tribe that returned, Judah. But many people from other tribes escaped from Assyria. Certain of them traveled to Egypt, but this remnant displeased God and incurred his judgment. A local king named Gathelus, however, who had taken the sacred stone into his possession for safe keeping, because he honored sacred memory, seeing God's judgment on these apostates, left them in order to find a better kingdom and a better way. He and his queen, Scota, sailed around the Black Sea into the Danube valley, taking with them a harp and the sacred stone, and eventually came with it to our land. Gathelus told his queen that the people who lived here should be her people, and he would call them Scotti, after her. The king drew to him a prophet named Ollam Fodhla and his scribe, Breack. They carried these and other ancient relics they had brought with them in procession to the sacred hills and groves of our land. They had a harp and an ark, in which was the stone, the Lia-Fail, which means Hoary Destiny. "Years went, by," Micha droned on, as in a trance, repeating what he remembered from his cousin's account of the bard's story, "and the heirs of Gathelus and Scota, Ollam and Breack took the Stone of Destiny to the sacred high places. At Tara the harp, which some said was the harp of King David himself, was buried, and the High King was enthroned on Jacob's Pillow. But then the true faith came to our land, and our people spread across the sea to Alba and established the true faith there. The Stone of Destiny was brought to them."

"Micha," Aidan said, "that is an interesting story but what has it to do with this place?" "I will tell you," Micha said. "That stone in front of us became my pillow. And as I slept, I, too, dreamed, like Jacob of old. And in my dream a ladder went from our village up to heaven. But instead of angels going up and down on the ladder, you were on it." Aidan was shocked, and dubious, and guilty that his parents would wonder where he was, but he stored Micha's dream in his heart.

Aidan's parents were indeed disturbed at his unannounced disappearance. They talked to Dara about it. Beyond Crag Liath, and half as high again, was the mountain of Moylussa. It was mysterious, dark, and the changing clouds and light made it look never quite the same. Dara hiked with Aidan to its summit. They left the world of meadow and green. Their breath came hard as they ascended the skree and the air grew thinner. The thought of getting to the peak above spurred Aidan on. When they got there, however, Aidan realized there was another peak beyond, and then another and another. "Life is like this" said Dara, "sometimes God gives us mountain-top visions, but when we get nearer, we see only rock and forget the vision, and give up. Always, always keep the vision of the distant mountain in your mind, and it will help you to keep going when life gets rough, and when the low-lying attractions lure you." Eventually they reached the summit. Something moved in Aidan's spirit. Below them the world seemed different. His village looked so small, and his worries fell into perspective. Even if there were mountains ahead, he could and would climb them.

Dara arranged for Aidan to do things that tested his powers of observation and initiative. If Aidan returned after a set-back and announced that he had failed, Dara would say it was an opportunity to learn. They would discuss what he might do differently if he found himself in a similar situation again. And Dara would arrange a similar situation!

A love of adventure had also been born, so he was delighted when his father, too, took him on trips, in his boat. The river Shannon passed by beautiful scenery and islands where Christian hermits had settled. On their first, short, trip they went to the island a few miles away where Mo Lua had started a community of hermits. They welcomed local inhabitants to hear the Gospel stories and share in meals. Mo Lua loved the animals, too. He was old, and died a few years after their first visit. Flannan, who came to assist him, was a missionary of royal blood, and Aidan got to know him on subsequent trips.

On their first long journey they rowed all the way downstream until the sea came into view. In the Shannon's mouth is an island called Innis Cathaig. "Let's go there," Aidan said. "It is not allowed," said his father, "hermits live there who do not welcome strangers." Aidan learned that this little island had once been inhabited by serpents, and no human had dared live there. But Saint Patrick himself had prophesied that a holy man would make this island his own, serpents would be banished, and it would become a place for God. A farming youth from the nearby mainland named Senan established villages of God on islands in the mouths of several rivers. His reputation as a man of God grew. Once two thieves paused to rob him of corn—but waited until his companion left. He never left. Next day they asked him who his companion was. "What if he were God?" Senan said. They say that Senan was moving his cattle across country south of the Shannon when he was stranded by an incoming tide. The local fort owner refused him shelter. In the spirit of Moses who led his people across the Red Sea, Senan led his herd across the Shannon to that island. There he stuck his spear into the ground and dedicated the place to God. He settled there and it became his place of resurrection. Senan may have been a man of God, but he was a stern one, and he allowed no woman on to his island. Lugar said they should respect other people's boundaries, but, to assuage Aidan's curiosity, agreed to circle the island in the boat before they began their homeward journey.

A long journey north took them to the great monastery of Clonmacnoise, founded by Ciaran the carpenter. Eventually sheep, pigs, and goats came into view in the monastery fields. They moored the boat and were welcomed for the night. A brother explained the plenitude of plants and creatures that inhabited that bog land "Not many plants can survive in bogs," he explained, "since there is little nourishment in either the soil or the water. So what does nature do to overcome this problem?" He took them to a sundew flower and another with wax leaves.—"they get nourishment through their leaves." This brother showed them Rosemary, Bog Asphodel, and Bog Cranberry. He took them to the slopes of the esker ridge, where orchids and thyme grew. He introduced them to fishermen who caught salmon, trout, pike, eel, and sturgeon. He explained how the winter and summer floods created a fertile plain which attracted birds such as the sedge warbler and corncrake.

They visited the tomb of Ciaran. While he was being mentored by Abba Enda on Aran Isle, they both had a similar vision. A large and fruitful tree grew beside a river in the middle of Ireland. The tree protected the entire island, its fruit crossed the sea and the birds carried off some of it to the world. Enda interpreted this vision to Ciaran thus: "The tree is you. All Ireland will be sheltered by your grace and many people will be fed by your fasting and prayers. In the name of God, go to the center of Ireland and found your church on the banks of a river. The tribes who make war each side of it will become one family there." God led Ciaran to that spot. Despite the fact that he died only seven months after establishing the community, it had thrived and grown in the two generations that had followed.

They returned. The cold set in. Memories faded. The passions of youth again competed for Aidan's heart.

608

Theirs was a farming but also a warrior society. Chiefs sent well-equipped raiding parties to fight border battles, take loot, and capture slaves. These warriors were richly rewarded. Some, like Finn MacCool, became the heroes in the sagas that the bards told. In the winter months warriors boozed and bragged about their exploits in battle and with girls. Christianity had introduced an alternative vision. Some who had become monks were among the greatest warriors, and were known as soldiers of Christ, but often, when youths bragged, they belittled this holy calling. Marriage was the norm for settled people, but adolescents, like warriors, were not settled, and many a girl willingly, or unwillingly, became the prey of males.

Aidan wanted to be all things—strong like the warriors, successful in love-making like his older friend Donnacha, skilled in farming like his father, and a hero for Christ like Patrick. Finn, who was a few minutes older than Aidan, was named after the hero of all heroes; he was a touch taller, confident in practical skills, and more popular with the girls. At times Aidan wished he could be like his brother. Did a streak of jealousy lurk somewhere, half buried? Would he, as the elder brother, take charge of the farmstead when their father aged and died?

Two boys used to run to the top of the crag and down again. One was Donnacha, the other Rianh. Rianh's name meant Little Prince and Donnacha's meant Brown-haired Fair Warrior. Shortly before Aidan's eighth birthday they challenged him to run with them to the top of the Crag. Aidan felt proud to be asked, but, being younger and less fast, he did not wish to be shown up as a loser. He created an excuse by starting after them. Donnacha reached the top first —the fast and furious one always did. When Rianh reached the top he ran back to Aidan and they jogged gently together to the top. Rianh was the gentle one, and Aidan learned from him.

Although Donnacha could sprint like no one else, Aidan made a discovery that made him feel good. If they ran a long distance, Donnacha faded and could not finish, whereas Aidan kept on at a steady pace. It was through running that Aidan learned perseverance and a sense of satisfaction in achievement.

Boys wrestled. Aidan greatly desired to wrestle, but shrank from making a fool of himself. He was astonished when Dara said she would teach him how to wrestle well. A woman teach wrestling? Some woman! He must always keep his eye on the other boy; she told him; whenever he saw a sign of movement he should move faster, so that his opponent could never get hold of him. A second skill was the way he held his body. He learned it was useless to stand upright, or to drop his hands; he had to crouch so that his opponent could not push him over, and he could leap easily towards him. She taught him how to clinch the opponent so that he could not wriggle out of it. A person cannot win unless he holds his opponent down. If the opponent arches his back, they have another chance. Aidan did many back exercises. He learned that even thin people can greatly increase their strength by lifting and throwing rocks, by pushing the body up and down with the arms, by hand springs, and neck exercises. That was when he began his life-long practice of pulling the body up and down on a tree's outstretched branch. Aidan could become a warrior if he chose.

Donnacha, Rianh and most of the boys their age started to behave strangely. They acquired things for which they had no money. They ran past dwellings with their faces painted, yelling, and holding spears such as Aidan had seen only in the fort at Kildare. Aidan pieced together the reasons for this. The major and minor clan kings were always vying for greater influence, and their fortunes waxed and waned. Alliances were formed and battles fought. Since the spread of the church seven large kingdoms had emerged who had agreements with local kings. The dominant people in Ulster were the northern Ui Neill. Now, however, the southern Ui Neill were flexing their muscles, and looked for allies in Aidan's part of Ireland. This was protected by Cathal, King of Munster, who dwelt on Saint Patrick's great Rock of Cashel. Cathal wanted an area between Munster and the southern Ui Neill that was a friendly, independent area. So he offered inducements to Aidan's people to support and fight for them. When this came to the notice of the southern Ui Neill they tried to draw the people to their side, in the first place, by claiming that Saint Patrick had founded the See of Armagh and that their churches should therefore give allegiance to that northern See, but there was always the threat of battle in the background. That is why Cashel's emissaries had been showering the young people with weapons, fine tunics, and even horses.

Aidan disliked their boasting and secrecy, but agreed to ride with them into a forest training ground. He felt a mixture of admiration and horror as he watched the first skirmish. One lad fell from his horse. At first they thought he had broken his neck. He was carried off the field. Another was covered in blood. From that time Aidan had no illusions about the life of a warrior. He granted that a people who were attacked had the right, perhaps the duty, to defend themselves, but had not Christ introduced a better way to conduct human affairs? Two parts of his being vied with each other—both parts yearned to give everything. His heart desired to give all to Christ's way. His gut desired to spill blood into a field of battle—and sperm into a woman's body.

At first it was Saoirse who was all over Aidan. Sensuous and lightly dressed, she had gone through several boy friends. To begin with Aidan kept her at a distance. On one occasion she followed him to the river. He waded in and forbade her to come nearer or he would drown himself. Later, he agreed to accompany her to the Shannon where they swam and relaxed by the water's edge. As she touched his body, passions that had been caged exploded. A raging inferno of desire convulsed him, and seemingly uncontrollable sexual energy. It pulsed through him, on and off, day and night. Aidan masturbated, but this did little to assuage this mysterious force. It was like a runaway horse, and Aidan feared lest it destroy him.

Soon it was Aidan who burned for Saoirse. He knew nothing of how an adolescent male should be with a girl. It was Donnacha to whom Aidan turned, for advice, for Donnacha, he thought, knew about lying with girls. "Be confident in your body," Donnacha said, "and do not assume she knows what she wants. Stroke her hair and face, then her breasts, and her lower body. Find out what she most enjoys. Give her small kisses, and if she likes them, make them bigger, until maybe you are sucking in her mouth. Did you know that women become frightened when a man makes love? They fear they will lose control of their body, or that the man might think they are ugly. Make her laugh. Fondle her a lot. Don't be like me, I rush in too quickly in order to make my kill." Donnacha laughed. Aidan did not. Donnacha was going too fast for him. "Lie on top of her, with your organ erect, but at first do nothing more. Savour the scent of her body, and learn to enjoy it." "Have you put your "sword" in a woman's sheath?" Aidan asked Donnacha. "Of course," he replied. "Is it easy?" he asked. "It is easy, but it is also easy to hurt a woman," he told Aidan. "I have learned to ask a woman to guide my sword so that it fits into her sheath at the right angle." "And what does it feel like?" He hesitated. Aidan sensed that Donnacha's sexual encounters had not made him happier.

He sought Dara's advice. "Be natural" she said, "God has put this in people. Follow your heart. Do not try too hard, do not be frightened. Let trust grow. Think of yourself as a house with the doors and windows open," she said. "The other person will appear as sunshine that sends unexpected warmth upon you. You will bask in this delight. But then sun will give way to rain and wind and cool breezes, and gusts that upset your belongings and send your pottery crashing. Welcome the rain and wind—if you can keep the door open, the rain will dry up and the winds will settle. You might close the shutters around your heart, but if there is true love you can look out again and see those rays which first caught you. You might, on the other hand, discover different, stronger rays of sun, until the memory of the first sunshine fades away. And you might fall so much in love with the True Sun that you desire that every energy of your being should reflect a ray of that Sun to every person you meet. Whichever way it is, be open to the sun, and to the cloud and learn from them."

"Soirsese definitely wants me, but she also demands me. I am definitely infatuated with her, but how do I know if this will die away or last for ever?" he asked her. "Do what you most want" she said nonchalantly. Aidan was shocked. Disappointed. But intrigued. What did he most want?

* * *

Choices. Choices. Aidan's twelfth birthday approached. His father asked to talk with him alone. It was unusual for him to set aside a specific time—they usually said whatever they wished in the course of the day. "The monastery at Durrow in the territory of Tethba has become large ", his father said. "It offers better education than any other place. We want you to go." Aidan drew in his breath. What about Soirsese? What about the life of a warrior? Why should his brother remain to assume responsibilities on their farm but not him? Why not a monastery closer to home? What if he could not take to monastery life?

The Irish Church had absorbed the clans, so that some children of many families joined a monastery school at the age of twelve, if not at seven. Pupils were provided with manuscripts of the Gospels, Psalms, classical Latin poets, Euclid, and sometimes Homer, by the extraordinary production of the monastery scriptoria. They could attain to seven "degrees" of which to gain the first, they had to recite all 150 Psalms. They were taught divinity, classical poetry, philosophy, Latin, Greek, science, and general literature. None took vows until they were at least seventeen, or twenty if they were to be ordained.

Lugar felt it was time Aidan learned about holy Columba and the Ui Neills. Aidan already knew that his people had become a client clan to the southern Ui Neills and that Columba, of the northern Ui Neills was looked upon as a spiritual father by them. In 553 Columba had met with his relatives among the southern Ui Neill. Aed Mac Brenainn, King of Tethbae, granted him the Great Plain of Oaks where some of them established a small community. The monastery grew quickly. Columba sent his cousin, Laisren, to supervise the expansion. Lugar told Aidan that once Columba was copying a book across the sea on Iona when he shouted "Help! Help!" Two brothers asked him why he shouted. "There was an angel of God standing between you," Columba told them, "whom I have sent as fast as possible to help one of our brothers who was falling from the top of the great house being built at Durrow." Later, Durrow brothers confirmed that a monk had indeed fallen from a great height, but had miraculously been unharmed. "One cannot describe, but only wonder at the speed with which an angel flies," Columba had said, "for it is as fast as lightning. How amazing is this most speedy and timely help which can be brought so quickly though so many miles of land and sea lay between." Aidan had to admit he was intrigued by Columba's relationship with angels.

He learned that Columba had established a line of midland monasteries which lay on a major route from Munster into the north of Ireland (Tihilly, Lynally, Drumcullen, Kinnitty, Seir Kieran, Birr, and Roscrea) and then stretched from Derry across the sea to the mother house at Iona, and that Durrow was the keystone that fed hundreds of hungry people every day and attracted students from over twenty lands, even a Saxon prince in exile from Northumbria. He learned of Durrow's fine reputation for illuminating Gospel manuscripts and that Iona abbots began their training at Durrow.

He warmed to what his father told him about Columba. He was a big man, a big thinker, poet, and pioneer. He had flaws, yet nothing could daunt his missionary spirit. Columba made friends with God's servants in many parts. Durrow honored these in their festivals, and kept alive their memory. And he had been born on Columba's Day. Even so, he was far from sure that this was the life for him.

He talked with Dara. "Think of your life as a journey" she said. "You have come to a crossing point. Several roads lie before you. You can traverse only one. One road is already well-traveled—along this you may go hand in hand with Soirsese. A second road is well trodden by Ireland's men—the road of battles and feats of bravado. Then there is a third road that passes through Durrow—that is the road less traveled." "And how shall I know which of these roads I must tread?" he asked. "You could think of your name," mused Dara. "Imagine yourself far down each road in the years ahead: where does the flame falter, where does it grow stronger?" As he tried to visualize himself on these possible future roads Aidan thought of the road Donnacha had chosen. Donnacha had to be first in everything, whether it was the conquest of a mountain or of a girl or of a tribal skirmish. The conquest mattered to him more than the mountain, more than the girl, more than the combatants under whose armor beat human hearts. He thought of the passions that both Soirsese and warrior exploits evoked in him. Although they could flare up fiercely, they flickered and faltered the further he journeyed in his mind. Did not Jesus say the kingdom of God would be taken by violence? A force for good could spread further than their tribal battle fields, it could recruit those with even greater passion than that of physical warriors. He felt he could burn for that vision to his life's end—and if he were to marry, there were monasteries with manaig where married monks could live. As for Clonmacnoise, it stood alone. Columba's family of monasteries, stretched like a trail with endless horizons. He decided he would learn more about Durrow. When his father told him that he could go for a trial period, and could return home to help with the harvests, Aidan agreed to go. He might yet become a warrior, a lover or a farmer.

Lugar accompanied his son to Durrow. They again stayed overnight at Clonmacnoise. Clonmacnoise is the great crossing place in the heart of Ireland. There the longest river which runs north to south crosses the longest series of eskers which run east to west. As they trudged along the esker road eastwards towards Durrow, he sensed that his life was at its crossing place. His heart was a mixture of excitement and fear.

chapter 2

DURROW

609

They entered the Forest of Oaks whose swaying branches, which offered strength and hospitality to earth and creatures, moved Aidan. Dara had told him that there is as much of an oak below ground as there is above. "As below, so above" she used to say, meaning that wise people who grow deep roots in the soil of virtue also survive the winds and draughts of human life. "The oak ripens patiently while lesser plants blossom and die," she said, "sometimes this enables the oak to flower twice in one season and remain leafed for longer."

The monastery came into view—the church and the brothers cells, the scriptorium and library, rows of huts where the junior students lived, the cells of the tutors, the refectory, the tables and log seats in the open air where in good weather groups gathered round their tutor. Further away were workshops where they made objects in metal, pottery and wood, book covers, crosses, shrines, and bridles for the horses. Beyond these were fields, the granary, and the mill. Aidan's heart leapt at the sight.

A brother in charge of the boys' dormitories named Canice welcomed them. He showed them round first the brothers and then the boys quarters and sat with them during supper. He conducted Lugar to a guest room and introduced Aidan to the boys who would sleep in the nearby dormitory beds. Aidan felt tense. Suppose they rejected him? When he thought of the friendships he had made at Crag Liath, however, he told himself that there was no reason why he should not make similar friendships at Durrow. He smiled and opened his heart to them. He slept well. The following morning his father said good bye. He hugged Aidan and had tears in his eyes. His son had flutters in his stomach.

Durrow's abbot was Bechan. Aidan doubted whether Bechan could remember everyone's name in a monastery of more than a thousand, so he was touched that he took the trouble to personally greet him. Bechan possessed order and dignity, but there was something else. Often what you see is all there is of a person. Not so with him. He had something in reserve, a space within which the deeper workings of Providence could grow. Aidan liked him.

Aidan was already missing Dara, but he was doubly blessed in the new mentor he was allocated. The foundation of the boys' spiritual formation was to live under the authority of an anamchara, to share every thought with him, however much pride resisted it, and to carry out whatever disciplines he gave. In smaller monasteries the abbot was the anamchara, but in a large monastery such as Durrow this role was delegated to senior monks. Aidan's anamchara, Micah, was a senior monk, but he was sprightly, his eyes twinkled and he saw deeply. Aidan felt free to ply him with the many questions that raced through his mind in his first weeks and as he grew through puberty into a man. "Can I be myself here? Who would be my friends? Do I really want to serve Christ above all else? How can you serve Christ if you are not happy?" He learned To share his hopes and fears, his desire for God, and his confusions. Trust grew, and with it stability.

Aidan had to become acquainted with many new practices. Two principles Dara taught him served him well: "observe what others do and find out why they do it: ask, if you are not sure of something." What stood out most among these new practices was the psalms. At Crag Liath all they had was the old priest on Sundays reciting a line of a psalm in a frail, sing-song voice, which they haltingly repeated after him. At Durrow, hundreds of toned voices chanted them several times a day; a precentor chanted the first half of a verse and everyone chanted the second with joy. In the school they were taught to write Psalms and Gospels on long strips of wood covered in bees-wax which they called tablets. They memorized a psalm from a tablet and then recited it to the tutor. At Durrow, Aidan learned that psalms carry within them all the feelings of which human nature is capable: Christians do not say them, they breathe them. The Psalms and Gospels became trusted companions. He maintained and commended the practice of memorizing them to the end of his life.

The text books for the school, chapel, missions, and library were produced in a large building named the scriptorium, which required many tables and chairs. In due course Aidan took his turn to learn to script there. Everyone worked in silence, though at times the youngsters conversed or made jokes in a low voice. Sometimes they expressed themselves by scribbling little notes on the margins of the manuscript they were copying. Every student was able to transcribe verses on to a wood tablet covered in wax, but only seniors who achieved a required standard were permitted to use vellum, or copy an entire Gospel. The school prepared its own vellum from the skins of goats, sheep, and calves. The damp skins were stretched upon a frame, scraped to the required thickness, and sometimes chalk was added to whiten them. The skins were then cut into sheets to form double pages of the book. The scribe pricked holes to create the shapes he wanted and ruled lines with a stylus. Aidan observed all this. Once, he asked a brother who cared for the cows how many calves were needed each year to provide the vellum. He learned that many hundreds were required.

All kinds of pigments were used for the illuminations of the text. Blue was drawn from woad and lichens, yellow from arsenic, red from toasted lead, green from verdigris, made by suspending copper over vinegar. White was made from chalk, and black from carbon. Other pigments were purchased from merchant ships that came from the Mediterranean. The scribes fixed and preserved these beautiful pigments with beaten white of egg. The ink was made of fish-bone black. All kinds of birds bequeathed quills, mostly geese, swans, and crows. They sharpened these often with a knife. Although many learned to transcribe, only those few who had completed manuscripts of outstanding craftsmanship merited the title "Scribe."

Aidan learned in the Scriptorium that God is worthy of the best that human art can offer, and that some people are drawn to God through beauty. Once, a student with a stammer named Feth asked if he could attempt to transcribe a Gospel on to vellum. He had been refused by his previous tutor. When he repeated the request to Mael, his new tutor, Mael said that first he must solve a riddle. "When you find a quill that Love gives for you alone to use, then your work will become more beautiful." Feth scratched his hair many times, trying to think what these words meant, but he could not understand the riddle. One day, when he had almost given up hope, he decided to stop worrying and sit by a pond. The geese were moulting. Feth gave them crumbs and they gathered round him. The mother goose then did something unusual. She took in her beak one of her feathers that had just fluttered to the ground, a fine feather that would make a perfect quill, and came close to Feth until the feather touched his outstretched hand. Feth took it. "I have found my quill," he thought, "the quill that is given in love and is just for me." That was a turning point for Feth. From that time he made his marks with tender, loving care and gradually became a skilled scribe.

In the great library opposite the Scriptorium many satchels hung on pegs in the wood beams. Each satchel was made of embossed leather, beautifully adorned with interlace designs, and each contained one or more volumes. A few of Durrow's most treasured volumes were kept in embossed leather covers. One of these was named "The Durrow Gospels." The most boring chapter in Aidan's life had begun. Yet if one bores deeper than the chores and chants and learning, we see a character being forged that will make possible a hero's journey.

611

Aidan returned to Crag Liath for the harvest in 610, and again the following year. The life he had known there had gone. Rianh and Donnacha had become warriors, as boys could when they reached the age of fourteen, and were off on some border skirmish. Fionnula had moved out. She had married into a family a few miles away. She was graceful and happy as ever, but was pregnant with child and occupied with her new life. Aidan's mother was unwell. Finn now took equal responsibility with his father for the farm.

Aidan agreed to meet Soirsese. He did not ask her what boys she had been out with since he had last seen her. They walked to the mountain. She chattered on about her hair and her wash routines, her breasts and her food tastes, her family and her admirers, her exploits and her dreams. She did not cease to chatter when she had nothing to say. The chatter washed over Aidan; it seemed less substantial than the life at Durrow. He knew now there was no going back. They lay down on a stack of hay. He informed her that one day soon he might make a vow of celibacy. He wanted to be joined to God even more than he wanted to be joined to a woman. She was angry at first—she felt betrayed—but within a few years she was happily married.

The Ui Neill thought better of taking the settlement by force. Aidan's people entered into years of uneasy self-reliance, strengthened by their southern neighbors. Their church neither repudiated nor endorsed the claims of Armagh that it had rights of allegiance, instead it quietly made links with Flannan's monastery that grew steadily on the isle in the Shannon. Aidan was pleased for his village, but wider horizons now beckoned him. Back at Durrow Aidan told Micah all these things. Micah began to probe into deeper things that Aidan only half knew. Blessed Columba taught "Forgiveness from the heart towards everyone." "Who do you need to forgive today?" he asked. Aidan said he could think of no one. Micah said, "Then let us stay in silence so that you can become aware of what is going on inside you." During the silence Aidan thought of his brother who seemed to be so effortlessly emerging as the head of the family; he thought of a Durrow brother who he felt put him down. He thought of another who often swept past him and made him feel excluded. These people re-inforced the idea that he was a Number Two person. In this way he began to understand who he should forgive. He told Micah the names of these people he needed to forgive, and added "and I do forgive them." Micah advised him to place in his heart the words he had spoken with his lips, and to wait for his heart to fill with a feeling of forgiveness.

Aidan grew in stature. He filled out physically. He would stand with feet apart, firmly planted, a discerning presence—and he undoubtedly had a gift of friendship.

* * *

In his third year in the school Aidan was introduced to Bishop Cassian's account of his visits to the spiritual fathers of Egypt's deserts. From these fathers he learned to analyze the thoughts which arise in one's heart, in order to know which thought he should yield to and which he should shun. He learned how Cassian returned from his desert conferences to his monastery at Bethlehem, which then released him to become abbot and bishop of the Christians in Marseilles. Aidan wondered how this community fared now. Bishop Athanasius' Life of Antony, the founder of those desert Athletes of Christ, was the most sought after of all their books. Aidan was allowed to copy some of Antony's words. Throughout his life Aidan urged people never to forget this saying:

> Keep God always before your eyes,
> keep Scripture always in your heart,
> and keep yourself where you are long enough
> not to move on in a rush.

He learned about holy Morgan and Bishop Augustine of Hyppo. Did these theologians misunderstand each other? he asked himself. Augustine thought that their Irish brother taught that people deserve God's grace. Aidan was not so sure that he did. Did not Morgan, whom the Romans knew as Pelagius, mean that we can choose to put ourselves in a position either to receive it (to "merit" it) or to refuse it?

The Irish had their own theologian, named after Augustine, who wrote about the order of creation. The Durrow library had copies of several works of Isidore, Archbishop of Seville. Aidan was allowed to copy from Isidore's Book of Maxims. In future years he would commend this maxim to many:

> If a man wants to be always in God's company,
> he must pray regularly and read regularly
> When we pray, we talk to God; when we read, God talks to us. .

The Commentaries on Scripture written by the Greek and Latin church fathers, pagan authors of Greece and Rome, computation and astronomy were included in the curriculum. Aidan was permitted to study a book entitled The History of the World Beginning with Creation. It explained the different orders of creation: angels, human souls who have departed this life, celestial waters, the various heavens, the terrestrial waters, the earth and its creatures, and human beings. Durrow had, of course, copies of the works of its founder, Columba, such as his Altus Prosator. Several senior tutors taught history in the form of poems which they composed, and which their students had to learn. One tutor named Ailithur taught them in that way about the sites of the world, of Alba, and their own land.

Columba had been a friend of the bards and the law-makers. The Brehon Laws (the Laws of the Judges), were first drawn up many years before Christ, but Laoghaire, the High King at the time of holy Patrick, appointed nine learned people, including Patrick, to revise these and commit them into Latin writing. Every three years lawyers gathered at the Festival of Tara to revise the laws in the light of changing needs. Columba was proud of these laws; he said that they gave women protection and rights— more than in any other country he knew of. Certain brothers at Durrow were versed in the Brehon Laws, though if a dispute arose with neighboring farmers it was necessary to appeal to the dalaigh, or advocate of the courts employed by the local ruler.

The course of studies could extend from seven to twenty six years for monks. The tutors had a saying: "Good teachers praise the understanding of their pupils that they may love what they hear." Tutors would spend time with a slow student in his cell, so that each could increase their understanding at their own pace.

"There are three labors in the day," their founder taught, "prayer, work, and study." The farms and gardens were mainly looked after by married members of the community, and those not in vows, but every able monk did some physical work. This could be cooking or cleaning, fishing or fire-making, plowing or picking fruit. At times Aidan helped to construct a new building or carriageway. If he was there at harvest he would help to cut and stack corn. Certain brothers brewed ale and others kept bees. They all took a turn in the kitchen—they learned to welcome guests as if they were Christ himself and to make each chore an act of devotion to God. They were mindful of a visit of their founder to Durrow who, when a boy spilt milk he carried in a pail, asked "Did you bless the pail before you poured in the milk?" They were sent out on missions. That was a different kind of work. They were allowed only one day's supplies. They learned to make friends with the inhabitants, to "think on their feet" and to depend upon God. Song and poetry graced social gatherings.

Columba had loved the bards, and indeed was a bard himself. He campaigned to keep their training schools open, and to maintain the rule that a bard be given three days free hospitality. It was quite usual for bards to stay at his monasteries. If brothers met a harpist on their travels he would play and sing with them when they stopped for food or rest. Many learned to play the harp and other instruments at the monastery. They copied and sang hymns from their Irish poets, including Columba. They put Christian words to some of their battle marches. There were disagreements as to how much they should incorporate the traditions of the bardic schools. Some believed that the transcribing of stories and laws from old times, which the Druids passed on from memory but never wrote down, was as important as the transcribing of Christian texts.

The brothers worked hard, but also made time for rest and fun. They perhaps owed this light touch to Columba. One cold winter's day a brother at Iona noticed Columba in tears. On asking what troubled him Columba replied: "I see in my mind's eye our monks at Durrow worn out with heavy work, yet still Laisren drives them on to finish building a great house before Spring." Columba thought they should not let work destroy the rhythm of their prayer and the joy of their life together. Laisren came to realize that he had fallen into a trap, for he told the brothers to stop their work, have a day of rest, and he ordered a special meal to be prepared. From that time he decided that whenever the weather was harsh they should lighten their work. That remained the custom.

The aim of their spiritual formation was to replace self-will with God's will. They learned to eat whatever food was placed before them; to perform every task without complaint; to arrive punctually, and to accept criticism without answering back. Various seniors gave talks about the aims of a monk. They understood that the monk's chief aim was to serve the Triune God, and that they showed this by treating each person as if they themselves were Christ. They were trained to fight daily against the eight vices: Gluttony, avarice, violence, self-pity, lust, sloth, vanity, and rebellion. They understood that vengeful words or feelings against a brother were out of place. If they had a grievance, they went to the brother concerned to compose their differences. If it was not resolved, it could be taken to the abbot. If a brother was openly at fault, another brother could reprove him, and he would ask forgiveness. Grumbling was forbidden.

Obedience was essential, for without it a community cannot maintain its harmony. Stories circulated of extra-ordinary feats of obedience. Scribes left a letter unfinished in their manuscript because they were so keen to set off at the call of the bell to prayer. In Carthac's monastery, many students were named Colman. As they worked beside a river the brother in charge shouted "Colman, get into the water." Twelve Colmans immediately threw off their clothes and jumped into the river! Durrow had links with Comgall's monastery at Bangor. The brothers were never quite sure whether one of their favorite stories was a joke or really happened. Some monks at Comgall's monastery were crossing the sands while the tide was out. A member of the community reproved a youth for some failing. The youth gladly prostrated himself on the sand as a sign of submission. The monks forgot about it. When they returned to the monastery the youngster was missing. They sent people to search for him. He was found still lying prostrate on the sand, in imminent danger of death, since the tide was rising. The monk who had rebuked him had neglected to tell him to rise up!

The Irish were less formal than the desert monks, but that did not mean that they were lax. They could laugh at themselves—which could be as effective as any punishment, though they did have punishments. When they yawned in chapel or said something un-Christ-like they would cross themselves. If something they did wrong was brought to the attention of the abbot he might tell them to fast from certain things, or spend extra time in a vigil, but this was always in a spirit of friendship. There were times, when the weather made them shiver or they were in low spirits and lost their keenness. On those occasions, more often than not, the seniors would encourage them to eat well or relax a little.

Aidan embraced this rich new tapestry of monastic experiences. At Durrow he saw holiness at close quarters—an unconcern for self and an eye for others' well-being. He took his time to decide whether he would choose that path, but in the end agreed to take novice vows.

At the age of eighteen a person could be ordained. Everybody—Bechan, Micah, Aidan himself—assumed that Aidan would take to ordination as a duck to water. It was not an issue. On Saint Peter's Sunday, he was ordained along with twenty three others. Senior monks from Iona came. Aidan's father came. Finn stayed at home to care for the farm, but Fionnula came with her children, and two cousins from Kildare. His mother was too ill—she died within a year. Dara sent a gift, and friends sent messages. The children told Fionnula she must tell Aidan a story she had made up—they said it was the best story they had ever heard.

Following ordination Aidan was made an anamchara to several of the boys. From time to time he deputized for a tutor who was on leave or unwell.

Aidan had crossed a threshold, though fantasies plagued his mind, which might suggest there was more to be addressed. Would he, could he, journey further and deeper beyond the boundaries of his by now familiar life?

chapter 3

EGYPT

617-619

Two days before Passion Sunday in the year of our Lord 617 Bechan asked to see Aidan. He required that "nobody must hear even a whisper of this." Aidan gave his word. "We need a brother who will undertake a secret, most significant but dangerous mission. We need someone with the energy of youth and whose absence will not be thought strange, that is, someone who is due a new role. We need someone who can travel as an everyday person, not as a monk or a wealthy merchant. And we need someone with discretion. Few people meet these requirements. I think you do"

Goose pimples formed on Aidan's arms. He said nothing. "A merchant ship arrived from Alexandria and sold us wheat. The merchant told us the city has been ransacked. The much loved Patriarch John is doing everything he can to serve the poor who are left. He gave the merchant a message in his own hand writing. It informs us that Alexandria's world famous library has perished. The patriarch needs help to re-start education almost from scratch. In neighboring lands Arabs are pouring in. They are joining a new movement, led by a prophet who is a good man, but he cannot read and only knows the Gospels second hand. John wants to reach out to the followers of this prophet, and to the remaining Christians who are in danger of losing the knowledge of the Gospel. They need support from the church here. They need books, and Gospels. He begged us to help in any way we can."

Thoughts flashed through Aidan's mind: of the seven monks of Egypt who established the first of Ireland's many desert sanctuaries at Ulaig; of the books Cassian wrote at his Marseilles' monastery describing his meetings with Egypt's desert fathers, of Bishop Athanasias's Life of blessed Antony.

To him, these books were the jewels in Durrow's library, and Christian Ireland owed its inspiration to the stories of those athletes of the Spirit. "The Christian world is falling apart," Bechan continued, "we can't behave as if we are a little finger divorced from the universal body of Christ— if we were to be divorced we would be nothing. We have a debt to the Christian world which gave us our Faith. We must send them gifts, money, but there is something more. Let us take them our most prized Gospel Book, with its beautiful illuminations and bejeweled cover. After all, it is locked away between festivals. For now we will simply say it has been taken elsewhere for safe keeping. Will you go?"

Aidan plied Bechan with questions. "Are not the pilgrim routes blocked—no one goes even as far as Rome now?" "You will not go overland. You will go the usual way of pilgrims to Marseilles. Cassian's monastery is now unsafe to visit; you will stay at the Bishop's fortified residence on the hill which overlooks the harbor until a ship that sails direct to Alexandria is ready. Our gifts will be carefully concealed inside blankets, and must not leave your quarters. On arrival at Alexandria you will take a donkey and make your way immediately to the Patriarch's residence. You will dress as a lay person."

"Why should this be so secret?" Aidan persevered. "Because," the Abba replied, "pirates rule the sea routes. If one whisper reaches any merchant ship that something so priceless as the Durrow Gospels is being carried to Alexandria, neither the Gospels nor their carrier will be safe." "Is this a command or do I have a choice?" Aidan asked. "We cannot impose something as daunting as this on any brother," Bechan replied. "We feel impelled by God not to refuse this plea for help. But the brother who goes must equally feel impelled himself."

Pilgrimage was in the Irish blood. They had heard of pilgrimages to Jerusalem and Rome. St Jerome had written that Judea overflowed with pilgrims, and that, round about the Holy Sepulcher were heard sung, in divers tongues, the praises of the Lord. The subsequent barbarian occupations of mainland Europe had halted overland pilgrimages to places like Rome. They had heard stories of pilgrimage nearer home, such as of Columba's relative, Cormac, and of Columbanus's travels as far as Italy, and they knew that trade by sea routes to and from places such as Alexandria continued.

Nevertheless, Aidan was rocked to his foundations. This extra-ordinary request brought him face to face with his identity, his name, his passion. What was the flame that burned deepest within him? If he said no, where would the flame go? He somehow knew that the flame was for passing on, and that if he refused this challenge, the flame might falter and fade.

That is how he embarked on the most far-reaching pilgrimage imaginable. It would take nearly two years of his life.

The journey to Marseilles was uneventful. From time to time Aidan allowed himself a wry smile. "No warrior has embarked on an adventure as far from home as this" he told himself. Upon his arrival at Marseilles Aidan was shocked at the extent to which barbarian pillaging had reduced that once great city to a shell. He clambered up the steep, broken steps of St Laurent Hill to the bishopric. A high wall surrounded it. He pulled the rusty bell chain at the barred, rusty gate. A wheezing little man named Morvan led him through the large, hollow building to his room, and returned with a pot of tepid water. On hearing the bell for vespers Aidan found his way, after several wrong turnings to the chapel.

There were a mere three people besides the Bishop, who rushed through the words in a monotone, and walked out without giving Aidan a glance. This church fortress was not only deserted of people, it was deserted of warmth. Aidan's heart bled when he thought of Cassian's once great community. A worm of dread crept into him, lest anything like this should ever befall Ireland's beloved Christian communities.

On the second day the bishop thawed a little and Aidan asked him about church life in Gaul. The late Bishop Gregory of Tours, the Bishop said, had lamented "unhappy our days, for the study of letters is dead in our midst, and there is to be found no man able to record the history of these times." Aidan began to value the Durrow scriptorium all the more.

He did manage to learn a little more about the Patriarch of Alexandria, and pieced together a compelling picture of this servant of God. Evidently he was affectionately known as John the Merciful. In his youth he had a vision of a beautiful woman, who said that her name was Compassion, the eldest daughter of the Great King. This had such an influence on John that he himself became famed for his compassion towards the poor. He called them his lords and masters, because of their great influence at the court of the High King of Heaven, and he had taken several thousand of the most poor under his care. He visited the hospitals three times every week, and freed many slaves. Three years earlier, barbarians had attacked Jerusalem, and John sent the fleeing Christians generous supplies of food, wine, and money. Now there was talk of the Persians threatening Alexandria. Patriarch John believed the only thing to do in a crisis is to make disciples of people who could emerge the other side of the crisis and become leaders. A respect for the Patriarch grew in Aidan and he longed to meet and support him

Eventually a ship arrived that the Bishop felt happy for Aidan to board. He knew and talked with the captain, and Aidan sensed that all would be well inside the ship, though what attacks they might suffer from hostile sea marauders, God alone knew. They had a few scares, at times Aidan felt sea sick, but at last Alexandria came into view and Aidan's excitement mounted. He was bringing the flame of the Gospel to a far-off land. What a privilege to contribute to a re-Christianizing of this ancient center of Christianity where Latin could be learned and the Gospels be memorized. He wondered if their glorious Durrow Gospels might even become the center-piece of the holy liturgy at the patriarchal church.

He obtained a donkey, and almost felt at home as he wended his way through the city. He began to image in his mind what he might do. He had a good memory, so he would turn the Patriarch's requirements into a mnemonic. As he proceeded, however, unease began to grow. The road that ascended towards the patriarchy became empty. The people he passed looked different. Were they really Egyptians, he wondered? In the distance the patriarchy came into view. He had expected to converse in Latin with a priest or monk, and was surprised that none were in sight. He had almost reached the main gate when he saw someone driving a donkey laden with food and noticed, half hidden under his sleeve, a tattoo of the Coptic cross. It was similar to Coptic crosses that Egyptian monks had brought to Ireland. Aidan took out the cross that was hidden under his tunic and showed it to him. They smiled and gestured Christian greetings. Aidan used sign language; he knelt as if in prayer and pointed to the patriarchy with a questioning look. "No, no" the donkey man gestured vehemently, and pointed Aidan in the opposite direction. After further sign talk, it became clear to Aidan that the patriarch was no longer there. Invaders now occupied his house.

Seized with horror, Aidan was tempted to run. But he did not, for that would have drawn attention to himself. He returned by a roundabout route to the port, where the ship would still be anchored. Dark had descended and he was near exhaustion, but he reached the port with relief. A moment later the relief vanished. The ship had gone. He found out later that the captain had set sail as soon as he learned that the city had been occupied.

Aidan was stranded in a strange, newly occupied land. His mission was a failure. He could not speak the local language. He had no way of return. Would he be left to die there, either by the sword, or by illness contracted from the scraps of filthy food he eked out from the streets? Or would he half live the rest of his life in some human backwater, there to nurse his hurts? Lord, what shall I do?" he cried out. "Ask what I would do if I were in your shoes" said a voice deep within. He thought of Jesus, born in the Bethlehem stable, and of his disciple, John the Merciful, making the poor his own in this city. The poor were the ones who could not flee, they were the ones who would be allowed to stay in order to serve their new masters. This is what he would do: he would seek out the poorest of the poor.

He wandered past endless roadside huddles and street stalls, and then into the area where people live off the rubbish dumps. There he saw two smiling faces, and a hand tattooed with a cross that waved a welcome. He, too, smiled and waved, and showed them his cross. They embraced. Their names were Mahmoud and Symeon and they each had loving families. They shared their meager scraps of food and invited Aidan to sleep on a blanket on the floor. He went to sleep looking into the night stars, wondering whence help might come.

Simeon had an intuition. He was absent when Aidan awoke—he had gone to fetch an old man, who by mid morning had returned with him. This old man was too frail to have fled the city, but he was learned. He spoke Latin. Aidan's Latin was limited to the Bible and religion, and perhaps the old man's was too, but slowly he came to understand Aidan's story. Aidan asked his advice as to what he should do next. The old man's advice was this: the city was unsafe for visitors, it was essential that Aidan leave and that he draw no attention to himself. The only way to do that would be to join a caravan on the trade route to Syria. Many kinds of people joined these long caravans, and there were usually new people among them. A caravan was leaving in three days. Until then he must stay with Mahmoud and Simeon. On Friday Mahmoud take him early to the caravan and introduce him to somebody he knew. "God will help you" he assured him. Aidan wondered.

FLAMEBEARER ON THE SILK ROAD

So began Aidan's long caravan journey along the silk road. The old route had begun by sea, from Alexandria south to Tyre, in Syria, but now they had to skirt the sea on land. Jesus, when he worked in his father's carpenter's shop, looked down on a similar caravan route, and no doubt at times mingled with the traders. Aidan decided to do likewise. Mahmoud recognized a familiar group and spoke to them. They let Aidan join them, albeit as a silent companion, and the trek began. Days passed into weeks. Aidan's feet became hard, and his heart sometimes felt numb. At stopping places silken and wool items were traded for food and spices. At one stopping place, in the Syrian region of Howran, trading groups who had traveled north from Arabia joined the caravan. There, also, a member of Aidan's traveling group pointed him out to someone—a Christian who spoke Latin. He invited

Aidan to his home where they spent an evening in deep converse. Aidan learned much.

The Christian told Aidan about the once wealthy Abd Al-Muttalib, whose fortune had waned and who left his sons only a little for their extended families. One son, Abu Taleb was really poor. His nephew, Muhammad, felt obliged to do what he could to earn his own livelihood by pasturing sheep and goats on the hills. His uncle took him with him on his trade travels, and when Muhammad was about twelve he went from Arabia on one of these caravans north to Syria. At Bostra, near where the Meccan caravan always stopped, there was a cell which had been lived in by a Christian monk for generations. When one monk died another took his place and inherited all that was in the cell, including the Gospels, and some other old manuscripts. One of these manuscripts contained a prediction of the coming of a prophet to the Arabs.

Bahir, the monk who then lived there, was well versed in the contents of this book, and felt that the coming of The Prophet would be in his life-time. He had often seen the Meccan caravan of Quraysh come into sight and stop near his cell, but as this one drew near he noticed a small, low-hanging cloud hover between the sun and two travelers. As soon as they halted, the cloud halted. When they took shelter under the tree, it seemed as if the tree lowered its branches to give them shade. Was this, Bahir asked himself, a sign that the Prophet had come? The cell was newly stocked with provisions, so Bahir sent a message inviting everyone in the caravan of Quraysh, young and old, bond and free, to share food with him. They came, but despite Bahir's invitation that everyone should come, they left the young Muhammad behind to look after their belongings. Bahir sought to discern which of his guests might be the Prophet, but God showed him that none were. So he asked, "Are you sure there is no one else who was with you?" "There is none, but Muhammad, who is looking after our belongings" they told him. "but he is only a boy." "Do not treat him like that," Bahir said, "please invite him to share the meal with us." So Muhammad came. Throughout the meal Bahir watched Mohammed with utmost attention. After they had finished eating, the monk asked Mohammad searching questions. He then asked Abu Taleb "Are you his father?" "I am his father's brother" Abu replied, "his father died when he was in his mother's womb." Bahir then said to Abu Taleb, "Guard him carefully. Great things are in store for your brother's son"

Aidan was not sure he had understood accurately all that his Christian acquaintance said, since Latin was the mother tongue of neither of them, but he did understand that on a second, quite recent trip, Mohammed, now fully grown, met the same monk again. This time Bahir told Abu Talib that he saw signs of a great Prophet in his nephew and that he should protect him from harm. "Now," the acquaintance told Aidan, "I hear reports that Mohammed has received revelations, and that Arabs are flocking to his teaching." Aidan enquired of his new friend how he might find the monastery of Bahir. He resolved that he would ask for hospitality and there form a plan.

For what should he plan? For a safe return? He still had in his possession the gifts from Durrow, including the priceless Gospels. The original mission was certainly aborted. His heart was heavy that Christian Alexandria had lost the knowledge of Christ, and that the attempt to help restore the Gospels there had come to nothing. Were the Syrian monasteries in need of these precious Gospels? He did not know, but one thing was certain, the Arabs were, even though they knew no Latin. Aidan began to wonder whether, in the deep mysteries of God, the real purpose of his visit was to bring the Gospel to the pagan Arabs, and even to the God-fearing followers of this new prophet, Mohammed.

THE SYRIAN MONASTERY

Aidan succeeded, with much weariness, in finding his way to that monastery. Guests thronged it, but they found him a cell. He asked if he might speak with Bahir who, he learned, was now very old. This request was granted. Aidan laid before Bahir his story, his predicament, and his prized possessions. When he removed the blanket from the Durrow Gospels Bahir's eyes filled with tears, and he prostrated himself. "We will put this in a safe place, and we will meet with the Abba and discuss what is to be done," he said. After a silence he asked Aidan "Where is God in all this?" Aidan listened to his heart, and his name flashed into his mind. "My name means Flame," he explained, "I do not wish the flame to return to my country having lit nothing in these lands—lands which gave us the bright spiritual athletes but which now face darkness." "I see," said Bahir, lost in thought. There was a pause. "Tomorrow I will introduce you to a guest. He is a follower of the Prophet. He has a similar spirit to yourself. I will be your translator."

THE PROPHET MOHAMMED'S DISCIPLE

Over the following days conversations took place that would for ever be etched in Aidan's memory. The guest, a young man named Ameer, was a former pagan who, since meeting the Prophet, had come to love God with all his heart. Ameer carried a prayer mat with him. Several times and in several places Aidan observed him unroll his mat, prostrate himself, facing east, and pray with deep devotion. This touched Aidan's heart.

On the first day they placed their sandals side by side outside the chapel. "Muhammad, peace be upon him, tells us that the prophet Moses removed his sandals when God was revealed to him in the desert, and that place became holy ground," Ameer told Aidan, as if Aidan could not have known this. "He says we, too, must remove our sandals before we enter a house of prayer, for cleanliness is next to godliness." "Yes," said Aidan, "in the churches founded by our holy Columba we remove our sandals before we enter the house of prayer. However, the winter in our land is very cold, and those who might become ill through cold are permitted to bow instead of removing their sandals."

That first day they talked about who are the chosen people. "I cannot read," Ameer confided, "but I know that the Jews' Scriptures say they are God's chosen people, and the Christians' Scriptures say they have now become the chosen people. This makes me hurt for my people. In my heart I believe we Arabs are chosen, too. God has confirmed this in revelations to the Prophet." "I know how you feel," Aidan told Ameer, "for we Irish are on the edge of the world, and we are not mentioned in any Scriptures." "What do you do with this feeling that your people are pushed to the edge?" Ameer asked. "We learn about the wonderful things God did through his prophets, through Jesus and his twelve apostles and spiritual foster mothers, to turn the people to God. We say: now God calls us to do the same in our land. We call our greatest teachers our Twelve Apostles, and our Twelve Spiritual Foster Mothers." "The Prophet says that the Jews were at first God's chosen people, but when they made a golden calf which they worshipped instead of God their right to be God's chosen was taken from them" Ameer declared. "I believe that is a truth for every people," Aidan said, "a people who turn to idolatry cease to be partners of the true God."

"Do you know the story of how Abraham offered his dearest son as a sacrifice, to prove that he loved God even more than his son?" Ameer asked. "The Jews say Isaac was that son, but the Prophet saw in a vision that it was our ancestor, Ishmael, whom Abraham offered." "Did God reveal the meaning of this vision?" Aidan asked. "I don't think so exactly, but without doubt it means that we Arabs are God's chosen people" Ameer volunteered. "What about other people who are neither Arabs nor Jews, but who are treated as worthless?" Aidan asked. "The Prophet says that God created all mankind. They can become God-honourers, too, and then they, too, are God's chosen people" Ameer assured him. "Yes, I believe that with all my heart," Aidan said, "God has a plan for every nation under heaven; each has its own dignity and calling."

They talked about tribal battles, the judgment, the next life, and the ceaseless struggle of good against evil. "Christ has taught us a new way to fight the spiritual war" Aidan said. Ameer said "I know that the Christians of Abyssinia gave refuge to Muhammed and his disciples." He wanted to learn more of this way of Christ. Aidan explained that no Christian is permitted to kill as an act of revenge, although some Christians were warriors, and would fight under the orders of their king in a just cause.

On Thursday they discussed prophecy. Ameer recounted how some years previously the Prophet had climbed a mountain a few miles from Mecca, and entered a large cave. There he received the first of many revelations. For over two years he vouchsafed these only to his closest friends, who wrote them down, but now he was making these public. Ameer, in common with growing numbers, eagerly traveled to hear Muhammad and his prophecies. Aidan was intrigued. "The founder of our monasteries, the late Columba, blessed be he, was a prophet," he told Ameer. "Sometimes he had revelations about heaven and the spiritual meaning of things, but often he foretold something practical that would happen to someone, or of a battle. These things always came to pass. He also prophesied about the land to which God sent him. Only once, as far as I know, did he prophesy about a land far away." "What was that?" Ameer asked. "On the island of Iona in the land of Alba, the blessed Columba told Luigbe moccu Min that sulfur had poured from heaven upon a city in Italy. Months later traders brought news that this was so."

Their last conversation was on Friday. Ameer explained that the Prophet had taught them to repeat the phrase "God is One," and to denounce people, like Christians they had met, who believed there were three gods, the Father, Jesus and Mary. "I love God," he told me, "when the Christians split Him I feel a terrible wound has been inflicted and I myself feel hurt." These words touched Aidan deeply. It caused him anguish that fellow Christians in Arabia—the ones the Prophet had met or heard of—had so debased the wonder of the Triune God, since for the Irish the Trinity enhanced the wonder of God and he longed to communicate this to Ameer. "We, too, believe that God is One," he assured him, "our discussion should not be about whether there is one God, but about what is the nature of God. If you have two people—one is self-sufficient, the other has a nature that has room for another—which would you say is the better person? Christians say that God is like the second person. God is not self-sufficient. At the heart of God is a communion of Loves." "The Prophet Muhammed taught that God did not beget a son" said Ameer. "Christians do not teach that God begat" Aidan said, "they teach that God eternally begets and is begotten. You have told me that God has ninety nine names. God can give expression to each of these qualities. Because God is the All-Compassionate One, the Uncreated enters the stream of created life without ceasing to be God; and because God is the All-Powerful One, He is not split in so doing. . ." The bell for vespers rang.

RETURNING IN A DIFFERENT LIGHT

Bahir and his co-elders discussed Aidan's aborted mission They agreed that their monastery should be the secret custodian of the Gospels until the situation improved. The Gospels would be placed in a cellar which would be locked. They would give Aidan sanctuary until a merchant ship bound for Britain was due to leave the nearest port, Tyre. The following night Aidan dreamed that he went with Ameer to be with his people; that he learned their language and walked among them carrying the Holy Gospels, translating the words from Latin and teaching them to learn and recite aloud Christ's words.

In waking life, however, tragedy struck. The Gospels were stolen— Aidan never found out how. The Gospel had been lost to the once Christian places of Northern Africa, and now it seemed that the Gospels that could have offered so much to the God-fearing Arabs were lost too. He was devastated. He carried this hurt to the end of his life.

The monastery asked a brother to accompany Aidan to the port at Tyre. Before they left Bahir came to Aidan and prophesied perhaps for the last time in this life. "The flame is not extinguished, it is lost" he told him. "One day in the far future the flame will spread through these parts as never before."

The journey across the wide ocean was wearisome, and hard to bear. Aidan occupied himself by repeating the Psalms, but also by reflecting on those conversations with Ameer. There was one question which, for the rest of his life, he regretted he had not asked him. This concerned the belief that Jesus' apostles were mistaken that Jesus was crucified and rose from the dead. There was no doubt they lived close to him for three years, they were present at his death, they talked with him after his resurrection, they died for their belief in his dying and rising—how then, could they be mistaken?

When he reached the land of the Britons Aidan transferred to another ship. More than eighteen months after his departure he arrived back at Durrow.

As Bechan reached out his arms to greet him, Aidan saw horror in his face. He had become used to his condition, but Bechan saw a gaunt, exhausted shell. He sent Aidan straightaway to the hermitage where a diet of good food and friendship began to revive him. On the second day Aidan told Bechan the whole, heart-rending story, at times with a breaking voice. The Abba understood, and because of this Aidan felt some relief. Micah often came to chat. Aidan was given light gardening duties for a time.

chapter 4

VISITORS REKINDLE THE FLAME

LIBRAN

The first visitor to help Aidan in the gardens was Libran, an aged and simple brother who had been sent with a message from their monastery at Tiree, in Alba, where he had gathered reeds for many years. As they worked side by side Libran's extraordinary story tumbled out.

As a poor youth in Ireland he had murdered a man. Before Saint Patrick came the penalty for murder was death, but afterwards two fines could be paid in lieu of death. One was the fixed wergild, and the other was the honor price owed to the kin of the victim. Should the murderer be unable to pay by himself, his family was normally responsible for paying any amount the murderer could not pay. Libran's wealthy uncle paid his death fine on condition that Libran worked for him as a slave for the rest of his life. This Libran promised on oath to do. Within a week, however, he fled. He made his way to the Isle of Iona where he confessed his sin to Columba. Columba gave him the penance of working for seven years at one of their nearest monasteries, at Monasteries, at Tiree, on a nearby island, after which Libran was to return to Columba for further directions. Columba believed that each person should make restitution, as far as they were able, to the person they had wronged. So he told Libran on his return that his penance was to go back to his relative, admit his wrong-doings and beg forgiveness. Columba gave Libran a gilded sword. "Give this to your master in return for your freedom" he said. "He has a wife with many virtues, and she will speak on your behalf." Columba warned him that he should then visit his ailing parents who needed care in their old age. "Your brothers will force you to make good the service due from son to father which you have for so long neglected. Though this may seem to you a heavy burden, know this: within a week of your new duties your father will be buried. After that your brothers will press you to give the same care to your mother. Your youngest brother, however, who has a good and sensitive heart, will understand your true calling, and offer to take on this duty himself." All these things, Libran told Aidan, happened exactly as Columba had said.

As they pulled up the weeds Libran told Aidan how he had profusely thanked his brother for taking on his responsibilities, trekked to the ferry near Derry, and returned to Iona where Columba welcomed him. It was then that Columba gave him the name Libran, which means "You are free." Columba prophesied over him: "You will enjoy long life, and end this present life in good old age. Nevertheless, your resurrection will not be here." Libran was upset by this, but Columba continued "Do not worry. You will die in one of my monasteries and you have reserved for you a precious place in the kingdom of God." "These words cheered me," Libran told Aidan, "and sustained me through the many years I served God in the monastery at Tiree. There they called me Libran of the Reed Bed."

"And now you are here—back in your own country but still part of the monastic family that has adopted you," Aidan told him, "and we shall hold hands and pray together as brothers who will share in glories to come beyond our ken." Libran became ill the next day, and died seven days later. His soul left his body, free from pain, with a smile on it like that of a cherub. Brothers gathered in the church to commend Libran to God, and Aidan was asked to speak words in his memory. As Libran's body was borne from the church to the cemetery they chanted "O happy fault that through decay and death comes a crown of eternal glory." Often, as Aidan wandered through the peaceful garden cemetery, he paused at Libran's grave and thought he saw a crown above it. He mused on the sin of Cain, who, by slaying his brother, brought curse upon their land. Libran had murdered someone of his own land. It was fitting, as Columba knew, that he should return to that same land for his burial and resurrection. For through the resurrection of Christ, and this man's obedience to Christ's prophetic words, the wound he once inflicted on the land was now being healed. Libran's story stirred him because a desire was growing in him to see broken, disadvantaged people raised up to their full stature.

Libran's death also touched something else within him—the fear of being trapped by monastic life. By making a commitment to one thing, we close the option to do other things. Yet passions and possibilities can emerge unsought. Aidan feared lest he would be like a man tied to a post who wanted to climb every mountain, cross every sea, and run to every place of mission. If Libran, who had stared prison in the face and undergone long years of penance could run his long course to the final hurdle with such equanimity, perhaps he could too?

COLMAN

Aidan went on to do other duties. He took turns as guest brother. The second visitor was an abbot. It was Durrow's custom to invite a senior monk from a neighboring monastery to stay with them during Lent and give teaching. Aidan was intrigued when he learned that Colman mac Beognai, the founder of the monastery of Lynally, would visit them for Lent, for he had heard stirring stories about his meetings with Columba under whom he studied when he was young. Colman was once sucked into the surging waves of the Corryvreckan whirlpool on his way to visit Columba at Iona. Imitating Jesus, he raised his arms to calm the sea in God's name. The prophetic Columba saw all this in his spirit. He smiled and said: "The Lord terrifies him in this way, not so the ship should be wrecked, but to arouse him to pray more fervently so that he may sail through the peril and reach us here."

Colman had studied under Columba, and had been developing tools for the training of monks which Aidan was keen to learn from. His Alphabet of Devotion was becoming well-known. He brought a copy with him and based his Lent instructions upon it. Colman taught that nature has its basic elements, and so does life as God desires us to live it. The elements, he taught, are like the letters of the alphabet. Their purpose is to ground us in what is real, to sift the false from the true. An alphabet of devotion provides a framework that helps Christians learn truths of heaven while they walk paths of earth.

Aidan often introduced this Alphabet to brothers in future years: "Faith with action . . . humility without favoritism . . . simplicity with wisdom . . . work without grumbling. . ." If the fear of being trapped by monastic life grew less at the grave of Libran, a passion to actively cultivate monastic life was planted in him by Colman. His time with the brothers made Aidan realize that a monk's daily plod need not lead nowhere, it can be the plod of life-long learning. He came to feel that even a life-time is too short for a person to learn, understand and communicate the sacred Scriptures and the writings of the Church Fathers and the meaning of the Gospel and the insights of the sages and the knowledge of people and of God. From that Lent a passion to grow in these things impelled him forward—for a time, at least.

THE BROTHER FROM SAINT KEVIN'S
GLENDALOUGH MONASTERY

While Aidan was still guest brother he was asked to welcome a brother from Ireland's monastic city at Glen Lough. He had walked for three weeks to bring the news that their much loved founder, the famed Kevin, one of The Twelve Apostles of Ireland, had died in extreme old age. Aidan was warmed by many new things he learned about Kevin.

A celebration of Kevin's life was arranged. A senior brother named Sinchell entranced them with stories of how Kevin blessed God's creatures and how they blessed him: trees sang to him and a deer left milk in the hollow of a log from which Kevin nourished his fosterling. When Kevin lay in Lenten vigil with arms outstretched, a bird laid an egg in his hand; people said he remained in prayer until the egg hatched. He quoted a bard:

> A soldier of Christ into the land of Ireland
> A high name over wave and sea
> Kevin the holy fair warrior
> In the valley of the two broad lakes.

Kevin, Sinchell concluded, worked miracles until he died well over one hundred years old, his life, like that of Moses, undimmed by age. Aidan pondered why Kevin lived more than twice as long as most of their brothers. Did he draw deep from God's good creation?

LOCAN

Locan's visit was a total surprise. He was the chief of a coastal area north of the Shannon which had nothing to do with the jurisdiction of the Durrow region. He was concerned about the hermits' island in the mouth of the Shannon which Aidan and his father had once circled in their boat. This was not really under anyone's jurisdiction north or south of the river. Because of this some difficult issues had accumulated which affected the mainland, and these had now come to a head.

Reports had become rife of strife among the hermits. Certain brothers frightened any stranger who set foot upon the island with their fierce words: others disagreed with that approach. Moreover, their abbot had died and the brothers could not agree upon a successor. Those things alone would not warrant Locan's interference in a religious community, but something else had brought things to a head: a body had been spotted on the shore, lying unburied. Moreover, it was a woman's body. That is why Locan journeyed all the way to discuss these problems with Bechan. Although Durrow lay outside Locan's sphere of influence, it was, like other larger monasteries, a resource for neighboring kingdoms. Locan was shrewd. He wanted to build alliances that could help protect and increase his base. He proposed that Durrow should appoint someone to have temporary oversight of the monastery, on the grounds that laws must be upheld, and he could not allow a lawless situation on his boundary to develop. Would Bechan send some brothers? If so, their first job would be to solve a possible murder mystery! Bechan was hesitant—he did not want Durrow to lose someone in a senior post, and yet, if he was to accede to Locan's request he would need someone with discretion. He went to bed with these matters in his prayers, but undecided.

The following say he asked Aidan to see him and laid the situation before him. "We are under no illusions," he said, "it is in Locan's interest to forge a link with us, yet I think he is telling us the truth. He wants us to solve a possible murder mystery, but the enduring task is to turn a collection of independent-minded hermits into a community who love the land and the people across the water as much as their own island." He looked hard at Aidan: "Would you do it?" "Why me?" Aidan asked, surprised. "For these reasons," the abbot replied, "you are available since you have not yet been given a new duty here, you have some slight links with the area, you are young enough not to be in competition with the senior hermits, but you are mature enough to soften them up gently. I want you to help them treat every person as a child of God. I cannot send an older brother; the hermits there are old, and they will not take kindly to someone their own age. I need someone who has a sharp mind and a steady hand, but who will love those hermits. Your first job is to solve the matter of the dead body. Your longer task is to befriend these brothers, to open them up to the outside world, to help them embrace Christ's call to hospitality. You will have our prayers, you must come back for retreats and to seek our counsel, and you will take a lad with you." "May I take young Ronan," Aidan quickly said, "he has the gift of friendship." Ronan was a smiling novice with brown hair and many freckles whom Bechan would find it hard to spare. Bechan paused. "This mission requires much sacrifice from you, Aidan, so I must make a sacrifice, too. You shall have Ronan."

chapter 5

SENAN'S ISLE

621-626

Aidan and Ronan strode across the esker and rowed down the river towards their daunting adventure, generously supplied with food for body and soul, books, a bell and a water timer. "It is an impossible task" Aidan thought to himself, thinking not of the body on the shore but of changing those hermits' habits. Humanly speaking, nothing attracted him to that lonely ordeal; he went there out of obedience. On the other hand, a holy man had founded the community, Senan.

Aidan passed on to Ronan what he had learned about Senan as a boy. He recounted the faith stories his father had told him on their boat, and how Senan had sought out teachers in Britain and Gaul and had become a learned teacher. Some had regarded him as one of the Twelve Apostles of Ireland. Even though this God-guided founder of villages of God in the mouths of rivers had not permitted women to live on Scattery Island, he had encouraged his sister Canera to start a community on the mainland nearby.

What had gone wrong, Aidan wondered? Was it that the first generation had pioneered in dependence upon God and the next generations had preserved things in dependence only upon themselves? His tenure here would be his first experience of a community whose stated purpose, although it had not changed, had been subverted by unconscious needs to possess and to defend. Could that be why hostility to change and in some cases dependent relationships had grown?

As for the dead body, in most places where a dead body was unaccounted for a dalaigh would be sent for to find out the facts and apply the Brehon laws, but because no one was clear under whose jurisdiction Senan's

Isle came, no action had been taken. In any case the dead body was the least of his troubles.

During their journey down stream Aidan asked God to give him love for Senan's heirs. Ronan was a delight—and he bubbled over with theories about who might have murdered the woman on the shore!

They soon learned that there was indeed more than met the eye behind the request that Durrow should take spiritual oversight of Inis Cathaig, as the hermits called the island. Locan was being squeezed by the southern Ui Neill, who had become the dominant rulers of most of Connaught, but not of the south east corner, and certainly not of Senan's Isle. The balance of power in that region was constantly shifting, and Senan's Isle was rather like a fortress without walls, for its inhabitants seemed impervious to what went on even just across the sound on the mainland. This Isle always had been a law unto itself; it had little strategic or economic value to the powers that be, but Locan had used his brain: the church was now a shaper of peoples without using the weapons of worldly power such as the sword and the fines. It had a symbolic and moral power. If Locan had an arrangement with Durrow, his authority was more likely to be honored. Locan's staff had informed the hermits that, because there were questions about the laws of the land, they were now under the protection of Durrow, that Aidan would have temporary spiritual oversight, but that he had come to serve and would respect the elders and the ways of the island. He was also under orders to sort out the mystery of the body on the shore.

The two brothers arrived with their gifts, but they received no real welcome, mostly just silent bows. No cell had been prepared for them. Aidan wondered if he should commandeer a cell, or gather a group to build a new one. He decided, instead, to ask a passing monk if he knew of an old cell or two that had been discarded for better ones. The monk led them to a place which was open to the full force of the east winds. "Will these do us?" Aidan asked Ronan, and they gathered rocks and wood to repair them. The old hermit had intended to leave them to fend for themselves, but seeing that they demanded nothing, he gathered a few stones, and showed them the nearest spring.

They did not, however, go to sleep at the usual hour. If any brother had curious eyes they would have seen Aidan and Ronan glide soundlessly to the shore in their bare feet to the place where the woman's body had lain. It had by now gone with the wind and the waves. Aidan said some beautiful heart prayers that entrusted that dear sister, whoever she was, into the mercy and love of God. He prayed peace upon her soul, and asked that her resurrection would be in the place of God's choosing. That night, they slept as Jacob once slept when he wrestled with God and a ladder enabled angels to move between heaven and earth.

"Do you say prayers at each of The Hours?" Aidan asked the old hermit in the morning. "We have no means to measure the hours" he informed him, "We say the prayers in our own place when we remember to." Aidan placed Durrow's water clock in a visible place. It consisted of a jar of water, having a small hole in the bottom so that the liquid dripped out drop by drop. As the level within the jar was lowered, it showed the time upon a scale. Aidan had been taught that the Roman senator Cassiodorus had advocated the water clock in his rulebook for monastic life the water clock as "a useful alarm for the soldiers of Christ." The clock was a useful reminder, but nothing was said.

"What about the murder—I thought this had to be solved first of all?" Ronan asked. "That can wait," Aidan said, to Ronan's surprise, "the body has gone with the sea and there is nothing we can do about it." "But what is the explanation of her death?" Ronan asked, "what if she was murdered?" "I strongly suspect we will find the answer by listening to the island folk tales," Aidan told him. "The folk tales also hold the clue to how we can turn the island round. Today, our priority is to establish a pattern of prayer." Thereafter Ronan asked every hermit he could engage in conversation, which was not many, to tell him a tale of the island. This disarmed some of the hermits, but Ronan still could not figure out the answer to the mysterious body on the shore.

"Shall I ring a bell shortly before we pray so that others will know to join us?" Ronan asked. "Not yet," Aidan replied, "lest they think the bell is taking away their freedom. Let us walk past their cells on our way to the chapel, so everyone gets to know the pattern we follow, and let us hope that someone will join us simply because they want to." In time, several hermits did join them. Once, more than half the hermits joined in for a festival It was then that Aidan asked if they thought it would a good idea if the bell was rung before the times of prayer, and one of them offered to be bell-ringer. It was a proud day when, for the first time a bell was rung for communal prayer.

Gradually the island spirit improved. Aidan realized this the day he spotted a visitor rowing towards the island. He went to the shore and welcomed him. Since they had no guest cell, he offered the visitor his own cell, and he himself slept on the chapel floor. No one complained. After that Ronan helped Aidan build an extension to his cell to use for future guests. After two years several guest cells had been discreetly built, and this met no resistance other than a mutter here and there.

During a return visit to Durrow Bechan said he had heard reports that Inis Cathaig was now a community, and he wished to offer thanks for this with the Durrow community. Further years of consolidation passed quite quickly. One evening Ronan asked "Do you remember the mystery of the body on the shore? Years have passed and I still have no idea who did it." With a twinkle in his eye Aidan said "I will give you a clue. Find an old hermit who will tell you the story of Canera."

"Ah, the tale of Canera," the old hermit reminisced with Ronan. "It was fifty three years ago now. Canera the holy hermit lived in a valley beyond yonder mountain range. She had aged, but was certain that valley was not her place of resurrection. She saw in a night vision a pillar of fire soaring into the sky above each of Christ's communities in Erin. The fire above Inis Cathaig was higher than all others. "Then that must be my place of resurrection" she said. She set off by foot until she arrived at the ferry across the Sound. The ferryman rowed her over and returned, leaving her alone on the shore. Holy Senan, our founder, went to the shore. "I have come to live on this island," she told him, "for God has told me this is to be my place of resurrection." "No woman shall ever live on this island" Senan replied, "this is my island and only brothers shall share it." "How can you say that?" Canera answered. "A woman was good enough to be Christ's mother. Christ revealed himself to women after his resurrection before he revealed himself to men. The women looked after Jesus wherever he traveled on his missions, and women were the first members of his church." "No woman shall live on this island" Senan insisted, "and you will not come beyond this tide mark where you now stand." "You have no power to thwart God's will" Canera told Senan. "God has told me that you will give me Holy Communion on this spot and that this will be my place of resurrection." "The story goes," the old hermit went on, "that Senan gave her the chalice on the shore, and that as she drank the holy blood she fell down dead. He would neither touch nor take her to be buried. She stayed there, lying where she fell, until wind and waves carried her away."

"An amazing story," Ronan thought as he lay down to sleep, and over following days he began to piece things together. Their mystery woman had died through an accident, or natural causes, and had been swept up on the shore. The hermits, conscious of that tale about Senan, had thought it best for the winds and the waves to take her, and so avoid questions, even scandal, at a woman being buried among monks vowed to celibacy. When Ronan confided his theory to Aidan he was assured that discreet enquiries had confirmed that this was indeed so. "Do you think?" Ronan asked, "that now ordinary guests are welcomed the brothers might accept women, too?"

To Aidan, Ronan was a delight—open, friendly, happy—but he now needed to grow more mature in the handling human conflict. Aidan assumed the role of a mentor. "You know," Aidan said, "I don't think some of our brothers have been fair to Senan. Senan had a beautiful friendship with his sister, and he encouraged some women to found a sister community on the mainland. Senan was a prophet. He saw things very clearly, in black and white. Some of the finest leaders, such as Brendan, from Birr, and Ciaran, from Clonmacnoise, brought brothers here to consult with him. He insisted on the Rule that women should not come to the island because, unlike our mainland monasteries, where everyone mixes with one another, only men vowed to celibacy live here, I think some of them have not understood where their loves really reside. They have run away from their feelings, and they might just as easily run into a woman's bed. I think this idea that Senan was hostile to women came from more recent brothers who have fears and shadows they have not faced. Our Lord had similar experiences with Pharisees. We can learn much from those experiences. We shall work at increasing openness to women here, but I think it will not be in my time that women and men share this one small island."

Both Aidan and Ronan thought more about Canera's apparently prophetic vision. Was it her human desire which surfaced in that vision, or was it God's will that the island should be a place of resurrection for a woman? Was Senan's resistance God's will, or did it stem from his desire to control? Was he afraid of women or was he concerned to safeguard the purity of the vows? And was the more recent episode of the woman's body on the shore a co-incidence or a sign? A desire grew in Aidan that one day this isle should be a place of welcome to men and women pilgrims alike. But that would be a work for his successor, for his term as Abba of Inis Cathaig ended after five brief years.

chapter 6

FIRES OF CONTROVERSY

626–9 THE EASTER DISPUTE AND THE TRANSFER

After the dramas of the Pilgrimage and the challenges of Inis Cathaig, Durrow never quite regained the color it once had for Aidan. Moreover, a new abbot named Cummian was appointed who, although his prestige and ability was widely admired in Ireland, resonated less well with Aidan than had Bechan. Cummian had been abandoned by his parents, and brought up in the community at Killeedy led by saint Ita, "the foster mother of the saints of Ireland." Later he studied at Findbarr's school at Cork where he learned a love of poetry. His brother became King of Connaught, and between them they exercised great influence. Cummian's old tutor, Colman, wrote of him::

> Of Erin's priests, it were not meet
> That one should sit in Gregory's seat,
> Except that Cummian crossed the sea.
> For he Rome's ruler well might be.

Instead of assigning Aidan a new role, he asked him to take temporary charge of some aspect of the work when a senior brother was on leave or unwell. Aidan took on these tasks gladly, and truly believed that God was as much in the daily chores as in the occasional excitements.

Although Aidan's own life was uneventful, changes were taking place at Durrow and in the Irish churches which were anything but. Throughout the churches in the Irish midlands intellectual and spiritual learning experienced a burst of new life. Their libraries accumulated books by the great teachers of the Christian world. Brothers wrote tracts of all kinds, some in Irish as well as Latin and the monasteries began to attract students from as far as Francia. Eminent among these teachers was Cummian. He wrote poems and penitentials, a commentary on Mark's Gospel, and much else, drawing extensively from many theologians. He established regular contact with Segene, who became Iona's abbot in 623, thereby restoring the abbacy to Columba's clan, the Ui Neill. Segene was emerging as a strong leader and began to take an active interest in the affairs of the Irish church. The two abbots agreed to increase the flow of brothers between Durrow and Iona.

Cummian took it upon himself to take a lead in a dispute about the date of Easter. Roman missionaries in Britain wrote to Irish church leaders asking them to change to the Roman dating of Easter. This was followed by a letter from Pope Honorius 1. He pleaded with them not to celebrate Easter on a date different to that agreed by the synodical decrees "of the whole world," and never to celebrate it on the same date as the Jews celebrated Passover. Some of the Irish objected to that first phrase. Were they not part of the whole world? It was not their fault that they had not been able to attend any of those synods that had changed the customs they inherited, as they thought, from Christ's apostles. The pilgrim routes to the great churches in Rome and Gaul had been cut off to them following the vandals' invasions, but their absence from these synods was not intentional. And the Irish had nothing against Jews—they knew no Jews.

This was a complicated issue. Cummian decided that before making rash statements he would undertake a year's investigation into the methods of computing the yearly cycles which determined the date of the Spring Equinox, and therefore of the Passover and Easter. He retreated to a cell not far from Durrow to do this. Following this year of study Cummian consulted Irish church leaders. They assembled near Durrow, and decided to celebrate Easter with the universal church the following year. Until the outcry! First, the Clonmacnoise brothers refused to accept this decision, then Cummian learned that Segene was against the change, and expected the Columban monasteries throughout Ireland to follow Iona's practice. There was such a fuss that the plan was postponed and Cummian sent emissaries to Rome to discuss this matter further.

Aidan began to think through this whole, vexed issue. He knew that the first Christians had celebrated Christ's resurrection on the third day after the Passover. He knew that, according to the Old Testament method of fixing the date, the Jewish Passover was the fourteenth day of Nisan (March in Ireland), as stated in Leviticus 23:5 and that this was to be a "perpetual ordinance." He knew that, according to the Gospel of John (for example John 19:14), this was the day that Jesus was crucified in Jerusalem, even though the other Gospels placed it on 15 Nisan. He knew that a letter of Irenaeus (who was born in Smyrna and became Bishop of the church of Celts at Lyons, d. 202) stated that Polycarp, the bishop of Smyrna, observed Easter on the fourteenth day of the moon, whatever day of the week that might be, following the tradition which he claimed to have derived from St. John the Apostle, whom he knew. Since then the Irish had gladly changed Easter to the Sunday after Passover, but Aidan agreed with Bishop Irenaeus who had begged the Pope to allow people to follow their local customs in such matters. Worship was a matter of the heart; it was in essence voluntary—so why spoil it by uniform regulation? Surely the Irish should be allowed to celebrate Easter in the way that was natural to them? If they went on pilgrimage to Rome, they would, of course, celebrate Easter on the same day as The Romans, but if a Roman came to Ireland, why should they not do the same as the Irish?

As discussions in the monasteries became more detailed and intense, Aidan and his brothers began to realize that there were different ways to compute the date of the Spring Equinox, from which the date of Passover was calculated, and that these computations were complicated.

The 325 Council of Nicaea decided that Easter shall be the first Sunday after the first full moon on or after the Spring Equinox, but if Sunday coincides with the Jewish Passover it shall be the first Sunday after that. The Council made no ruling about the different ways of computing the date of the Passover. It might seem simple to wait until a day when the hours of dark and light are equal (the Spring Equinox) and wait until the first full moon after that. But to compute this in advance, in order to prepare for the festival, is a complicated process that involves calendars based on the movements of both the moon and the sun, and these calendars and computations diverged from one place (for example Antioch) to another (for example Alexandria). The Irish thought the equinox happened on 25th March, the continentals on 21st March. To the Irish, whose faith reflected God in creation, it was nonsense to celebrate the resurrection of Christ, the Light of the world, on a day when there was more darkness than light.

Various tables were produced that attempted to calculate Easter for a series of years. British and Irish churches used a calculation table (Celtic-84) that was similar to one approved by Saint Jerome, based on an eighty-four year cycle. However, by now it had become obsolete and had been replaced by those of Victorius of Aquitaine and, more accurately, those of Dionysius Exiguus. This 84-year cycle gave way to the Alexandrine computus in stages

As the Celtic world established renewed contact with the Continent it became aware of the divergence. The first clash over the matter came in Gaul in 602, when Columbanus resisted pressure from the local bishops to conform. Most groups, like the southern Irish, accepted the updated tables with relatively little difficulty, with the last significant objectors being the monks from Columba's monasteries. The southern Irish accepted the common Easter calculation at the Synod of Mag Léne around 630

But one thing the Irish were sure about: they observed the Equinox on March 25th, not 21st as did the Romans. If they moved it to the 21st they would find themselves celebrating Easter in certain years on a day when there was more dark than light. What a nonsense: Christ, the True Sun, rising in glory, and his very own creation not reciprocating!

There was one more thing about which he had a niggling sense of unease. Why did Honorius think it would be so dreadful to celebrate Easter on the same day as the Jews celebrated Passover? The tone of his letter reflected a disdain for Jews: Aidan thought that they, like everyone else, should be treated as children of God. Yet he was conscious of the apostle Paul's injunction "let there not be disagreements among you." If Durrow had accepted the new calendar Aidan would have observed it for the greater good, though with sadness. Since, however, their mother monastery at Iona seemed set to uphold what they had always maintained, Aidan could not deviate from its path. He thought that the focus of a Christian's energy should be the Gospel—sharing it and living it. Administrative matters, even such an important matter as the date of Easter, should never displace the pre-eminence of the Gospel. John, the loved disciple, and the Celtic peoples, had always treated rules as servants, not masters, and he had no desire that the church should become rigid. The issue remained unresolved during Aidan's lifetime. It came to a head a decade after his death.

A summer and winter passed. The dispute was simmering on and Aidan found himself thinking more about the apostle John. He stopped by at the scriptorium where a talented brother was illuminating the eagle, the symbol of John's Gospel. As the eagle alone of all birds could gaze into the face of the sun without being blinded, so John, alone of all apostles, could gaze into the face of Love. Aidan longed that their churches might reflect the ways of John.

Brothers brought some goods they had downloaded from a ship that had come from the Mediterranean—these included pigments for the scriptorium. A crew member had given them a message from the monastery in Syria. This was confused, but the gist of it was that the lost Gospel had not been recovered. That night Aidan dreamed. He dreamed of the Gospel of John a brother had been illuminating. The eagle flew from the page to the Jews in Rome, and they saw as John saw. The eagle then flew to the Prophet Muhammed and his God-honoring friends, and the same thing happened. Then the eagle changed its shape.

It turned into a key.

Another winter passed. They were uneventful months. Aidan fulfilled his duties thoughtfully, yet, if he was honest, he pined for something more, though he knew not what. Segene was keen to sustain a circulation of brothers between Ireland and Iona. Aidan had the impression that Cummian had mentioned him when the two abbots discussed the Easter question and practical monastic matters.

After Easter, in the year of our Lord 629, he and three others were asked to transfer to their mother monastery across the sea in Alba. They traveled north to their sister monastery at Derry by horse. Aidan's love of horses pulsed through him anew. They rode over two hundred miles, staying overnight with various communities, until they came to Derry. There they stayed a week before two Derry brothers accompanied them to the ferry across the sea to Iona.

Aidan left Durrow a capable, trustworthy person who could cross new frontiers. He had equipped himself adequately as a scholar, but was not the sort to spend the rest of his life buried in books. He would never again see his beloved Ireland. He would, however, have to visit places he did not yet know within himself, and be would be tested almost to destruction.

PART TWO

TESTING FIRES
Iona and the Middle Years

chapter 7

THE FLAME FADES

629

The sky growled as Aidan and five brothers traveled north to their monastery at Derry and then crossed the sea to Iona. During the five days of hard rowing, with nights spent on the islands of Rathlin, Islay, and Colonsay they rehearsed what they knew about Iona since Columba had established its monastery two generations previously. It was a legend in Aidan's head years before he set eyes upon it. Older Durrow brothers had regaled the younger monks with stories about it.

Hunters and gatherers had lived there from ancient times, stepping lightly from site to site as the seasons turned. Fort dwellers had once peopled the hill that tops the Machair. Locals knew Iona as Innis nan Druinneach, meaning Isle of Crafts People. They said the Isle's school of carving was famous long before the Christians arrived, and a burial ground had been set aside for them.

They knew that before Columba had disembarked at Iona he had stopped at Dunadd, on the mainland, to meet with his cousin, Conall, king of the Irish colony of Dalriada in Britain. It was Conall who had offered him the island. Columba was not at first convinced that Iona should be the site of his new monastery. His heart was in Ireland. He felt that if he could see his beloved homeland from Iona, his affections would for ever be torn between the two places. He had asked God for the gift of purity. The pure can only serve one master, so Columba climbed Iona's highest peak: if he could see Ireland, he would not settle there. He could not see Ireland. He named that peak "the Hill of Never Looking Back," and he and his twelve brothers began their great monastic task.

Aidan recollected that although Iona graced the far edge of Dalriada, it was on the strategic waterways which linked Dalriada to the northern area her Irish and Christian rulers hoped also to colonize. The Picts had inflicted a serious defeat on the colony in 560, three years before Columba came. Could they do it again? Columba, the supreme strategist, made sure they did not attempt that in his day. He led a peace mission north through the Great Glen to the court of the Picts' King Brude. There, beside Lough Ness, he prayed for Brude's son to be healed. Would those bonds still hold, Aidan wondered? Columba ended his days on Iona amid spiritual signs and struggles and shapings of peoples. Two generations had since passed. Was Aidan coming into a period of decline or renewal for Iona?

Iona came in to view and they landed. They were welcomed, fed and taken to their cells. The monastery was more compact than Durrow. Around the chapel clustered the monks' wattle and thatch cells, and facing the west door of the church, on top of a rocky hillock called Tor-Abb, commanding a view over the straits, was the Abba's cell. Everyone had their food served from a great flat rock in the refectory. Bread and milk, fish and eggs were the daily diet, with some meat on Sundays and other special days. Hospitality, of course, was a sacred duty, and the guest house was being further extended.

The Seniors had oversight of the five daily services, the copying of Scriptures and the teaching of students. The workers, or lay brothers, hunted seals, cultivated barley, milked cows, slaughtered beef cattle, and fished in the river Shiel. Horses were used to carry things. Fertility was increased by prayer and importation of rich soils from other places. These "island foot soldiers," as they were called, marched out at dawn pulling the foot plough to the cultivatable land, singing God's praises. It took a week for a man to plough one acre. The younger, fitter men worked the farm, fished, milled, and cooked. Like Durrow, Psalms and Gospels were copied in the scriptorium between the hours of prayer. There was a baker, an herb gardener and so on, and there were no less than sixty who could, if need be, row the boats. A bard once wrote of them:

> Wonderful the warriors who lived in Hi
> Thrice fifty in the monastic Rule
> With their boats along the ocean
> Threescore men a-rowing.

The brothers slept in single cells. They bred seals on the nearby Isle of Erraid for food, skins, and oil. Some of the six hundred monks were skilled as blacksmiths, glass makers, wood turners or shoemakers. Some used querns to gruel the grain by hand. There was a granary and the mill for drying out the grain before grinding. The brothers wore tunics with hooded cowls of undyed wool, similar to those worn at Durrow, but as the sheep were mostly black, they had a darker color. The Abba, in contrast, wore a white cowl. Sandals were worn out of doors, and the ancient Christian courtesy of washing others' feet was practiced. As at Durrow the monks in life vows wore the tonsure that Irish bards had adopted from of old: they shaved the hair on the forehead, but let it grow long at the back.

Two very aged brothers had known Columba. His influence could still be felt. They called one of his poems "The Quern Song" because he sang it as he milled the corn, and they, too, still sang it—Aidan liked to encourage people to sing songs in the work place as well as in church. Columba had slept on a stone pillow and made sacrifices. The current monks were tough, too, and they were righteous men.

Before Aidan and his brothers had disembarked an old fisherman had told them "they say Iona lays a blessing on every eye that sees it," and excitement had mounted within him. Yet gray cloud and gray, gray granite blanketed his eyes and dismantled his imaginings. Encircled by dark mountains, Iona felt glum compared to Durrow. Where were the jokes and sounds of laughter, and the families? Iona's climate, its terrain, its occupants all seemed to frown. Some inexplicable grayness entered Aidan's soul. He was vowed to obedience and would give it his best, but he feared lest his well should run dry.

* * *

Grayness was there, but so also was Abbot Segene. He was the fifth abbot of Iona from 623 for twenty five years and of the same tribe, the Ui Neill, as Columba. He reached out. He established a church on Rathlinn Island, and extended the hermit cells on Hinbar Isle. He invited Aidan to take turns at different duties in order to get to know how the monastery worked, and so that Segene might get to know where his gifts lay. Aidan had little time to grovel in the grayness. Over a period of nine months he assisted in the chapel and at the altar, in the guest quarters and the scriptorium; he mentored novice monks, and was anamchara to several brothers. Gradually, his determination to do his duties well, and the satisfaction this brought him, pushed negative feelings into the background.

Under Segene the monastery began to record sayings and stories about Columba. Stories were recounted aloud during the silent evening meals. They lifted Aidan's spirits above the gray. Each Sunday Segene would take one of the founder's sayings and show how it applied to some matter that had arisen. Although Columba himself had not written down a Rule, Segene thought it important that novices in all the Columban monasteries were taught what he called The Rule so that it would stay with them for life. Some important parts of the Rule were:

> Three labors in the day—prayers, work, and reading.
> Forgiveness from the heart towards everyone.
> If you are given something, give something away.
> Offer constant prayers for those who cause you trouble.
> Only sleep if you are tired; only eat if you are hungry.
> Love God with all your strength and your neighbour as yourself.
> Have a mind prepared for red and white martyrdom.

By the last words the brothers understood that they should often rehearse in their minds how they would give all to Christ if ever they suffered the pain of being killed because of their faith, as were the early martyrs in Rome who shed blood. By white martyrdom they meant that they were willing to leave behind home and comforts and lay down their lives to serve Christ in another people, if God should so call them, as had Columba. There was a third martyrdom, that of prayer and fasting from home comforts, which everyone could aspire to. Aidan thought much about these martyrdoms: would he be willing to lay down his life for another people?

The story of Columba's death was etched in their hearts. More than once Aidan fell asleep re-living that story: Columba waited until the busy Easter period was over, for he did not want his death to detract from those celebrations. In May he toured the island in a cart, spoke to the workers on the land, and blessed the island. Six days later he visited the barn and thanked God that there was plenty of grain for all his monks. He told his attendant, Diormit, "His day is called the Sabbath, which means rest. It is indeed a Sabbath for me, for it is the last day of my life. After midnight, when the Lord's Day begins, I shall go the way of our fathers." On the way back Columba sat down to rest. His white packhorse came to him and, sensing his master was about to leave this earth, laid his head on Columba's chest and made loud cries of grief. Then Columba ascended the hill and gave a prophetic blessing over the community. He returned to the monastery and transcribed, as was his custom, some more verses from the Book of Psalms. The last verse he completed was Psalm 34:10, "They who seek the Lord shall lack no good thing." He gave some final words to his brothers, and remained some hours in silence. As soon as the bell tolled for midnight, in a last burst of energy he ran into the unlit church. It was bathed in a heavenly light. He knelt by the altar. Diormit raised Columba's hand and he died blessing his brothers. Their faces were full of grief; Columba's was transfixed with joy.

That night some friends were fishing in the valley of the River Find. They saw an immense pillar of fire, which seemed to illuminate the whole earth like the summer sun at noon. After that the column penetrated the heavens and darkness followed, as if the sun had just set. Aidan re-awakened with a start. That was when he was born. That was why he was named Little Flame!

One thing Aidan loved was the horse circling, the feel of flesh against flesh, the panting, pulsing thrill of movement, and the bonding. The story of Columba's pack horse renewed his craving for a horse he could call his own. In April Segene asked Aidan to join a working party to prepare the nearby Isle of Hinba for summer retreats. Aidan knew that blessed Columba had spent weeks there alone. Once some brothers landed and heard singing in unknown tongues and saw light brighter than that of any lamp pour through the cracks of his cell door. Later they built a cell on the small hill for Columba's mother, Eithne, who lived there in her final years. Since then more cells had been built. Usually about five brothers went by boat to repair the cells and tend the meagre crops ready for the first group to make retreat. Each new task made Aidan envision some further dimension of light, as it were, streaming through cracks.

Segene's demeanor remained calm amid many visitors, many pressures. Roman emissaries continued to urge him to change the date on which they observed the Paschal Feast. Segene re-iterated their contrary view. Segene took time to relax. He liked nothing better than to sit on the rock they called Columba's seat, looking out to sea. They said it was here that Columba wrote the poem which the brothers delighted to repeat:

> Father, do not allow thunder and lightning,
>> Lest we be shattered by its fear and fire.
> We fear you, the terrible one, believing there is none like you.
>> All songs praise you throughout the host of angels.
> Let the summits of heaven, too, praise you with roaming lightning,
>> O most loving Jesus, O righteous King of Kings.
>> The flame of God's love dwells in my heart
>> As a jewel of gold is placed in a silver dish.

Aidan observed Segene and aspired to remain calm amid competing pressures. He, too, sat on that seat, and pondered those words: "The flame of God's love dwells in my heart."

Segene's concern to build good relations with other peoples was not limited to those in Ireland and Pict lands. Columba's descendant ruled Dalriada from Dunadd, which on a good day the brothers could sail to in four hours. The fort had grown into a bustling community. In 616 it took in a significant number of refugees from the Saxon royal family of Northumbria and the Dalriadan king offered them a treaty whereby they had the rights of foster children. Segene arranged that several brothers should reside at Dunadd to lead the prayers and to teach and assist the Saxon royal party, also that some of these exiles would spend periods with the monks on Iona. Aidan would soon get to know them, but not quite in the way he would have hoped.

chapter 8

THE EBBE AFFAIR

Occasionally Aidan visited Dunadd. He was introduced to Acha, the exiled Queen of Northumbria whose husband had been slain, and to her staff. Her children were now part of the Dalriada ruling family, who had offered them fosterage in return for treaty obligations. The men served Dalriada as warriors. Oswy, the oldest of Acha'a children, seemed to Aidan somewhat distant. Aidan warmed to his younger brother, Oswald. He was a robust horseman, a devout Christian and a warm human being. On visits to Iona Oswald sometimes lingered in the chapel, praying with his hands open to heaven. A Saxon warrior would never let their hands wander from the hilt of their sword, so Oswald's praying hands spoke much about his changed values. Aidan had little opportunity for personal conversation with Oswald, however. There was an elder half brother, Eanfrith whose mother was their late father's first wife, Bebba. Eanfrith fled to the Picts further north, and married a sister of the Picts' king Gartnait. They had a son named Talorcan. They occasionally visited Dunadd, but Aidan never met them. He was briefly introduced to their sister Ebbe.

During these visits to Dunadd Aidan thought about how God revealed to Columba in a dream that he should appoint Aidan McGabran as King of Dalriada even though Columba himself preferred another. His namesake was the first king in Britain to be anointed in Christ's name. When King Aidan's heir, Eochaid Bude gave Oswald and Oswy refuge, they were minors, aged 12 and 4 respectively. Eochaid gave them fosterage, which both Saxon and Irish laws upheld. Eochaid stood as godfather for the children, and made his son, Domnall Brecc, Oswald's foster brother. Oswald married a relative of Eochaid Bude. She bore a son named Ethelwald, but the birth damaged her and she died not long thereafter. Oswald's fosterage, baptism and marriage formed a kind of healing bond between Dalriada and Northumbria, strengthened now by greater spiritual input from Iona under Segene.

As for their sister, Ebbe, Aidan felt sorry for her. While her brothers hunted, fought battles and married, she had to stay at Dunadd with her mother. She had a far away look in her eyes, which were set in an oval face, with a pronounced nose and chin and flowing, black hair. Her body was well-proportioned, fit for a princess. She used to walk up and down Dunadd's halls in her long, thistle-purple dresses, lost in thought. Aidan wondered what was really going on underneath her royal finery. In late Spring Segene asked to see Aidan, and he found out.

Domnall Brecc was the suitor of an Irish princess, but secretly he began to have doubts about her and to harbor thoughts of Ebbe, who knew nothing of this. At the same time a fine young man of the west Saxons was given shelter at the garrison. He was a cousin of the West Saxons' king, a keen hunter and a man of adventure. As young men do, he had wanted to explore the world beyond his kingdom. His name was Aelfride. He fell madly in love with Ebbe, and she with him. This was the last thing either her family, or its Dalriadan protectors had in mind for their two peoples, for the west Saxons were pagans and potential enemies. Oswald had long talks with Ebbe and Domnall Brecc. He discovered that Ebbe had no feeling for Domnall Brecc, that her feelings for Aelfride were indeed passionate but that she was confused, for she had also felt drawn to take vows as a nun. Oswald had asked to talk over the situation with Segene.

Segene informed Aidan that Oswald had asked the monastery to take Ebbe under its protection. She needed distance and time apart. Since Iona allowed no women in the monastery, Segene had decided to open up the little isle between Iona and the Mull ferry as a refuge for Ebbe and her attendants. "We require an experienced brother, with discretion, to have spiritual oversight of this women's isle, and especially of Ebbe herself. I ask you to provide this" he informed Aidan. That was not all. Someone Segene refused to name had forced himself upon Ebbe and now she hated herself. Worse, she was pregnant.

Aidan grieved. He knew that women who become victims of rape feel violated in the deepest parts of their body and often dislike, even loathe themselves. He knew that they lose trust in men and shrink from touch. Would Ebbe feel this way, or would she just feel guilt he wondered? "Many women blame themselves," Segene said. "Blame is a way of avoiding the pain, but it also prevents the healing. The deepest wound that needs healing is the shame."

Weeks of hard labor transformed that rocky isle into a place of welcome. The task of digging the ground, cutting and transporting logs, and constructing buildings fit for royal women required the help of many, at first from Dunadd, but as word spread, married people from Mull joined in the enterprise. The private dwellings were larger and more modern than those at the monastery. To create the communal building a large oak beam was secured deep in the ground. String was tied to its top, to make a circle around it on the earth. Posts were secured at six points in this circle. Supple branches were inter-twined between these to make the walls.

Ebbe arrived with a blank stare, and went to her chamber without a word. In due time, she delivered a girl. She was given a nurse. Aidan decided that they should create an herb garden outside her chamber, in the hope that she would begin to take an interest in it. She asked about a plant named Inula Helinium. Christians from Gaul had brought this and it had flourished at the church dedicated to St. Martin some miles south of Dunadd. It had a yellow daisy-like flower, and its roots had medicinal qualities. Ebbe began to care for the herb garden.

She liked spinning—at Dunadd she had made beautiful dresses and covers for the chalice. Aidan outlined a project for new altar cloths, and consulted her about the designs and materials. Ebbe liked to read, and they agreed on the books that would be brought from the monastery library. Some unseen barrier still remained, however, until one day Aidan confided in her his childhood secrets, and his heartbreak when he left Soirsese for Durrow. It was then that she asked to talk with him. "I had set my heart on being a bride of Christ, she confided, "but now I have a child. I must be a mother."

Weeks went by and Aidan returned to the monastery—until this affair took another unexpected turn. "Ebbe is acting in a strange way again" Segene informed Aidan, "and it was reported to me that her bed was empty all night, not for the first time, and that she refuses to talk about it. As you know, the Northumbrian exiles are our honored guests. We cannot require them to adopt the full monastic Rule; we must not alienate them but neither can we afford to let any cause of scandal go unchecked. This whole affair needs intelligent but sensitive handling. I assign you to Women's Island for another season. Get to the bottom of this affair. It is important that there is a godly outcome."

The question always in Aidan's mind was how he could get Ebbe to tell him what was troubling her. On the feast day of Mary they arranged to go by boat to some hermit cells on Mull. As they ate their lunch Ebbe confided in Aidan. "Aelfride, Prince of the West Saxons met me at Dunadd. Recently he came to the island. . He took me to Mull on his boat. We spent the night together. He begs me to marry him. He is a pagan."

"Tell me more about him," Aidan asked. "He is strong, handsome, and kind," she said. "Could he love God?" Aidan asked. She hesitated. "Oswald made a friend of him because he wants to build goodwill with the west Saxons and to introduce them to the Faith. They talked of a visit, but not at this time. The Dalriadans would not support that." "Would Aelfride agree to meet with you and me together?" he asked. "I will see" she said.

That was how Aidan came to meet Aelfride. He liked him. He had a mop of tousled hair, and his face laughed. He delighted in adventure and noticed little things. The strength in his body was tender; he was a good man. Setting aside the monks' Rule they enjoyed an evening with good food and ale, they shared experiences and told stories. Aidan talked about his home in Ireland and Aelfride told about his family and their farm. It was near Ox Ford, or Ohsnafordia as the Saxons call it. They grew crops that Aidan knew nothing of, for they had more soil and sun.

Before night became day Aidan asked Aelfride some hard questions. "Many warriors leave their wives while they fight and hunt, and often they lie with women while they are away. On their return they use their wife for pleasure and to bear heirs, but that is not how we Christians understand marriage," he said. Aelfride grasped him by the arm "Believe me," he said, "I do not want a marriage like that. I love Ebbe, I will cherish her as my own body, I swear it." They talked about Ebbe's desire to be a bride of Christ. "I think your people are pagans?" Aidan asked Aelfride. "Ohsnafordia is a burgeoning town on a trade route to Mercia," he said. "Christians travel through. Some of our thanes have married Christians from other kingdoms. Some of us can read a little Latin. I have seen a copy of a Christian Gospel in Latin." "And what did you make of that?" Aidan asked him. "It stays in my heart—especially the stories of Christ, the Son of God. I believe they are true." "Can I help you in any way?" Aidan asked. "Yes, teach me to pray." Aidan felt a rippling of the wind of God. They repeated a prayer until Aelfride could remember it and say it each day of his life.

As the darkest hour drew near Aidan asked Aelfride "Would you, if Ebbe became certain she was called to be a bride of Christ, let her go?" He paused a long time. "I would" he said. "And in these circumstances would you be willing to let Aelfride go?" he asked Ebbe. There was a longer pause. "I hope so," she said. In the end, they did let each other go, and Aelfride departed for his home without her.

Sixteen months later Ebbe married Aelfride in Ox Forde in the presence of Oswald, and Domnall Brecc married an Irish Princess Aidan had yet to meet. Ebbe's refuge at Iona was ever after known as Women's Island.

chapter 9

"KING" ARTHUR

Arthur. The bard's words those years ago at Kildare about the warrior who "led the legions of Christ" had faded from Aidan's memory. Until Segene asked him to be responsible for the monastery's work at Dunadd for a season. There, at the royal garrison barely a day passed that did not bring some new tale of this man. A legend was in the making.

A fort had existed at Dunadd for long ages. Once small, it was now a little city encircled by a stone wall. King Aidan had gathered round him his sons, his warriors and their families; at Dunadd, in contrast to Iona, talk flowed as fast as did the mead. Returning warriors bragged about their exploits on the battle field and with women, but stories of heroes who had given their lives in battle, and even of prophecies, also circulated—no doubt changed by many tellings.

"Have you heard the prophecy that Berchan the bard made about Arthur? He has not died, he only sleeps. The people will wait for him many years and then he will return." "Have you heard about Arthur and the Round Table?" Aidan had not. "He gathered Christian men from four races round this table—Britons, Irish Scots, Picts, and Saxons—there they made plans for a kingdom fit for Christ, where no woman would be molested and where no child would come to harm." Aidan enquired where this Round Table was, and who were the people who gathered round it, but no one knew. A desire grew in Aidan to sift the real from the imagined facts of Arthur's life. This was not just out of curiosity. Since coming to Alba he had pondered much on the arts of leadership and the myths that shape peoples. He wanted to discover the real Arthur. He determined, when opportunity came, to seek a meeting with the king.

65

It was the custom for Peadar, the Latin Scholar, to inform new brothers of the history and myths of their people, and to make sure they grasped the background of those they served. Aidan knew that the Irish had colonized the kingdom of Dalriada and that Columba's cousin was its first king—the first-among-equals of various sub kingdoms led by different branches of the clan. He knew that Columba had been regarded as its spiritual leader, and that his anointing of Aidan was the first Christian consecration of a ruler in any land known to them. He knew that Columba had questioned King Aidan about a successor to his kingdom. The king answered that he did not know which of his three sons, Arthur, Eochaid Find or Domangart would be king. The far-seeing Columba said that none of them would be—since they would all be slain in battle. Echoing the biblical Samuel's choice of the youngest of many brothers to be King of Israel, Columba urged King Aidan to send to him his younger sons. The one that rushed into his arms first would, he said, become the new king. Eochaid Buide was first, and it was he who was now their king. But it was Arthur about whom he wanted to know more—especially why a man of their race should be so loved by Britons.

He learned that in the years before King Aidan came to Dalriada there had been a falling away from the Faith among the Britons, and even among the few Christian Picts. Pagan ways had returned. The poor were oppressed, women were badly treated and God was despised. Bishop Kentigern, grandson of the great King Loth who had ruled the Orkneys as well as his own Britons by the river Forth, had to flee to the Cymry in the south west. The Christian parties were defeated and in disarray. Aidan wanted to know how the tide had been turned, and what part Arthur had played.

After a much delayed meeting with the king, and many conversations with Peadar, he pieced the following picture together: Arthur's father was crowned king of Dalriada in 574, but before that the Irish had settled in other parts of Alba; in fact King Aidan already ruled the small but strategic eastern kingdom of Manann that lies between the river Avon and the Forth. Picts to the north, Northumbrians to the south, and the battered remnants of the Britons to the west panted like hungry dogs to devour one another. Upon his move to Dunadd, Aidan put Arthur in charge of Manadd. There Arthur strengthened the fort of Camelot that the Romans had built a short distance north of their Antonine wall. Arthur was not only a warrior of skill and courage, he also had a gift of friendship. He built up alliances with any tribe that showed good will. His devout father wished to be a monk more than a warrior, and did in fact end his life in a monastery. He deputed Arthur to lead many battles in his name. Thus, although Arthur was never king in name, he became commander of the combined forces. Although Arthur was a man of the flesh, he shared his father's strong faith. He made it his aim to rally the Christian parties among the different races, and reclaim lands ravaged by greed and violence that had once been Christian. These he did not occupy himself, but bequeathed to allies of other races who would rule them in the spirit of Christ.

A superb horseman, Arthur built up defenses on strategic high places and fought twelve decisive battles between the two great walls built by the Romans—the southern wall built under the Emperor Hadrian and the northern wall built under the Emperor Antony. The Britons, before their defeats, had called their commander in chief "Dux Brittanorum." That was why he had heard Arthur being called "Dux Brittanorum" in the chatter of the mead hall.

Arthur won his battles in alliance with the Christian Britons in the west. The first battle was by the river Glen, the following four were fought by the rivers of Douglas, near the Lough Lomond. The sixth was won against pagan Picts and Saxons by the eastern river that leads to the great Rock of Bass where hermits pray. Then Arthur fought the pagan Britons, aided by the Saxons, in the inland forest near the river Tweed. Many pagans were slain. Their famous bard, Merlin, escaped into the forest where he wandered like a man who has lost his mind. Hearing of this, Bishop Kentigern led a search party into the forest. He sat with his old friend for many hours. He prayed for him and baptized him in the name of Christ, though only God knows whether that poor shell of a once mighty bard understood, for not long after he was found alone, unkempt and dead. The eighth battle took place further west, by the fort near the river Gala. The pagan Britons had joined with the Saxons to extend their territory northwards. This was the battle in which Arthur rode ahead with a great banner of Mary, mother of Christ. People said he had brought this back from Jerusalem, but Eochaid Buide told them that Arthur never went to Jerusalem—the image of Christ's mother had been painted on his shield by a thane skilled in art. That place is now called The Vale of Woe because so many were slain. The ninth battle was fought by the river Leven which flows from the Lough Lomond. The next two battles were fought near Dun Eidyn, near the mouth of the river Forth and at Iuddeu, a day's journey away. The twelfth battle was on the Hill of Badon near the river Avon. Arthur was generous and far sighted in victory. He gave the lands he had wrested from the Saxons to three brothers, for he perceived they were true and trustworthy leaders who would be worthy servants of the King of kings. He returned Rheged to Urien, who married Arthur's sister, Morgan. To Llew he gave Lodoneis, which had once been the land of King Loth of the Picts. To Arawn he gave the northern part which they called Yscotland.

Aidan was bemused to learn that sailors from merchant ships had heard tales of Arthur's exploits among people as far away as Gaul, and southern Britain, whose land the Saxons call Wales. Aidan asked Peadar how this could be. "When Bishop Kentigern was exiled far south among the Britons," Peadar explained, "he told them stories of our battles and the faith of our heroes—especially of Arthur. It is no wonder they took him to their hearts, for Arthur included the Cymri among his trusted circle. During the mass migration caused by the Great Plague these Britons took these stories across to the land in Gaul they call Little Britain. It is like this, each land wants its heroes. We Irish have our Twelve Apostles of Christ, and we imagine our holy Brigid to be the nurse who was present at Christ's birth. They, too, want their Christian heroes. I think you have only heard the half of this yet. You mark my words. In the ages to come many will be the stories and songs of Arthur among the Britons."

In time Aidan cleared up the mystery of the Round Table. "You have the wrong idea of a table in your head" Peadar told him. "The truth is that Arthur more than once gathered his allies to meet with him at the great fort at Iuddeu. At the foot of the fort is the circle of grass they call The Knot. These leaders included Britons and Scotti, one or two Picts and even a Saxon. They were not just warriors, they were friends, bound together by their faith in Christ, and by their hopes of God's kingdom. They sat around the Knot to confer, to eat, sometimes to jest—and to pray. Arthur had no secrets—he liked to meet in the open—and the people loved him for this. I think it was one of the locals who joked "That's their round table," and ever since, that's what people have called it"

There was one legend that Aidan could neither fully believe nor completely dismiss. He had heard tales of Arthur's death, of a magical sword, and of his being taken on a royal boat to burial on an Isle of Avalon, which no one could now find but which would one day appear again. He found one further opportunity to ask the king about this. "It is quite simple, and, I am sorry to tell you, rather unpleasant" Eochaid replied. He told how in 582 Arthur led his forces against the invading Picts at his fortress at Camelot, in Manann. They were put to flight and, just as blessed Columba had foretold, he and his brother Echoid Finn, and over three hundred others were slain. Warriors brought their bodies back to the Camelot fort. His sister Morgan, who dearly loved her brother, came to the scene, washed and embalmed his body, dressed him in finest clothes and placed him on a bier. Below the fort is a stretch of bogs and streams known to the locals as Avalon. Morgan sang songs of faith as they pulled the boat across these, threw his sword into a pool of deep water, and buried him on a mound amid the bogs. There the priest and the bard laid him to rest. "He is but asleep" intoned the bard, "on the day of resurrection he will return." "That, my friends," Eochaid concluded, "is all there is to these stories about my uncle. That is no doubt why the Britons say that he will return. We Irish know the true meaning of this legend. It lies in our belief in the resurrection. Those who do not suffer the second death shall arise from their first, earthly death. As surely as the glorious gold-bright sun, though it be hidden through the night, dances in joy at its rising, so the glory of the resurrection of the Christ of the elements, even though his children sleep for a time, dances up and down as they rise in their bodies, each in their own place of resurrection, entering into the glorious rule of the beloved Savior of victory. And Arthur's place of resurrection shall surely be like none other."

A sense of gratitude for Arthur grew in Aidan. Here was a man who dared to give a lead, to stand up to the tyrant, to rally the forces of good, and to live out Christian values; a man with a Christ-centered strategy for his nation during the period after the Roman troops left, when brutal Saxon invaders were taking over; a man who built a chain of defended towns to protect the people from the invaders. Arthur was thwarted by quarreling Celtic kings, yet he revealed rare qualities of joy inspired by hardship and deepened by adversity. He had a vision of a land where each man protected his brother's dignity and all races lived under God's law of love and honor.

The stories of Arthur's great deeds expanded Aidan's horizons. He pondered the destiny of peoples and the qualities required of leaders. Arthur laid good foundations and made great friendships between peoples. It dawned upon Aidan that this is a great art, to be learned through much practice, and never to be taken for granted. His admiration for Columba also grew. Columba had set aside his worldly preferences and accepted that God wished the prayerful Aidan to be king, not his more thrusting brother, and that the child-like Eochaid Buide should be his successor, not his warrior brothers. Arthur had been freed by this divine choice from the protocols and pressures of the court, to become a mighty man of stature in his field of strength. Christian leaders must surely continue to guide rulers and their warriors.

The Irish were interested in the idea of the great and wise king. Aidan pondered the wisdom for leaders taught in the Scriptures, and in their own folk lore. Cormac was thought to have been a High King of Ireland some time between 2nd and 4th centuries who ruled from Tara for forty years. He was famous for his wise and generous judgments. He was once asked "What is best for a king?" He replied:

> Composure rather than temper
> Patience rather than contention
> Geniality rather than arrogance.
> Military action for just cause.
> Justice without bloodshed

Leniency within the integrity of the law.
Goodwill to tribes
Distinct guarantees
Just judgments
Fasting against neighboring territories.
Glorifying the sacred
Respecting poets
Adoring God.
Productivity in his reign
Attention to every unfortunate
Many charities.
Fruit on trees
Fish in estuaries
Fertile land.
Let him visit the ailing
Let him improve the condition of the poor.
Let him have legitimate claim to truth
Let him rebuke falsehood.
Let him love justice
Let him quell fear.
Let him knit every peace treaty together
Let him declare every clear judgment
Let him speak every truth.

Before he returned to Iona Aidan drew up in his mind Ten Rules for Kings:

1. Dedicate your life and your country to Christ.

2. Respect what is noble.

3. Raise up the poor.

4. Expose evils.

5. Be honest about your mistakes.

6. Bond your people in struggle for the common good.

7. Be calm in crisis, decisive in action.

8. Earn the trust of your thanes.

9. Order your kingdom so that the strong have something to aim for and the weak have nothing to run from.

10. Seek the counsel of a soul friend.

The first thing he himself would do upon his return was to seek out his new soul friend at Iona.

chapter 10

CRISIS

633

If Dunadd fanned the flames of high hopes and great ideals, Aidan's return to Iona quickly dampened them. He delayed a visit to his soul fried. He hardly dared admit to thoughts he had. Too many brothers were small-minded. Gone were the open hearts and the smiling welcome for each new day that marked life at Durrow. Here, the third generation after Columba had dug in rather than reached out. Aidan even sensed echoes of Senan's Isle hermits. A long year passed. The days darkened.

At Michaelmas the brothers went to Sithean Mor, the grassy knoll visible from the Machair, which they circled on horseback in the glowering gray. Aidan pined for the gentle greens and the smiling faces of Ireland; he even pined for Dunadd with its stories of heroes, and its energizing Northumbrian exiles. As the cattle were driven through the ritual fire to ward off the ills of winter the thought crossed his mind: Did not these monks need a fire that would burn out the comfortable accretions of the years and blaze a new trail? The priest's words at his baptism about the sparks that would come from this baby flame came to mind, but his own flame was burning low, too.

A DIFFERENT SOUL FRIEND

Abbot Segene had asked Tomas, a senior monk of insight, to be Aidan's soul friend and he did at last get to see him. Tomas was calm, erudite, but less spontaneous than Micah. Micah had helped Aidan to deal with sins he was aware of: Tomas drew out things he was as yet unaware of. Tomas had two aims: to help Aidan to be willing to do anything, however menial, with all his heart; and and when he had learned that, to discover what callings lay buried within him that needed to be brought into the light. "I wonder whether you advanced too fast at Durrow," he said one day. "You leapfrogged into new initiatives, but was there insufficient opportunity to live an ordinary life, to find your well-being in everyday tasks, to be anonymous? Try not to let the world revolve around your own needs" Tomas suggested. Aidan worked hard to do this, but he had a question for Tomas: "What is the place for initiative in monastic life?" They discussed this at some length.

Before they had gone far along the path of bringing things to light, the frustrations caused by these buried callings festered and manifested themselves in Aidan's uncharacteristic behavior.

"What is worrying you?" Tomas asked. Aidan thought. He worried that someone might be late for duty; he worried lest an action he took might upset a brother; he worried that this or that was not finished, that the winter might come before they'd enjoyed summer, that someone he valued might be moved to another monastery, that he would forget to do something, that this or that person would leave things in a muddle. He worried that he had an ache in his joints. He worried about being worried. As if these were not enough Tomas drew out of him worries deeper still—things he missed at Durrow:

> The sound of the wind in the elm, making music to us
> The startled cry of the pleasant gray blackbird when she clapped
> her wings
> Listening early in Ross Grencha to the stags
> And to cuckoos calling from the woodland on the brink of the
> summer.

Tomas unearthed something more—an underlying unease. In Columba's time the island only had brothers as residents, but since then a number of fishermen had come from Mull. Aidan had taken pains to sit with a fisherman named Eddie as he cast oatmeal on to the waves. He had found out why fishermen did this. They hoped that in return, the sea would cast up its treasures for them. It seems that in olden days the fisherfolk invoked Mhannannkin, the god of the sea. Since the Christians had been on the island, the fishermen spoke not of this in their presence, but still they cast their oatmeal. This prompted Aidan's unease. The monks had become too busy—with the demands of prayer, work, study, and of the ever increasing hospitality—to spend time with the islanders whose home this was. Although the monks were friendly to islanders, a half buried feeling that their space had been invaded cried out to be noticed. Aidan had made it his job to listen to the likes of Eddie. Two islanders had taken him fishing in their boat. How little the monastery knew of their lore—that frustrated Aidan.

Other things also nagged at him. He was fascinated yet appalled by the story of the first Irish monk on Iona to be buried in its Christian cemetery. His name was Odran. As his brothers shoveled the earth upon his corpse he moved. Someone urged that they get him out; another cautioned this brother to wait. According to the story, Odran whispered "Leave me here, I want to be the first martyr on this island." And so, in due course the shoveling resumed. Aidan had tried to make death his friend since his puberty. The Irish admired the martyrs, and Odran had found a sneaky way of being a physical martyr. Aidan admired his determination, but he still had an unease about it; suicide, after all, was a sin. He did not like the mind-set behind it; it was far different from the free and easy ways of his child hood.

During subsequent meetings Tomas drew yet more out of him. Most of Iona's monks came from Columba's northern Ui Neill clan, but Aidan did not. Leadership was hereditary: a new Abbot had to be the most suitable person among the few who were next in the founder's blood line. The feeling that he was a number two person as he was to his elder twin, came back to haunt Aidan. He felt he was an outsider. He had kept his head down and served Christ as best he might, or so he had thought, but a frustration was building up.

And then there were no women on Iona. He missed women. He felt only half alive on an island in which only half the human race was represented.

"You are hiding anger," Tomas said, "you smile rarely and you cut short others' words—those are tell-tale signs." He suggested Aidan spent a day on Mull and expel his anger by shouting with all his might. Aidan rowed across one morning, and walked two hours into a thick wood until he came to a large, uprooted tree trunk. There he let out the loudest, longest scream of his life. Unfortunately, two people were making love the other side of it. Greatly startled, they ran for their lives. Aidan decided he would not use this method again! Angry at his thwarted exercise, he ran to a bay and plunged into the foaming waves. There he ranted and raved to his heart's content. He felt much better for it and returned with a lighter step. But it did not last.

Tomas sensed that Aidan was carrying yearnings larger than Iona could contain, and that, if they were not expressed, they would wear him down. He suggested that he wrote on wax tablets those things that burned within him. These writings revealed to Aidan that his frustration was not caused by worldly ambition, as he had wondered; it was because he was carrying something, like a woman with child, and whatever this was it needed to be recognized, and nursed, and brought to birth.

Was it something to do with the lost Gospel in Alexandria? Visitors to Iona had sailed off in search of an island of promise: was it something like that? His thoughts returned to Aedh, whose premature death as a pilgrim had stirred him as a boy. He recalled Columba, whose soul friend had advised him to go on pilgrimage away from his homeland for the rest of his life. Pilgrims who left behind home comforts to enter the obedience of monastic life indeed took a big step. But the greatest heroes were those who went into exile from their homeland, for ever, abandoning themselves to God, not knowing where they would be led, and laying down their lives for the people among whom they found themselves, that they might learn the ways of Christ. That was total dedication. Giving one's all until the very last breath on this earth. Columbanus and many, many others had gone far across the seas to do just that. They were as much martyrs as were those who had shed blood rather than deny Christ. He and Tomas agreed that he would store these things in his heart, and be open to whatever God might bring.

Assumptions Aidan had grown up with but never questioned were discussed, and the possibility of moving beyond these negative grooves. For example, that he was a Number Two person, that he had to hold in feelings and aspirations without trying to discover if God was in them, or that he could make the wellspring of his life, not the inadequare well-spring of his family love, but the infinite well-spring of the love of the Blessed and Holy Trinity.

For a time Aidan improved, but too much lay buried. Aidan was experiencing a crisis in the middle of his life. His seasoned shell was beginning to crack. Tomas could not live his life for him.

CRISIS

Winter came and went. Only grim duty kept Aidan going. He received a message that his father had died. That night a frenzy of desperate images tore at him through sleepless hours. He saw himself as an immature youth who fled to the snow-clad mountains: there he lay down and froze to death. He became an abbot who could not bear the burdens of his office, so he walked over a cliff top to his death. He returned to Ireland and began a new life as a farmer. He returned to Alexandria and sought out some hermit's cave in the depths of the desert. In the morning he stumbled into his clothes and into another meaningless day.

Others noticed that he was not his normal self. Tomas had words with the Abbot, who asked to see him. "You are not your usual self," he said. "Tell me how you are feeling?" "I feel," Aidan said, "that I cannot make one more decision. I am too exhausted to think. I feel that my brain is a running away like a horse, and I feel panic lest I can never rein it in." "Then you must cease all duties at once and go on leave," said Segene. "You are in the middle of your life. It is likely you have reached a crossing in the road, and you do not know which road you should take. You need time to discover this. We will call it a pilgrimage, or a compassionate leave to see your family, anything. You can stay, of course at any of our daughter communities here or in Ireland. Come back when you are ready, before next winter begins, and we will talk again." Aidan was given supplies, and left on the first ferry to Mull.

"Let your feet follow your heart until you find your place of resurrection"—this much-loved Irish saying played in his ears like a tune that a harpist constantly repeats. Sometimes, however, all a person knows is the place where they must not be. As he trudged across Mull he knew that his place of resurrection was not on a small island cut off from the mainland, cut off from the warp and weft of ordinary people's lives, cut off from the tides and fortunes of God's great world. His heart took him to the shore, for shores bring us to the borderlands of possibility, to fresh horizons. He slept on the sands in peace. As he waited for the ferry from Mull to the mainland he thought of Columba. He had lived on Iona and yet he had not been constrained. He had gone north to the Picts, but Aidan's heart did not take him there. He would walk southwards to the furthest tip of the Mull of Kintyre, to the place where Columba first set foot on Alba. He would place his feet in Columba's footmarks, and there, perhaps, he would know what his next steps should be.

It was a long journey, but it passed quickly. The great man's first foot marks on his arrival from Ireland had been clearly preserved in a rock as a way-mark for pilgrims. Aidan placed his feet in these marks, unconscious of time. He thought how Columba had mourned for his beloved homeland:

> I stretch my gaze across the sea
> From the great oak beams:
> Many are the tears of my tender eye
> As I look back upon Erin.

Should he return to Erin the same way Columba had left it? If so, for what? No. His feet did not wish to go there, they searched for some other part of the great heart's terrain. He would return north by the eastern shore of the Mull of Kintyre. At first he thought he would avoid Dunadd, but the more he walked the more his thoughts dwelt upon people he had met there. To his surprise, it was the Northumbrians who stole the largest place in his heart. These English—sometimes they reminded him of a juggler who kept different colored balls in the air without losing their foothold—that was a trait he admired. They were brave—as were other races—and their speed of horse and love of sport he respected; but something else drew him too. Was it because in their company he no longer felt constrained? His time with them had been like coming out of a dark place into sunny uplands. Were these thoughts selfish, or foolish? He did not know; he knew only that his feet were following his heart to Dunadd.

What would he say when he rang the bell at the gate? He told them the truth: he had been unwell and had been given leave; and he asked if he might stay for a few days. He was given a bed. As he lay down he looked forward to meeting again with Peadar and some of the English contingent, and he fell into fitful sleep. He learned in the morning that Peadar was away, and so were the young English warriors. Acha was there, and the attendants and a few other English, but none that he knew well. He was especially disappointed that Oswald was not there. A hollowness engulfed him. There was nothing there. He felt a fool and a fraud.

After he had broken fast he made his way to the chapel and sat in a corner. He began to shake, and then to sob. They were quiet, fast, little sobs, which he could not stop. He sat there for hours, sobbing with his head in his hands. He was a broken man. Dimly he became aware that someone else had entered the chapel. This person sat on the opposite side, in silence. Only when, at last, Aidan took his head out of his hands and sat up did he say something. "There may be a reason why you are here," he said, "would you like to talk, or even if you would not, to come and drink something with me?" The man beckoned, and Aidan followed.

His name was Sorley. He was not an Iona monk, and he had not been present at Dunadd during Aidan's term of duty there, but he exuded a deep spiritual presence. "I was training to be a Druid," he told Aidan, "when I embraced the Faith of Christ. I am now a counselor to the King, and although I belong to no monastery I have taken vows." Aidan felt that this man had compassion and understood.

Over the following days he unfolded the story of his life to this man whom he had never met before, and who asked him questions that none had ever asked. "What do you think is the worst thing that could befall you?" Sorley enquired. "That I would be declared unfit to be a monk and that I would return to my family who would think me unfit to be a farmer" he said. "Why would that matter? If, in fact, those were not your callings you would then be free to follow whatever is your calling" he said. "Why do you think God gave you pride?" he asked. Aidan had not thought that God did give people pride. The answer Sorley hoped for was that God gave people pride in order that it might be broken, because only when we are broken can that for which we are born emerge. Sorley described, in detail and with beauty, the process by which a creature is conceived and is born. Nothing can be born that has not been vulnerable. "Why do we feel pain when people hurt us?" was another of the questions that came like spears from this wise man's mouth. As they discussed this, Aidan realized that he liked to surround himself with nice people, nice conditions, so that he did not get hurt; that the place of refuge to which he liked to return within himself was a place free from hurt "The center of the Son of God's life was not that," Sorley said, "it was the place of suffering compassion."

"I have come to the end" Aidan told Sorley, "I have reached my limits. I cannot go on as I was before." "That is very good," he said lightly, with a smile, "for perhaps your real life can now begin." Aidan became angry, and lashed out at Iona. He went through a list of complaints and concluded by saying that Iona was like hell. "The hell is not in Iona, it is in you," said Sorley. That remark went deep. Aidan wrestled with it for a day and a night.

He was permitted to stay longer at Dunadd, but he did not see Sorley for several days. He sensed that he could not put off his departure too long, for things inside him were coming to a head. Sorley took him to a cave by the shore. He asked him to think, in silence, of each thing in his life that had been driving him like a horseman's whip, and of each thing that was now nearing its end. Each time something became clear Aidan was to take a stone and hurl it into the sea. The throwing of those stones lasted almost until the end of the fast, the ninth hour, when they took Christ down from the cross.

At last Aidan sat still in the cave. No more stones were needed. Silence descended. Sorley broke it. "What is left?" he asked. "Is there something that you do not strive for? Something that is a pure gift?" Silence resumed. "Whatever is left, lay these on the altar" Aidan heard the voice say. There was a further silence. Then he knelt at the altar of the ocean. "There are three things that are left," he said, "the call, the Gospel, and the flame—these I now lay on the altar."

They lingered there in silence. "Earth, air, water, fire—the elements remain. If you are fire—be who you are," said Sorley. He lit a candle he had brought. He gave it to Aidan and laid his hands upon him in blessing: "God bless your call, and open the door; God bless the Gospel, and the peoples who await its coming, God bless the flame, and kindle it in a hundred thousand hearts."

Aidan returned to Iona. It was harvest time.

chapter 11

KILLING FIELDS AND ANGELS

Some brothers trudged back from a hard day's work in the fields, somewhat dispirited. As they passed a grassy mound a beautiful scent wafted over them for which they could find no explanation. The Abbot told them "This is the place where holy Columba often communed with God. He knew you were tired and he came to meet you. Let this be a sign that our saint is still among us and wishes to encourage us." They named that spot The Hill of Angels.

Aidan decided to pray there. Columba had seen innumerable angels: Aidan had seen none, but he was intrigued by them. As he sat on that grassy knoll the oft-repeated story of how Columba spent a day fighting the spiritual war against innumerable demons flooded into his mind. The demons attacked Columba like legions of little black darts. Columba fought them by proclaiming scriptures and repeating prayers. As some demons fled, even more attacked. Finally, at close of day, realizing he could never repel this attack with his own prayers alone, he commanded the angels to disperse them. The demons fled. On his return to the monastery, Columba announced that the plague would sweep the land, but because of that day's encounter, Iona itself would be spared. That came to pass, as did so much else that this man of God prophesied. Aidan did not see an angel, but he did feel a presence. This presence drew his attention to the little uninhabited islets that were scattered around Iona. He could see one or two from the Hill of Angels. Less clear was a faint impression of another island further away. For some reason he started to pray for these bare islands.

The monastery continued to gather other memories of their founder. A story that fixed itself in Aidan's mind was that of a crane from a foreign territory. Blown off course by wild winds it collapsed, exhausted on Iona's shore. Columba deputed a novice to become a kind of guest brother to the crane, and to treat it as an honored guest for three days. As Aidan recovered against a background of such stories he became more aware of each person and thing around him; hospitality of the heart towards all, including foreign people and creatures grew strong in him, and he thought often of the Scripture that says many who have welcomed others have welcomed angels without knowing it.

Aidan was able to make certain of these stories his own.

A transfer of several brothers between Iona and Durrow took place. One of those returning to Durrow was related to the Crag Liath clan. Aidan asked him to take a gift and a message to his brother when he was able to. Aidan had ceased to compare himself with Finn. He now had no desire to be in charge of the family farm. He was content in his own calling. Along with these shifts in his feelings had come a wave of warmth towards Finn. Although they were so far apart, he felt closer to him now than he had ever been.

During his time of testing Aidan had come to terms with not having seed of his own. Nevertheless some part of him longed to reproduce. The longing was not now for physical seed. Was it, perhaps, something to do with God's birthings or with some race of people in whom Christ had not yet been born? He could not articulate it—there was just a dim awareness.

* * *

In the summer of 633 grim news began to percolate through to the brothers. There had been a mass slaughter of the Northumbrian people by the British King Cadwallon. The Northumbrians' king Edwin was slain. Deira, the southern sub-kingdom, called Edwin's son Osric to its throne. Then they heard that Eanfrith had raised an army of Britons, Picts, and Saxon supporters, and secured himself at Bamburgh as king of Bernicia, the northern sub-kingdom. Many of the Northumbrians who had become Christians under Edwin went back to their pagan gods. They said that since Edwin's Christian God had not saved him, the old gods must be better. Eanfrith, sensing this, and wanting to quickly draw support from as many of his people as possible, adopted their pagan practices as if he had never so much as heard of the Christian Faith. Oswald and others felt dismay and hurt.

Worse still, Cadwallon destroyed Osric and continued his relentless campaign in both sub-kingdoms for a whole year. He inflicted unspeakable atrocities upon those fractious, shepherdless peoples. Their kingdoms became killing fields. They were a sea of blood. The scheming Eanfred, believing he had secured the promise of a peace agreement with Cadwallon, went to him with twelve chosen warriors to negotiate. The treacherous Cadwallon had him killed. Was there nothing left to these Northumbrians other than treachery and rule by terror? Aidan's heart bled for the wounded men left to die, the women and children left prey to death by hunger, disease or sword. Jesus had foretold that there would be wars and rumors of wars. How many such hells would the world have to endure before God's kingdom came? What was the path to salvation in the middle of such situations?

During this year of sickening news from the south, Oswald spent periods at Iona in prayer and in conversation with Segene. They developed a deep and lasting friendship. Aidan sometimes chanced upon Oswald. He told him he wished to pray for him with understanding. Oswald's face stayed in Aidan's mind even when he was not at the monastery. Aidan sensed he saw in it the face of Christ.

Months passed without a sight of Oswald. Then the monastery received a message from Dunadd. Oswald had recruited a small army of Irish and Northumbrian warriors. He requested their prayers that, "my army, though small in number, strengthened by our faith in Christ, may overthrow the impious commander of the Britons." He had also requested that he be accompanied by several brothers who would lead them in their prayers. This Segene granted. That night the bell summoned the brothers to special vigil on behalf of Oswald and his companions on their unique and dangerous undertaking.

Anxious days followed as the brothers waited for information. News arrived that Oswald had gathered his army overnight at Arthur's fort of Camboglanna (which some English now name Birdoswald) before marching next day to the battlefield by the Roman wall. There Oswald and his warriors had knelt on the earth and placed themselves in the hands of Christ. They secured a victory against the fiendish Cadwallon despite his much larger army.

The brothers at first knew only that Oswald had secured the throne, over time they learned that many of his Irish and English warriors followed him there, soon to be joined by their families. Oswald then sped to Lindsey, just south of the river Humber on Northumbrian's southern border, and secured an alliance. He wanted to assert from the start his right not only to be king of both Northumbrian kingdoms, but to be recognized as over-king of the English. His most significant act of all, however, was taken before he left for Lindsey. He sent a senior aide to Iona with this request: "Please send a mission to convert my people to Christ."

Segene gathered the community together. He described the events leading up to Oswald becoming king of Northumbria, and wanting to strengthen his alliance with Dalriada. He spoke of Oswald's request that they send a mission to his people, emphasizing that this request marked perhaps the most significant opportunity in the history of all Columba's monasteries. He recalled some of Columba's missions. He explained that to begin with the community would send a mission leader and twelve brothers—a familiar pattern to the Irish that reflected Christ and the twelve apostles. Segene announced that the leader would be Corman. Corman was a senior brother who was of Columba's clan, and a fine scholar and teacher.

On the day of their departure Corman's tall, gaunt frame stood out among the other twelve. These represented a range of skills that would be needed in Northumbria; they had all been taught by Corman. The Abbot blessed them, the community prayed for them, they sailed south, skirting the mainland by the Sound of Jura until they came to the Roman Wall. They walked eastwards along the wall to the river Tyne, and then went north by sea to Bamburgh's garrison. There, Oswald gave them quarters, and their mission began.

Aidan and the rest of the brothers returned to their duties. Although it was the same monastery that Aidan had once left in the distress of crisis, now it no longer felt like a cage. As water, when it is blocked, sooner or later finds a way to flow round the blockage, so Aidan was now content to let the water of the Spirit take its time to flow wherever it wished.

A year or two after Oswald's victory, Oswald personally told Segene what had happened the night before his fateful battle. As he slept in his tent he dreamed that Columba stood among his field of warriors, mighty in stature, his head reaching into heaven, and his cloak covering them all. He used the biblical words that God once spoke to Joshua: "Be strong and of a good courage for I will be with you." Columba continued: "March out tomorrow, your foes will be put to flight, Cadwallon will be slain, and you will return in triumph, for this is a just cause." Oswald assembled his senior warriors and told them the vision. He won the victory, commanded that a large wooden cross be made, and personally held it as his warriors secured it in the ground. He asked them all to kneel in prayer. The Saxons, who unlike the Irish were not Christians, vowed that they would return with him to the royal fort at Bamburgh and embrace the Faith. Oswald named that battle site "Heaven's Field."

When Aidan heard of these divine interventions he knew that heaven could come into any hell. He went to the Hill of Angels to pray.

chapter 12

THE CALL
Flame among the Ashes

The brothers at Iona settled down after the departure of the thirteen missionaries. Several, including Aidan, were invited to fill the vacancies on the monastery's inner council left by their departure. Strangely, no news was received from their departed brothers..

Everything seemed normal except that Aidan became suddenly unwell. This was out of character—he seldom became ill. He felt pains in his stomach and extreme tiredness. He was short of breath and coughed so much he had to miss the prayers. One or two brothers with similar symptoms had died, and Aidan wondered if he should resign himself to a decline followed by an early death. He was not upset by this—he was happy to let things take their course. During sleepless nights he thought much about death—his own, and also the deaths of those poor, war-broken English.

He was surprised therefore when Segene asked him, not to see a doctor, but to spend time with his anamchara, Tomas. Tomas asked him a strange question: "Did you want to go with Corman?" Aidan thought awhile. Since his transforming experience at Dunadd, he'd felt free to do whatever God wanted, so he had not asked himself such a question, since clearly God had not called him to go to the English. In any case, since he was not descended from the founder, he could hardly have expected to be the leader of such a mission.

Tomas said to Aidan "When you came to the end of your strength at Dunadd you let go of everything you were holding on to. However, things we let go of try to come back in another form. Be alert to this. Do not try and control events. Abandon yourself to the flow of Providence deep under surface happenings. As you do this a pattern forms that you will only notice as you look back."

Tomas had been reading the writings of Bishop Augustine of Hippo. "Love God and do what you like was Augustine's advice," he told Aidan, "what do you want to do?" Eventually, Aidan came out with it. Something deep within him had in fact leapt when Segene had first announced that they would send brothers to Northumbria but, since he had not been chosen he had thought no more about it. "Perhaps you have pushed down what you really want," Tomas suggested, "and perhaps that is why you have become ill."

Aidan tried to discern any symptoms of a conflict between unresolved desires. He thought of meetings of the monastery council when he had compulsively spoken on some subject he felt strongly about, and how he had gone to the opposite extreme and said nothing even when he had something worthwhile to say. "School yourself to be silent in such meetings," Tomas advised, "unless your heart burns with a fire that comes like a gift—then you must speak out." As Aidan and his soul friend bared their souls Aidan began to see that, although being willing to accept God's will was indeed the most important step, other steps were also required. God's will would not come ready-cooked on a plate from heaven. Aidan must take responsibility to communicate what he felt God was wanting of him; he must grow in confidence and assert his views when this became appropriate, without demanding that they be heeded. Tomas read to him the words of the apostle to Timothy: "Fan into a flame the gift of God that you possess through the laying on of my hands. God did not give us a spirit of timidity, but the spirit of power and love as well as self-control" (2 Tim 1:6, 7). He encouraged Aidan to pass on to others the thoughts God put into his heart, and to speak boldly when he burned within.

But what about Aidan's weak physical condition? A voice in Aidan's head said "You can choose between life and death: which do you want?" He was shocked by this thought. He was at first not sure which he wanted most. Half of him wanted to die and half of him wanted life. Several days later, in a flash, he knew that he had been born for something not yet accomplished, that he had more yet to give on this earth, that he had not yet fully lived but that he could and should live life in all its fullness. He knew that God could change his body and all that lay within him. He shouted out to God "I choose life." There was a tingling in his bowels. A wave of heat spread through his body. He saw himself as strong, fit, confident—every fiber of his being was flowing with God. He rose up in the strength of Christ and breathed deeply of God's good air for the first time in months.

Winter set in, and Aidan resumed full duties. Nothing outwardly had changed, but now each chore became an experience of Christ's presence. Whether any one else noticed he cared not—he knew something of eternal significance had changed.

Still there was no news from Corman, though Oswald sent a trusted aide on horseback to Dunadd. Segene conferred with him there for several days but the brothers were told nothing. One week before winter gave way to Imbolc and its festival of fire Segene informed the brothers he had some desperately sad news. Corman and his twelve brothers would arrive the following day. Their mission had not worked out as they had hoped. In fact, it had failed.

Corman's forlorn team disembarked declaring that the Northumbrians were barbarians, and it was not possible to bring the Gospel to such uncivilized people. During times of chatter such as Sunday lunch they belittled them. They explained that the Saxons had regarded them as foreigners, had refused to listen to them; they were not interested in their traditions, were impatient with their translators, and sneered at or avoided them. Corman asked why monks in vows should waste God's time on such people. Aidan flinched at his tone of voice. However difficult it had been for the brothers, surely those English peasants deserved respect?

Segene urged the whole community to use the remaining days of Lent to fast and pray about this sad turn of events and to reflect upon what they should learn from it. Aidan most certainly used the time to reflect. Corman's mission was the biggest missed opportunity in Iona's history. The chance to bring Christ to the English made Columba's mission to the Picts near Inverness pale into insignificance. What was the root of the failure? Was it prejudice—a failure to move out of one's own pattern of life and put oneself in the shoes of another people? If the eternal Son of God could dive from infinity into a human skin, surely Christ's brothers could move out of their inherited patterns and journey with Christ within another culture? Christianity, like any other religion, inevitably took the shape of the culture in which it was born, but the Life it nurtured was capable of crossing over from the Jewish people into the Greek-speaking world. It was true that the Greeks were part of the civilized world, but the brothers had heard stories that Jesus' apostles had gone to the four corners of the earth, even to places that knew no Latin and had primitive laws. Christians impelled by the love of Christ had learned new languages, new philosophies, new ways of working. If they had not, Ireland itself would still be pagan. Surely God did not wish the English to be barbarians for ever?

Segene convened the new council. He invited Corman to give a full account of their activities. Corman described how, first the nobles and then the peasants had been invited to the royal garrison to hear them preach. Translators did not understand their words. On each occasion their listeners returned as they were before they came. He concluded by describing these people as intractable, obstinate and uncivilized; in fact, they were barbarians beyond the reach of the Gospel. Segene then spoke. He informed the council that Oswald's aide had talked at length with him at Dunadd. Oswald felt that although this was a major setback, if the right lessons were learned Iona should have a second chance to undertake a mission. Segene reminded the brothers of their founder's missionary impulse in seeking to win as many souls to Christ in a foreign land as had lost their lives in the battle of Cul Dreimhne.

He called for a period of silent prayer. Following this he invited any brother to speak if they had insights to offer. There was a pregnant pause. Aidan was aware that he was burning within. He rose from his seat and addressed Corman, lovingly: "My brother, it seems to me you have been unreasonably harsh upon your ignorant hearers. I think you gave them the meat of God's Word; perhaps with hindsight it would have been better to have fed them with the milk until, little by little, as they grew strong on the food of God's Word, they became capable of carrying out spiritual disciplines. You were zealous to lay upon them our spiritual practices. Perhaps it would have been better to let their own practices grow out of their newly found love of God, even if they seemed strange to us." Then he addressed the whole council: "I do not think we should make another plan. I think we should go on a mission of listening. Listen, learn their language, learn also the language of their hearts. We must not only take a message, we must model the ways of Christ. We must not confine ourselves to the royal headquarters, we must establish a community in a place where brothers and workers and students and visitors can feel at home. We must start slowly, sow seeds, and allow God to ripen them." Aidan's lips mouthed the words, but it was God's voice they heard. Their hearts burned within them as he spoke. They felt in their bones that from a man of discretion and spiritual authority their community had been given a way forward.

The sense of the meeting was that Aidan should head up the mission. Nevertheless, Segene waited twenty four hours. He believed it was never wise to make a decision in the heat of a debate. He consulted some senior brothers. Two days after the council he told Aidan: "We want you to go. Bring me your suggestions for the twelve brothers you wish to take with you. We have bishops with us for Easter. We will consecrate you as a bishop and commission you and our twelve new apostles to the English on the Day of Resurrection."

So Aidan would become a missionary bishop. Why? In Ireland the planters and pioneers were spiritual parents, abbas and ammas, to their people. Northumbria, however, had far more people. Aidan might in a sense be their spiritual father, but in practical terms there would need to be many monasteries, each with their abbot. The king of Northumbria, who was already widening his alliances, would need his missionary bishop by his side to oversee the entire Irish mission.

No doubt sniffy types thought Aidan was not well-fitted for this new work, but thoughtful people would see that was not so. Aidan would have to go into "the highways and byways" to reach the English: he had learned to be a long distance walker. He would have to suffer hard tests: he had suffered many. The ability to make friends would be more important than knowledge of the minutiae of documents and protocol. In his new role he would face pressures of the court and the courtly, expectations of the country folk and the uncouth, and the needs of his own brothers in a strange land. He would need stamina, discretion, compassion. Aidan did not realise this, but thoughtful people saw that these qualities were already becoming his benchmark.

Although this was a high call, Aidan had no sense of heady elation. He had been tried enough to know that this was a sacrificial calling—nothing less than his all and Christ's all would do it justice or see it through. This call to lay down his life filled him with awe. He did have a sense, however, that he was walking hand in hand with destiny.

THE TWELVE APOSTLES TO THE ENGLISH

One blessing, at least, flowed from Corman's failure: Aidan was allowed to select his own mission team. He thought much and prayed through one night. Segene had some suggestions, of course, certain of Aidan's choices surprised him, and he was very loth to lose two of Aidan's nominees, but in the end Aidan was in a strong position and took with him his preferred team. Jesus had chosen his twelve apostles. He had not chosen eminent Pharisees, he had chosen everyday people who made mistakes but who were willing to learn with an almost child-like trust. Aidan wanted apostles like that for the English.

He had to consider many things. He would need at least one brother who would always be an anchor, whatever storms might lash them—someone who could turn his hand to different things but who above all would be Aidan's rock of stability. He would need a brother who would earth the mission base in the daily prayers—someone with a praying heart, a good singing voice, and disciplined habits. He would need a brother who had served at Dunadd, who knew the ways of a court, for Oswald would surely require a senior brother at Bamburgh, and Aidan wished to avoid the trap of having always to be there himself. He would need several able teachers, the skills of the anamchara, one good organizer. For his first team of evangelists he needed brothers with a gift of friendship and speech, with health, vitality, and loyalty, and a brother who could be their leader when he himself could not accompany them. They needed at least one brother who was as strong as any Saxon warrior—it would take time for those warriors to understand other kinds of strength. They would need a reconciler—some one who could help people to resolve conflicts without blame and with understanding. They would need a brother who was quick to learn a language—a young brother perhaps. Nor must they forget the Celtic Britons who lived in Northumbria, and the Irish Scots. A brother who had trained at Whithorn would be an asset. Someone skilled in the scriptorium. . . and in cooking . . . and in tending crops and cattle. . . The needs were endless, but he could only choose twelve. God would raise up others and develop new gifts.

These were the brothers Aidan chose to be his "twelve apostles to the English":

1) *Foigall*—he had the gift of a wise bard. A distant relative of Columba, he would be Aidan's chaplain and serve the royal fortress at Bamburgh.

2) *Barr*—he had the gift of administration. Unflappable and happy, he would oversee the small monastery they would establish.

3) *Boisil*—he had the gifts of teaching, insight and devotion—he would oversee the school and be an anamchara.

4) *Cainnech*—he had the gift of cooking and would oversee hospitality. He also was an anamchara.

5) *Ciaran*—he had the gifts of prayer and singing and would oversee the worship.

6) *Killian*—he had practical gifts—gardening and building—he asked no questions and got on with things.

Then there were the six who would be sharing the faith among the people:

7) *Diuma*—he also had the gifts of teaching and oversight and could deputize for Aidan on mission journeys. He was a fine anamchara.

8) *Donan*—he had the gift of friendship, he laughed much and bubbled over.

9) *Declan*—he had the gift of speech and healing

10) *Ronan*—he had the gift of strength. He could wrestle and the Saxons would admire him. His heart was as big as his frame.

11) *Mael* —he had the gift of memory and knew the Scriptures.

12) *Jonas*—he had the gift of the child—he smiled, asked questions and made peace: the children and their parents would love him.

On Easter Day in the year of our Lord 635 Aidan and the twelve apostles to the English were commissioned by Abbot Segene, and Aidan was ordained a bishop by the visiting old Bishop Malchus of Armagh. Segene said "Out of desolation and death came the resurrection. Among the ashes of failure, let a new flame be lit."

chapter 13

THE JOURNEY OF THE TWELVE

635

They went a different way. It was longer, harder, necessary and Oh so fruitful. "Before you build, count the cost" Jesus had taught.

Aidan needed time to build a team who understood the cost of their huge and risky endeavor before they arrived and were swamped with conflicting requests. Before Jesus began his mission he spent forty days in a place far from his new mission field, confronting temptations. They, too, would take forty days for the journey in order to do something similar.

Corman had sailed south, walked from west to east along the Roman wall, and then gone by boat along the Tyne and up the eastern coast. Aidan would walk north, and then trudge east along the cattle routes beside the rivers Lionh and Tay until they reached the sea at Cell Rígmonaid, when they would sail south to Oswald's coastal fort at Bamburgh. Ever since Columba's trek up the Great Glen to King Brude brothers from Iona had from time to time pilgrimaged north, and a few had then veered west through Rannoch moor and Glen Fasach (or Lionh) and beside the river Tay to the eastern sea.

Aidan had thought intensely about this. He could see many reasons for taking this course: practical, human, strategic, and spiritual. A practical reason was that they needed to start from Dunadd, in order to pick up Foigall, who was on duty there, and some gifts from Eochaid Buide. Aidan feared that some of Oswald's most loyal warriors would think poorly of a last-chance mission sponsored only by the same religious community who had sent the first. If they knew that an ally warrior king also supported this mission it would create respect. So, at Aidan's request, they took a banner of

Christ which had been used in some of Dunadd's battles as a gift from one hill-top fort to another. From Iona they took a bell, a copper hand bowl for washing with "Iona" inscribed upon it, candles, Gospels, Psalms, and other books.

The human reasons for the long journey were obvious. These twelve brothers had never worked as a team before. They had differing temperaments, talents, interests, flaws. They needed to get to know each other, to work through disagreements, to laugh and cry, and pray, and be real, and to bond in a common vision before they went off in different directions after their arrival. Aidan had to argue hard for this with Segene: "Christ took three years to share with his twelve apostles all that his Father gave him; I need time to share with my new team what is in my heart" he told him. "We also need time to listen to what is in the heart of each brother. We need time to discover what irritates us about each other, to explain what we are thinking, to grow in understanding. When we arrive, I want the twelve apostles to the English to be like a choir that sings with one voice."

None of the twelve had thought about "strategic reasons": Aidan had. Northumbria had so recently been a sea of instability, and could be again, yet on its borders were small but established Christian communities of Picts or Irish Scots. Glen Lionh was the center point between the Irish kingdom of Dalriada and the Pictish kingdom of Atholl. If their mission to Northumbria was to be safeguarded, they needed allies among the Christians of these and other neighboring kingdoms. That route now had its first sprinkling of Christians—they would avail themselves of their hospitality, encourage their life and work, and ask for their prayers. "We need to extend our friendships with the Christian communities north of Northumbria," Aidan advised Segene. "If God grants us success we will need to call on many Christians to come and help us."

The spiritual reasons for choosing this different route came more from intuition than logic. Aidan recognized that warriors lost battles because they did not know their enemy, or did not prepare thoroughly, or were outnumbered, outmaneuvered or divided among themselves. Was it like this with spiritual initiatives? From his childhood days Aidan knew that those who became monks were known as soldiers of Christ, and that all Christians were supposed to overcome evil with good. But no one at Crag Liath, not even Dara, had explained the skills of a spiritual warrior. Donnacha and Rhian went off to train as warriors: how did soldiers of Christ train? The brothers did learn disciplines of body, mind and soul. They learned to pray, to think, to befriend, to create—but was there something more to do with the unseen forces of good and evil?

Aidan was wary of sharing such thoughts with his raw recruits. They had heard immature people speak about spiritual warfare—they behaved like lads who boasted about being warriors when in fact they had only played at it. Nevertheless, they would pass through borderlands between hostile groups where Christians now prayed and he sensed that these glens were thick with the unseen forces of heaven and hell. Jesus had gone to high ground to seek his Father's face and heaven's resources and to overcome "the Prince of this world" before he chose his Twelve, before he succumbed to over-eager crowds, before his final week of testing. They, too, would go to the high lands to seek God, to repel the unseen forces that opposed this mission, to secure the freedom of God's servants to achieve what God had sent them to do before they went down to the English people.

Aidan had learned some skills of the spiritual war from what he read of the desert fathers and their battles to replace the eight deadly sins with enduring virtues. He had learned from the stories of his founder the value of combat prayers and of harnessing the forces of heaven against the powers of evil. The truth was, however, that the necessity of engaging in spiritual warfare had only just dawned on him as he took on board that even Christ could not bring in God's kingdom without first overcoming his tempters in the wilderness.

The following morning the brothers sailed to Dunadd. The day after they sailed up the Loch of Awe, and trekked across the Rannoch moors. This toughened them up. They reached Clachan an Dìseart, the monastic community on the little island between the River Orchy and the Orchy Bheag. Believers were beginning to make pilgrimage there. They had a restful walk to Beinn Mhanach, the Hill of Monks, who gave them hospitality the following night, gathered their community to learn all they could about Aidan's mission, and blessed them with prayers and provisions. Then began their long trek beside the river of Lionh. As they walked Aidan began to shake. He felt that some mighty battle raged in the heavenly realm and a prophetic spirit came upon him. He interceded with groans for these people who could be allies or enemies; later he urged them to intercede that the Northumbrian kingdom might become God's kingdom. They stayed in dwellings by the Lionh crossing.

The following day they came to the great yew tree at Fortingall. A gnarled old man who tended the cemetery sat on the stone wall. "This is the oldest yew tree in the world" he informed them, "and that Pontius Pilate who put your Christ to death lived in these parts." The man claimed that the Romans had come so far north because the glen was replete with pearls, and the Roman s mined and traded them. According to him Pontius Pilate was the child of the Roman officer in charge.

Two of the brothers became unwell, so they walked gently on to Inchadny where they were made most welcome. They stayed several days. Aidan gathered and taught people on the Sunday and visited folk nearby. They prayed for the sick and left behind a man who befriended them and kept the flame of Christ alive in that place.

They walked on next day until they saw dwellings on the slopes. They called this place Dail, or Dull in English. Religious people had lived in those parts for many centuries—the pagans' standing stones bore witness to that. Some Christians had cells there and were overjoyed to receive them.

The next day's journey was long. Exhausted, they climbed to the fort at Dunkeld and asked for hospitality. Here Conal founded a settlement in 570. People told them that a young disciple of Columba drew crowds to hear the Gospel there, before he fell ill and died. Later holy Marnoc came, with the king's blessing, and founded a flourishing church. The Iona brothers shared their news and were glad of their prayers.

They then wound their way to the Picts' monastery at Scone. The monks there were serious about their faith, and their studies were of a high standard, but there was an aloofness that was not attractive. "I don't think they are interested in other people" said Ronan. "They are very interested in God" said Mael. "We are all different—let us remember them with quiet regard" said Diuma. They walked on beside the river Tay until at last they arrived at the estuary at Cell Rígmonaid where brothers received them overnight.

Next day they sailed south and then into the Firth of Forth. They used their time well. Aidan suggested that they practice a few English words that he had learned at Dunadd. An, twa, breo they chanted—one, two, three. Wes buhai—hello, literally meant Be you hale. God be mid sie was goodbye; and Ic bancie be meant I thank you.

On the north side of the Firth of Forth the Picts had become Christians. On the south side and on several islands, scattered here and there in caves and cells, Irish pilgrim for the love of God had settled and made friends with the locals. The mission band spent their last night by a cell dedicated to Mary, mother of Jesus, on the shore several miles south of Eidin. The Christians welcomed and served the brothers. Aidan learned from them the names of hermits in the region, and asked them to pass on his greetings and request their prayers. Aidan used this final resting place to rehearse with the brothers his vision, principles, and plans.

Aidan explained that they had used the journey to their mission field as a model for the journeys they would make once they were in their mission field. They had journeyed in a rhythm of withdrawal and advance. They had taken time to ask questions, think, pray, and grow good relationships with those they met on the way. They had got to know one another as never before. Aidan had used the time to think through many issues, sometimes sharing his thinking aloud

He then focussed on the big picture. He reminded them of previous missionary efforts. The Iona brothers knew about Columba's meeting with Bishop Kentigern of Strathclyde in 584. So concerned were those two leaders that pagan invaders were replacing Christianity—the Picts from the north, the Saxons from the East—that they agreed Kentigern should journey to Rome to seek help. At that time Gregory, who had recently been in charge of the city's affairs, had founded six monasteries, and had become a monk himself. Gregory told Kentigern how his heart had been touched by the sight of the Angles in the slave market. "Not Angles but angels," he had said. Aidan liked what he had heard about Gregory. He was the first monk to become a pope of Rome and the first pope to style himself "the servant of the servants of God." In response to Kentigern's pleading Gregory had sent a small delegation to Iona and a larger one to Kent. He had intended to lead the second delegation himself, but they made him pope before he could set out, so he sent Augustine and his brothers instead, followed by a second group led by Paulinus. "I sometimes wonder," Aidan said, "how much better things might have been if Gregory himself had led that mission," for Augustine never wanted to come, and in fact tried to return to Rome before he got to Kent.

Aidan shared something of the talks he'd had with Ebbe, and occasionally with Oswald, when they had told him about the mission those Roman monks had brought to Northumbria under Paulinus, and how it was aborted by the battle-field death of King Edwin, who invited them. The people had retuned to their gods, and the priests had returned to Kent, though old James the Deacon was still quietly fulfilling his duties down at Catterick. Paulinus had accompanied the king to his royal centers such as York and Ad Gefran, but he had not met ordinary people outside these centers; Corman followed the same pattern in Bernicia. Aidan explained why they must reach far beyond the confines of the royal centers, even though they would at first have to learn the Northumbrian language at Bamburgh. Aidan had learned that men everywhere carried a dagger, and he asked if the brothers were willing to share the faith along remote country tracks without protection. All twelve said they were willing. Aidan talked about the Irish monasteries. They were of the people and for the people. The English must have peoples' monasteries away from the royal centers, and within a generation these must be led by English people. That meant that they must create a monastery school for English boys. He talked about the Three Lents. The mission would suck them into endless activities: they must continue the discipline of going off alone in vigil. He spoke of the remnants of the Celtic Britons and of the Irish and Pictish believers on the borders: Aidan was now their bishop; he wanted them to feel valued and connected to the mission. At their midday prayers Aidan asked God for good beginnings. He prayed that he and his brothers would be given grace to become aware of persons, perceptions and possibilities, of places and their past, and he prayed a blessing on the community which had so generously received them, which the locals called the Lady's place."

Following morning prayers they took the boat south. Aidan and The Twelve sailed towards a war ravaged people whom their distinguished brother had dismissed as obstinate and uncivilized. The world held its breath.

PART THREE

THE FLAME SPREADS
The English and the Ripe Years

chapter 14

BUILDING FOUNDATIONS

The vast rock of Bamburgh which housed the king's garrison came into view. To their surprise Oswald, with his dark moustache and flowing back hair, stood on the shore, feet astride, to greet them, flanked on each side by his aides. Aidan had half wondered whether, after the embarrassment of the first mission, Oswald would let them arrive as unobtrusively as possible. In fact they were royally escorted up the steps and into their rooms and invited that night to a welcome banquet that would warm their stomachs and their hearts.

The brothers were impressed by the strange sights that met their eyes. Everything was on a larger scale than Dunadd. Beside the great hall were soldiers and staff quarters and a church—all made of wooden blocks set between upright posts. These were roofed with thatch—the crevices stuffed with moss and clay. Windows were few, small and high, and some had a thin skin nailed across them. Small sheds on the edge of the enclosure housed goats, swine, and oxen, and the serfs. A large enclosure in front of the great hall was used for gatherings, sporting contests and was a place where friends could stroll and talk. They met warriors, thanes, a minstrel and some children still panting from their games, one of whom was Oswald's son by his Irish wife. A tall warrior held a staff on top of which was the tufa—the waving feathers which signified the leading English king. Already Oswald had re-united Northumbria's two warring kingdoms of Deira and Bernicia, and as ruler of the largest English kingdom, with strong alliances with Dalriada and other kingdoms, he was recognized as first among equals.

The banquet proceeded in the great hall that was flanked on either side by kitchens, guest rooms and ladies bower. Meetings were planned for the next day at which both Oswald and Aidan would set out their proposals, so

97

for now Aidan could relax. As the banquet drew to a close, however, Oswald did something that took Aidan by surprise, and threatened to jeopardize the entire mission before it had begun. He announced to the assembled company that, as a sign of his welcome and support, he made a gift to Aidan of a precious royal horse, so that as bishop Aidan might reach as many people in his large kingdom as possible, in the shortest time. It would, he said, enable Bishop Aidan to travel as far as York and Carlisle and conserve his energy. He then placed into Aidan's hands, in a grand and generous symbolic gesture, the expensive reins that belonged to the horse.

Aidan froze. He had proposed to tell Oswald the following morning that he and his faith-sharing teams would always walk among the people and eschew the trappings of the court. He could not accept a horse for it would distance him from the peasants who could not afford horses. Yet, to refuse this gift in front of the entire court before he'd had the chance to communicate all this to Oswald would be an insult, a disaster. Aidan prayed. Words flashed through his mind: "Horse. . . You've always wanted this. . . Opportunity. . . Temptation." He jumped across an abyss into the Word of God, and he heard himself saying "We are deeply grateful for your welcome. This generous offer is a sign of your belief that God has called us here. We seek to learn lessons from the previous mission, to live simply, to offer a different approach which may surprise some, but we ask you to trust us. Until we meet to talk these things through tomorrow, may I lay these reins before the altar in the church, where it will be our practice to kneel before we retire to bed?" The king nodded. The mission survived to see another day.

The brothers had some days to explore the garrison and to mingle with the people whose language they could not speak. Jonas found himself playing with some children as if they had known each other for life. Killian wandered outdoors and tried out various implements as he gave some workers a hand. Several times during that first week Oswald gathered groups to hear Aidan speak about the Gospel, and introduce each brother by name, who told something of what was in their hearts. Oswald stood beside them and translated their words.

On the second day Oswald and Aidan had their first of many heart-to-heart meetings. They discussed the evangelization of the kingdom, a school for English boys, the spiritual needs of the royal centers— and first of all, a place where Aidan might establish a missionary monastery base. Aidan explained that, as with Iona and Dunadd, it was vital to locate the monastery near enough to the royal headquarters to be protected, but far enough to sustain its independent life of prayer and hospitality. Oswald, perhaps reluctantly, accepted Aidan's reasoning. He conducted Aidan to the highest point of the Rock. With their backs to the sea they surveyed the lush landscape—enticing blankets of undulating green encompassed by the Cheviot Hills. "Choose your site" said Oswald. Aidan took his time. No place called to him. At last he turned round. There was nothing except the sea—except for the Farne Isles to their right and in the distance to the left some rocky hill with a small hinterland. "Is that a peninsular or an island?" Aidan asked. "As the tide ebbs and flows," said Oswald, "that place is surrounded twice daily by the waves of the sea like an island and twice, when the shore is left dry, it becomes again attached to the mainland. At low tide we can ride to it from here." He explained that when the Saxon colonists came up from Lindsey and established their headquarters in this region, those Lindisfaren, as they were called, re-named that island Lindisfarne. The island represented a turning point in the fortunes of the English. "The Britons knew it as Medcaut" said Oswald, "which means Island of Healing." Then it was that Aidan recalled the bard he had heard as a boy telling the tragic story of Medcaut, and how his heart had been strangely warmed. Lindisfarne—the Rock of the English: Medcaut: the Healing Place of the Britons. "Can we visit Lindisfarne tomorrow?" he asked. "We were at home with our island monastery at Iona, but a mission monastery needs also to be connected to the mainland. If our visit reveals no contrary reasons, let us build our village of God there."

So they did. Oswald provided three skilled staff and four serfs to accompany the brothers to Lindisfarne there to build the simple huts of their first monastery. As they worked, Aidan surveyed its cliffside hill. At Iona, Columba built his cell on the little hill—should he follow his example? Aidan decided not. He would live on a level with his brothers, though they did build a watch tower on the hill, so that they could light a flare to warn their protectors at Bamburgh if they were in danger. They built a little wooden church in the inner rath. There they placed an altar and a copy of The Gospels. They erected the monks' cells to the right, and guest cells and a refectory to the left. A small distance behind the church they built cells for the boys they hoped to recruit for a school, and in due course they constructed a scriptorium between the church and the boys' cells, and a little hospital. All these were simply made of wood.

The outer rath stretched down to the harbor. There, over the ensuing seasons, they made a stone kiln for burning lime, a mill in which the corn was crushed, storehouses, and wattle huts for pottery, blacksmiths' work, and the building of the boats. Beyond were the fields.

Aidan taught the Rule of Columba but added to it, for things that the Irish took for granted, and therefore never needed in a Rule, were not obvious to the English. Simplicity and hospitality, for example. The English fought fiercely to possess things. Even the peasants treated their homes as if they were forts. So Aidan taught them the rule that God's earth is for all to enjoy and share with others, and that they treat each person as a child of God.

Columba had insisted that no work should be done on the sabbath. This had caused controversy, since other church leaders claimed that Sunday should be the Christian sabbath and that Christians had no obligation to cease from work on Saturday. Aidan advised that Monday to Friday would be the full working days, but if things needed to be done on Saturdays, he was happy. Fast days were another matter. He was resolute that brothers would fast from food until 3.00 pm on Wednesdays and Fridays, but he would not impose this rule on others. They fasted on Fridays because on that day the Lord was nailed to the Cross, without food or drink, until the ninth hour.

So they sought to model God's kingdom for the English by creating at Lindisfarne a place of prayer and hospitality, learning and work, where each labored according to their ability for the common good. It would be a village of God which could sustain the resident brothers, the mission brothers, the English students, the workers, and the many visitors who would come.

As the mission to the English developed Aidan was increasingly absent, but Lindisfarne was always the mother community which sustained him with its loving and dedicated life. He never forgot the day when a boy named Caoimhin who was cured after he prayed for him danced round the outer rath, throwing petals on the grass and singing. Boisil, helped by Barr, was a sound and strong prior. Under his leadership the monastery grew from strength to strength.

The memory of the Romans who had made Britain a colony of their empire was kept alive among the Northumbrians by the presence of the wall built by Emperor Hadrian. The Britons and the peasants needed no reminding that the Saxons had then invaded and made the land their own colony. Lindisfarne would not be a colony of invaders: it would be a colony of heaven.

BLAZING THE TRAILS

Within a month the first brothers hit the roads. They'd had a few weeks at Bamburgh and Lindisfarne mingling with the Saxons and they knew just enough English to get by. Some well-meaning people said that their walking unprotected into the byways of the kingdom was foolish. The mission brothers kept before them, however, the example of the Lord, who spent three years walking the tracks of Galilee, going with his disciples into villages, homesteads, and crowds, and then retreating to places of quiet. In order to steep themselves in the ways of Christ they had practiced washing one another's feet, and they had listened attentively to their Saxon friends tell of their homes and customs. They often recited Christ's words "In as much as you visit the sick, clothe the naked, and feed the hungry you do it to me." They learned a prayer: "Christ before me, Christ behind me, Christ in face of friend and stranger." As they walked they each tried to learn a Gospel passage or a Psalm, and to meditate upon it.

Before they set out Aidan took Declan, Diuma, Donan, Mael and Ronan aside. He explained that they might meet four groups of people. The majority would be English pagans. These would not warm to foreigners like them who wanted them to change their religion. Some would be British pagans, whose beliefs were much different to those of the English, for they were handed down from their Druids. They should not make them think that everything they believed was wrong. They would explain to them how the Druids' wisdom was a preparation for the Christian Faith. They might suggest to them that they, like Columba, could make Christ their Druid. The third group were English who had been baptized under Paulinus's mission but who had gone back to their pagan gods. They were the most difficult to reach. They must not urge them to change back to Christ just because they again had a Christian King—nor because it would bring them material gain. They would help them to understand that Christ does not remove suffering from us, but shares it with us. The fourth group were Britons, few in number, who thought of themselves as Christians, for their grandparents had been, though they had long lacked clergy, Gospels or churches. The Britons had a saying: "You cannot teach grandmother to suck eggs"—those nominally Christian Britons might resent them because they had been invited to their land by their foreign conqueror. They might be nursing hurts, and the brothers would do well to remember that they were Christians before the Irish were. As if all this was not complex enough, Aidan also alerted the brothers to an opposite danger. Some, knowing that he was close to Oswald, might rush to accept the new faith only in order to get the favor of the King.

At various times the brothers discussed how a conversation might go when they met someone from each of these groups. Following such a conversation Aidan always brought them back to their first principle: Greet each person they meet. Take time with each who returned the greeting. Befriend them and listen to what they had to say. Ask them what they believe. Ask them if they would like to know what they, the brothers, believed. Respond only if they invite them to. In such ways he prepared his teams. Nothing, however, had prepared them for what they actually met.

They met nothing. That is, nothing but sullen stares and silence. Most people avoided them. All were suspicious. The brothers had the worst of both worlds: they were alien foreigners on the one hand, and, on the other, although as allies of the King they might have had favors to distribute, in fact they brought none. They returned to Lindisfarne from their first journey discouraged.

Their second journey was to the slave market. Various landowners at court had given Aidan money "for the church." He refused to spend one coin on their personal needs or on buildings—he spent it on the poor. So at the slave market he was able to buy the freedom of three serfs, Ogbert, Okfrith, and Eddie. These liberated slaves were delighted, but some were bemused, for their lack of education offered them little opportunity. "Would you like to become part of our monastery at Lindisfarne?" Aidan asked them. "We can find out what work you are suited for, and even whether you have an aptitude to study." Eddie became a fisherman, Ogbert found himself at home in the Lindisfarne cow sheds, and Okfrith discovered a talent with the quill. As they journeyed together back to Lindisfarne, however, they became the brothers' English teachers!

Aidan had not thought that this simple act would have wider repercussions. Nor had he realized how fast news traveled across the large kingdom. One thane told another, and during the drinking evenings in their various halls, when half the world was present, gossip galloped like a horse. Soon the travelling brothers noticed a subtle difference in the way people looked at them. They took the brothers into their hearts.

On subsequent journeys the brothers waved a greeting to a passing farmer, and he returned the greeting. A group of people who were boiling their food shared their fire and the brothers' food. A woman brought her sick baby to them. They prayed for it and she took them to her home. Neighbors gathered. The brothers asked them to tell them about their concerns. Barely another month had passed when an astonishing site met their eyes: the people in the village they were approaching ran out to greet them. They knelt, and asked the brothers to bless them and make the saving sign upon their foreheads. They invited them to their homes and shared food. Soon the whole village gathered round to hear them read from the Gospel.

That kind of thing began to happen in village after village. It was an astonishing turn of events. Nevertheless, they had reached only a fraction of Bernicia, and they had yet to enter Deira, the southern sub-kingdom. More doors were opening than one faith sharing team could go through. Oswald agreed to send messengers to Dunadd and Iona asking for more brothers to come. Iona sent emissaries to all their monasteries and churches in Ireland and Britain, and so many more were enlisted, and continued to be enlisted for several years. Some of these were priests who baptized the new believers and gathered the people each Sunday.

A SHINE IN THE ROYAL CENTERS

Aidan was committed to a people's mission. He was determined that the royal center should not become a cage, as it had for Corman, and as had the royal centres for Bishop Paulinus under a previous regime. Yet he knew he must not fall into the opposite trap of siding with the people against the court. If they lost the good will of the court all else would be lost, too. He and Oswald had a good relationship but different agendas. For example, in Bernicia Oswald went along with Aidan's determination that all church buildings must be simple. In York, however, Oswald restored the damaged but prestigious buildings that Paulinus had established. He argued that if Aidan would not ride a horse he would not expect to oversee such distant buildings. He wanted to gain the respect of southern kingdoms with a Roman form of Christianity and to build alliances with them. Because both king and bishop were servants of Christ, their agendas both served the greater good.

Saxon kings traveled throughout their land dispensing justice and authority and collecting rents from their various estates. Oswald aimed to visit each royal center at least once a year. These included Ad Gefrin (Yeavering), Dunbar, Holystone, Carlisle, Easingwold, and York, each of which Oswald renovated.

He was keen to revitalize these, to put trusted colleagues in charge who would reach out to old and new friends, and improve the conditions of those who worked the lands around them. In this way he would earth his authority in the far-flung parts of his kingdom, and travel from these centers to establish ties with other English kingdoms. He wanted each center to have a chapel and a chaplain who would teach the Faith and lead regular prayers.

Aidan had always been clear that they must start their work at Bamburgh, open their hearts to everyone at court, share with them their vision, and ask for their help. He would always be grateful that in the first weeks Oswald, with great humility, translated beside him. Although Oswald had at first been disappointed that Aidan would not routinely reside at Bamburgh, Foigall had made a good impression. He had made a friend of one of Oswald's older thanes. They conversed daily until Foigall's English became quite versatile. Foigall learned about the antecedents of Saxon royal families, and drew knowing smiles when he wove their anecdotes into his stories from the Bible.

Oswald agreed to Aidan's request that he have a private chapel built just outside the busy inner compound, where Aidan could retire to pray, and think, and be. This was most used when Aidan was in royal residence for meetings or for certain Christian festivals.

While Oswald was on his travels several of his warrior thanes asked to speak with Aidan. They offered him gifts of land and money, but not without exacting their price. A Saxon people's territory depended upon victory in battle. A victorious king rewarded his warrior thanes with properties or hides of land, and this bound them to him. They, in turn, raised up warriors and tenants who were loyal to them by making them gifts. These thanes wanted the church, through gifts, to be bound to them. Aidan struggled with pangs of fear. He thanked these benefactors for their generosity. He explained that there can be two ways of making a gift. One way was what they knew already. Another way, which Christ and the first Christians practiced, was to make a gift because you wished to bring good to a person even though you received nothing in return. He explained that the mission brothers must be free to serve all people as God directed, and that they treated everyone, even a serf, as a child of God. He could only accept a gift if he was free to give it away to whomever he wished. One thane was so angry he stormed out shouting that he would complain about him to the king. Another became rather cold and said Aidan had given him cause to think; he quickly left without repeating his offer. A thane named Agilwald, who owned land by the river Coquet, took much interest in Aidan—too much. He gave him a large gift of money. Soon after that he informed him that some difficult neighbors were in a land dispute with him. He asked Aidan, as a man of peace, if he would ask them to desist—and he hoped he would then be able to make further donations to the church. Aidan took the trouble to find out the neighbor's side of the story. This man owned a much smaller estate, and to him Agilwald was a bully who issued threats if he did not hand over land which had always been his. Aidan urged Agilwald to be generous to his neighbor as he had been to him. Another thane gave Aidan a large sum of money. "You can build a new church with that," he said. Aidan told him he would give it to the poor.

Aidan asked that Foigall should be his representative at Bamburgh for the majority of the time that he was travelling or at Lindisfarne, and that Foigall should oversee the spiritual work in each of the royal centers in consultation with himself.

Oswald was always in residence at Bamburgh for the Nativity and Easter festivals. He turned these into significant occasions, to which many people, including royal exiles related to Edwin, who had deposed his father, were generously invited. Aidan led the celebrations at these times. The thing that most rejoiced his heart during his entire life work in Northumbria was what happened at Oswald's banquet one Easter. Rich foods had been placed on silver dishes. Just as Aidan gave thanks for the food, the officer for the poor informed them that a crowd of poor people was outside begging for alms. "Take this food to them." Oswald ordered. A moment later he ordered his staff to break into pieces the silver dish on which the dainties had been placed and give each of the poor a piece of silver. Aidan was so thrilled that he raised Oswald's arm and prophesied that it would not perish. Oswald's love of the poor sprang from his love of God. He could neither bear them to be hungry, nor that they should be turned from God by the greed of wealthy Christians. He was the first English king to appoint an officer for the poor.

During conversations with Aidan, Oswald recalled how they had both been present when Domnall Brecc was crowned king at Dunadd in 630, and how they were both versed in the Columban tradition. Before Columba's time, the kings of Dalriada had been subject to the rulers back in Ireland. Columba had sought God's choice of an independent ruler of Dalriada and had ordained him as king using a set form. He had preached, laid hands upon him and crowned him. Oswald, who was already king of Northumbria in law and in practice, had never been crowned. They held a coronation. Aidan laid hands upon Oswald, placed the crown upon his head, the scepter in his hands, and Oswald dedicated his life and his kingdom to the King of Kings and to the service of all his peoples. A shine had come into the royal centers.

SOUL FRIENDS AND THE THREE LENTS

Some strong foundations had been put in place: the values of simplicity, humility and hospitality, the daily rhythms of prayer and Scripture meditation, the sharing of friendship and faith—but one fault line in Aidan's own life remained. He was too busy. The mission was bursting forth in all directions. Impossible demands were put upon him, and he felt pushed from buttress to post. He was wanted at the court and at the monastery, he had oversight of faith sharing teams for which demand far outstripped supply, students' parents and the school pestered him as it expanded into uncharted territory, lands were being given for the building of new monasteries, thanes from Deira were pressing the church to start things there, and Oswald had a new idea every time they met! So much of it was good. It felt as if the mission was at a threshold. Yet the apostle Paul wrote about the evil one prowling about like a lion seeking whom he could devour. If he could devour Aidan, all else would fall into his lap, and Aidan was very near to exhaustion.

Until he left Iona he had always had a soul friend assigned by his abbot. The brothers here had soul friends, but he had not. Recognizing his personal needs, he asked Boisil to be his soul friend. Although Aidan was titular abbot of Lindisfarne, Boisil had grown in stature and was now its abba in all but name. He, too, was busy, but he delegated well and made a priority of his times for mentoring. Boisil had average height, dark hair, and piercing eyes. He did not engage in banter, but was warm and interested in people. Being well-read, he always had something new and something old to draw out of the riches of his mind.

At their first meeting as soul friends they discussed the role of the soul friend among the English. The Irish brothers had each been assigned a soul friend, and English boys at the school would be given one, but otherwise this custom had not become a practice of the English. Aidan said he thought it was a precious gift that in time some would ask for, but it was not something to be imposed or even expected of all. However, he would talk with Foigall. It would be good to spread awareness of this custom among his friends at the court.

Boisil's main concern was for Aidan. He recognized symptoms of exhaustion and being torn in many directions. It was a sign of the deep trust between these two men that Boisil felt free to challenge the man who could dismiss him from his post! He recognized that the building of foundations had been at a huge cost to Aidan. There was a real danger that the urgent would crowd out what was eternally important. So he asked Aidan "What about the Three Lents?" The Irish tradition of three Lents had been given a nod at Lindisfarne, but not among the new Christians. If Aidan did not model this, who would? The Irish tradition was that busyness was not a reason to forego a season of retreat, it was the reason why it should take priority. The third of these forty day periods of vigil followed Pentecost. Aidan went to a planned meeting with Oswald, who had many matters that required action. Aidan plucked up his courage and said "I have to cancel all duties and go on retreat, alone. I would like to do this on Farne Isle." Oswald was horrified, but only for a moment. "I will have my staff erect a shelter tomorrow," he said. The Farne Isle, though wild, was close to Bamburgh. Humans had never inhabited it. Local people feared it—they said it was the haunt of devils. Maybe they mistook the wails of the seals and the shrieks of the breeding kittiwakes for the cries of demons.

On his first full day on Farne Isle Aidan mulled over with the creatures and God the multitude of activities that crammed his mind. Deeper issues came to the surface. He resolved to delegate everything except those things that, at present, only he should do. That included spending several days walking among the people each month. Concerns that had lain, neglected, in the background of his mind, jumped into the foreground: Women, the Britons, and the healing of lands given by powerful people for new monasteries—that they might become villages of God.

chapter 15

VILLAGES OF GOD
Healing the Land

Aidan loved evangelism. He felt compelled to pass on the message of Christ, but he knew also that they had to model God's kingdom on earth or their words would mean nothing. Had not Bishop Irenaeus of Lyons taught that Christ had two arms? One arm was the message; the other was the embodying of Christ in a visible community.

The faith was spreading fast in the hearts of the people thanks to the proliferating mission teams; now they had to think what visible signs they could establish that would remind people of the Faith after brothers had left. Christian waymarks around which people gathered for prayers and teaching were erected in many places. These were formed of two large slabs of stone, or flint, in the shape of a flat cross. It became a custom for landowners to erect a Cross on the highest point of their estates. Others erected them at meeting places and harbors.

Now that the church had gained influence landowners gave sites for a chapel where they could pray, for a burial ground, or for a church. Some of these would house just a priest and a prayer cell around which the estate dwellers gathered. Others were large estates where the intention was to establish a monastic community. Certain donors used their land to bargain with God. They promised that if God gave victory in a battle they would give some land to the church; or if they did dark deeds they would donate land as a penance. Aidan disliked this. The spiritual dynamic of the great Irish monastic villages lay in the consecrated life of their founder, and of the founder's spiritual heirs, expressed in daily practices of prayer, study, work, and hospitality. Such things could not be commanded on the whim of a donor, they were the fruit of purity of heart and patient toil. Aidan wrestled with this issue on his Farne Isle Retreat. How could these communities be villages of God and not the pawns of powerful overlords? He decided on two initiatives. He would develop Lindisfarne so that it became a resource for godly living for a wide area, and he would require that every donated site would be soaked in prayer for forty days before one sod of turf was turned.

The forty days of prayer came to him on the Thursday of his retreat on Farne Isle. Thinking of Jesus' Supper on his last Thursday, he had prayed late into the night in obedience to the Lord's command to watch and pray. In the darkness it dawned upon him that Jesus' death—the cup that in his flesh he wished he would not have to drink—would have effects vastly beyond the petty drama being played out by the Jewish authorities. The land itself would be affected by Jesus' lived prayer. The sun would hide its light. The earth would open and raise up the dead. He prayed "Sweet Jesus, wash this land with your tears and ours." It was then he resolved that brothers would pray for forty days over each piece of land that was given to the church for a monastery

His first step was to recall his original twelve Irish brothers to Lindisfarne. "As a dog returns to its vomit," he told them, "so a place returns to its original spirit unless it is completely cleansed of ungodly influences and consecrated to the Triune God." A place might have accrued all kinds of unclean spirits or pagan superstition, but the spirit of possessiveness is what he feared most, transmitted through the landowner and imbibed even by the new Christian occupants.

"What should we pray?" asked Ciaran. "Everything, anything or nothing," said Aidan. "Cleansing takes place when a person comes to be soaked in God and soaked in that place until the soakings become one. It may be that tears will come—tears for the spirit of possession, hatred, belittlement, neglect. Then you pray that these spirits lose their hold. It may be that tears of joy will come for the harmony of nature. Then the birds and the streams will sing out more because you are there joining them to their Creator. It may be the Spirit will lead you to make reparation. Confess on behalf of those who have gone before you the sins in that place that have broken God's heart. If you are a priest, say the Holy Sacrifice. Place sticks or stones that represent these sins on an altar and afterwards throw them far and dance and sing. After forty days on a mountain Moses' face shone. We must pray that the faces of those who form a community in these places will shine too."

Declan could not understand how some brothers never seemed to pray. He was thinking of Killian. "Understand this," said Aidan, "God has made each person different, but each can serve God equally well. Everything Killian does, he does to God. Deeds are his prayer, speech is yours, silence is another's. Any of you can spend forty days in one of these places and pray in your own way. Your presence is your prayer."

Mael asked Aidan to teach them a prayer they could repeat in such places. He taught them:

> Circle this place, O Lord
> Keep evil out, keep good within.
> Keep fear out, keep trust within.
> Keep greed out, keep generosity within.
> Keep hatred out, keep love within.

There were times, in various places, when some agitated person would urge Aidan or his brothers to cast out demons from that place. They learned to be careful about these requests. If one devil is cleared from a place which is then left empty, seven devils may fill the vacated space, as Jesus warned. Aidan's practice was to heal a place through forty days of vigil only where it was to be inhabited and where prayer could be maintained.

Holy places adorned Ireland like scattered flower petals: Aidan encouraged all English Christians to hallow places through prayer. They prayed along the wall the Romans built from coast to coast in the time of the Emperor Hadrian. Remnants of the auxiliaries who stayed on when the Roman troops left and of communities that grew around the forts were Christian. Granaries had now replaced the turrets, and young men with trades, not only war bands, lived in these places. Aidan made a special point of visiting the Fort of Banna, where holy Patrick had his home. It was surely no accident that Oswald chose to spend the night there before his battle with Cadwallon. They met a man at Banna Fort who sat at his fire, making pottery. "Oh yes," he said, "Oswald came here and we liked him. The youngsters rode off with his warriors for the big battle. And would you imagine, that evening the birds flocked in a great arch over our heads and sang in a mighty chorus like they'd never sung before. Oh yes," he said, "my little girl said to me we ought to call this place Bird Oswald, because since King Oswald came the birds sing again. Just think of that, Bird Oswald—what ever next" he chuckled.

Many such sites were prayed over on Aidan's travels. Certain places, however, were resistant. The brothers discussed why this should be. "The land holds and reflects the human story sown in its soil," Aidan taught, "it may be that treachery and blood-revenge are embedded in certain places." He encouraged them to learn from local people the unhappy story of that place. When the time was right they might together make an act of confession, seeking God's forgiveness and a new start. They prayed like this in Dun Kaith, in Woden Hearh, and in Thunor Leah. Local people gathered with them around the pagan standing stone. They marked a large circle in the earth. Each brought a stone that represented some foul deed or curse which had scarred that place, or the name of someone who had been slain. As each named their stone, they hurled it into the circle and said words like these:

> I name this curse that was put upon this place . . ..
> I name this act of blood . . .
> I name this person who was killed here . . .
> I name this grievance we have carried in our hearts . . .

On it went, differently in each place, until the stones made a cairn. "We circle this place in the power of the Mighty Trinity" they would pray as they walked the bounds. Then they would cut two branches, tie them in the shape of a cross, and place this in the cairn. They would bless water and pour it over the stones. "The Tree of Death has become the Tree of Life" they proclaimed. They knelt and prayed "May the Cross of Christ set this place free—from the ill-intent of demons and mortals, from the bitterness of memories, from the power of the past to control the present." They chanted from the psalms the promises and praises of God. Before they left such a place Aidan proclaimed "The Lord is risen and is in this place" and everyone replied "He is risen indeed and is in this place for ever. Alleluia!" Many were the places where first Irish and then English brothers knelt, not just for a brief prayer, but for hours, days or a whole season.

LINDISFARNE

They had not waited forty days before the work on the Lindisfarne monastery began, though on the first day they blessed it, and invoked God's protection upon it. As stories were told of Medcaut's past, however, Aidan realized that here, too, evil as well as good influences can remain buried or be brought in by incomers. Betrayal and spilt blood, mixed with more recent pride, had seeped into the very earth. So they, and locals they had befriended, walked the boundaries of the enlarged monastic area to pray for healing and protection. They began at the ferry and ended at the place they call Mary's Gate. Old Ancram "the sour-faced seer" could feel things of which others had no knowledge. When the brothers were not far from Mary's Gate he said "a stream runs under here. It bears no good. It carries blood and filth and does not breathe. Mark my words, no good will come to people who dwell above it." Aidan stopped him, for the prophetic spirit had come upon him. "Christ descended into the depths of the earth to redeem all who were in thrall to evil, and all that was unclean" he told them. "Those who were imprisoned were set free and the earth could breathe again. In the name of that Christ, we say: Cleansed be the waters that flow under here. Freed be the spirit of all who live and visit here. In this place may the Tree of Death and stagnant disease become the Tree of Healing for the English people."

Aidan's first priority was to establish a daily rhythm of prayer and praise. They had no choir, but Ciaran could play a harp. They chanted the psalms in unison. Each time they gathered they had three periods of chanting. In the first two they sang together, but in the third they sang from side to side. Although the custom in Gaul, whose ways were becoming known among the English, was to have one reading from an epistle and one from the Gospel, the Irish loved the Old Testament too, and they introduced this to the English.

At Iona they celebrated Holy Communion on the mornings of Sundays and on the anniversaries of certain saints. Occasionally they rang the bell and summoned everyone to the Feast of the Saving Victim when someone had died or when grave news reached them. Aidan continued that custom at Lindisfarne, but added saints days that the Northumbrians felt drawn to. The liturgies the Irish used, though partly home grown, had been passed on from Basil and Gregory Nazianzen to the Egyptian Desert Fathers, and Comgall of Bangor adapted these in the light of Bishop Cassian's writings. Each monastery made its own variations and gathered its own collection of prayers for spontaneous use. At Iona they added songs Columba composed. Lindisfarne also reflected this approach. Brothers copied out such materials as they had, but gradually they added new prayers and songs drawn from Northumbria's emerging talent

No school for English boys existed north of that established by Augustine in Kent. Aidan determined to establish a school for Saxon boys at Lindisfarne that would train up the future Christian leaders of the English. It was a demanding but joyful task. Aidan asked the help of the English in recruiting. Oswald himself suggested some key families who should be invited to send their sons.

They would be versed in the arts of study and prayer, but also of discernment and discipline, friendship and leadership. The Irish teachers had improved their English, and the English boys had to learn Latin. A large wooden chamber served as a dormitory for the boys, and a smaller one for the daily lessons. The boys washed outside in a stone cistern of rain water. The manuscripts of the Scriptures and the Church Fathers were placed in a little library which gradually grew. New arrivals from Dalriada or Ireland brought further manuscripts and later visitors returning from Rome brought more. Copies began to be made once a scriptorium was in place, but the library was never large, for their mission was to give what they had to help establish other monasteries and churches.

The core of the syllabus was to teach the boys the Psalms and Gospels in Latin. Some struggled, but most managed to chant the psalms, at least, during the times of prayer. A brother recited the verses and the boys repeated them over and over again. The brightest pupils learned the Latin grammar, and were able to read Cassian and other Fathers. Every one learned the Creed and the Our Father.

Each boy received a set of tablets covered with wax, and a pointed pen of bone, quill, or iron. For ink they used a goat horn filled with a blend of charcoal and fish glue. There were relaxing times when the boys practiced a harp, horn or pipe, and sang the hymns. Aidan was mindful of the role the bards played in his childhood, and he encouraged them to tell their own folk tales as well as those of the Irish. The monastery often used the "glee-wood," as they called the harp, to accompany readings or stories at meals, especially on a festival or saints day.

They sought to utilize minds, hearts and bodies in the service of God and people. The boys took part in manual labor as well as study, and engaged in sports such as swimming, archery, and wrestling. In the summer there were races on the beach, and a tradition emerged of an annual climb up one of the Cheviot Hills. They did exercises that would prove most necessary when they made dangerous journeys on foot; it was essential that they could take care of themselves in the wild. They learned to look after the boats, whether rowing or sailing, and to guide the great floats from the mainland without grounding them on the reefs.

Although most of the farm work was done by the workers, the students learned to milk the cows, and fetch water and milk in pails. They swept their own dormitory. They were expected to consider the needs of others and to be punctual for the prayers; and they received punishments as was necessary. Each boy had his anamchara, and each was trusted to be alone, not only for the common vigils, but also to explore the dunes and think their own thoughts.

At first the boys came from warrior and landowning families. Some left behind the warrior way of life with ease; for others it was a struggle. They continued to love their horses and sports, but they no longer went off to battles, or bragged about their conquests in the mead halls. The older boys walked long distances, traversed the Cheviot Hills, and did physical labor even in winter when warriors often grew lazy and fat on their ale. The fire of Christ that burned within them transfused their natural energies.

Eata was among the first twelve students. He was one of the gentlest and simplest of souls one could wish to meet. He became a key worker of Aidan's mission. He did whatever needed to be done, and was the first to be entrusted with a major assignment.

Oswald introduced Aidan to one of his leading families, who placed all four of their sons in the school: Cedd, Cynebill, Caelin and Chad. Their father, Godwine, had become one of Oswald's most trusted supporters. He was a fine warrior but had larger aspirations for the land and for learning, and for his family. Chad, the oldest, regarded Aidan as an icon. He wholeheartedly embraced the idea of giving his life to God by learning all, living as simply and serving others as humbly as he could. In future years he would follow Aidan's example and walk everywhere, eschewing a horse. Caelin, however, had not experienced the choices that Chad had. He resented "losing" freedoms and fun times. His behavior, and that of his brother Cynebill, became erratic. On one occasion they ran away. Barr informed Aidan.

Aidan recalled the story of the desert ascetic Antony. When an archer criticized him and his brothers for having a relaxed recreation time, Antony asked him to shoot one arrow after another. Each time the bow strings stretched taut and the archer became tense. "You see," said Antony, "it is not good always to be like that. We need times to relax." Aidan realized that the younger boys needed to enjoy their favorite pastimes and to have fun if they were ever to choose disciplines out of a free heart. He asked Ronan to spend some months at the monastery and to coach the two younger brothers. They took to him at once. He challenged them to ride horses at low tide to Bamburgh, to beat him at rowing, and they told each other stories about their experiences.

As those two brothers shed their frustrations, their love of God came to the fore. Somebody nicknamed the four brothers "Mathew, Mark, Luke and John,," and they were often called "the four Evangelists."

They went on to do great things for God and became known as the school's "wandering scholars." Chad was a younger half brother whose mother was a Briton. Egbert, Jaruman and others also joined the first intake of twelve boys.

Barr proved to be an outstanding teacher. He held dialogues with the boys on matters of history and geography. The English believed the world was like a round, flat plate, and they had strange ideas of the Otherworld. Barr used his knowledge from traders, pilgrims, and books to give them a wider understanding. He tried to make learning interesting. He introduced puzzles, and he encouraged them to give accounts of their own travels.

Many kinds of visitor came to the monastery and Barr encouraged the boys, from time to time, to act as a visitor's guide.

The scriptorium began with the brothers, but most pupils were given instruction in the art of illumination, though only the most able were given a calf skin. These prepared with great care a service book for each new church in the kingdom. As skills developed, a person might spend many hours over one single letter. The manuscripts were bound in strong leather cases.

After the terrible battle of Medcaut the island had remained deserted, apart from a few fishermen's storage huts. Aidan determined that they would make friends with folk on the nearby mainland. Some of them helped in the work and in time settled on the island. As years went by a doctor, members of the nobility, and former slaves were drawn to live there. Others came because they were sick or aging, and brought their own attendant. Some came simply because they were hungry to learn the ways of God.

Chickens, cattle, and fish in their home-made ponds soon populated the tidal island as much as the seals. They, too, were part of the Lindisfarne community. As the years went by they created a cemetery. Families as well as monks were buried there. A Saxon named Ealfrith became a fine stone carver. His runes and Saxon letters graced their first funeral stone. It grew into a village where serfs and farm workers also flourished.

Aidan and Foigall had gained the good will of warriors, administrators, families, and workers at Bamburgh. They asked the Irish teachers to mentor their children, and they asked help in mapping the towns and villages, the local customs, the land and water routes of the kingdom. As a result they were able to establish communities like Lindisfarne in other parts. Melrose was first. Harts Pool, Holy Well and Carlisle soon followed

The English people were introduced to spiritual practices and rhythms of prayer that were nothing less than a way of life. Cruel Saxon war-mongers had all but extinguished the flame of the Gospel that a few Roman ecclesiastics had brought. Now Aidan had lit grass-roots fires that surely nothing less than wholesale ethnic cleansing could extinguish. The spiritual birthright of the English was becoming a Scriptural, people-friendly, and flexible way of life nourished by a network of villages of God.

chapter 16

BEGA AND THE BRITONS

BEGA

It was the only time Aidan felt extremely irritated by Oswald. In the busyness of his first year Oswald had asked if he had heard of Bega when he was in Dalriada and continued "She is by the western shore—I think you should meet her." Barely a season had passed when he asked "Have you been to see her yet?" Aidan had a mission to organize, a monastery to establish, a court to relate to and did not ride a horse. The western shore was not the priority for his mission—yet Oswald wanted him to give his attention to this Bega!

Aidan would have pushed this matter out of mind but for his retreats on Farne Isle. During one of these the word, "Bega" became insistent. So he found out more about her. He learned that she was a princess whom Oswald had met at his first wedding in Ireland. They were kindred spirits. She brought the warmth of Christ to everyone she met. She wanted to be a bride of Christ, but her father, as was usual, wanted her to marry a prince from a tribe he wanted on his side, who agreed to this. The prince refused to take Bega's No for an answer and raped her in a fury. Bega fled. Somehow, she managed to get a message to Oswald who arranged for the heirs of that wise and Christian king Urien to give her sanctuary at Rheged, and promised her a welcome in his kingdom if he should ever gain its throne. Bega sailed from Ireland, arrived at Rheged and explored places along Northumbria's southward shore that might be suitable for a hermitage. She found a bay and a friendly landowner in what was now Oswald's kingdom.

Aidan placed Bega in his prayers. He acknowledged that she should be honored for what she had done, and that he was her bishop. He sent an Irish priest to her. Now the time had come to combine a visit to her with a faith sharing mission to the Britons on the western shore. The Saxons called these people the Welsh, meaning the foreigners. Their language was not entirely foreign to the Irish, however, and there had been many exchanges between the early Christian communities in their two lands in early days.

He journeyed with six brothers, including three of the original twelve. They were astonished at what they found at Bega's place. A path bordered by herbs and scented flowers led them into an area enclosed by three superbly constructed beehive cells. The central cell was a chapel. A beautiful cloth was draped over a stone altar, where a candle flickered. John's Gospel, illuminated in bright colors, lay open on the altar.

Before they reached the enclosure children came as if from nowhere. "Come and see our kitchen," they said, and skipped them into a marvelous rectangular building behind the cells. A delicious aroma of freshly baked bread filled their nostrils. Pots, beautifully labeled, lined the shelves; each was filled with fruits, roots, herbs, spices, or pickled meats. Swiftly, noiselessly, the youngsters formed a circle around them and sang a song such as they had never heard before. It went something like this:

> Welcome and welcome—a thousand welcomes to you
> Friends of Christ, honored guests
> Here may you know peace
> May smiles touch your lips
> May cherries bloom on your cheeks
> May joy shine from your eyes.
> May you eat well
> May you sleep well
> May you be well
> Until for ever in heaven you dwell.

A young woman stepped forward, her hands stretched out in welcome. "I am Bega. These"—her hand indicated the children—"are my monastery. Bishop Aidan, you are our Bishop, we are part of your family, and while you are here, this is your home. May you and the brothers be happy with us." They ate a meal with them—it was tastier than any Aidan could remember since he had left his childhood home.

After the meal a boy said "Please may I take you to our school?" They walked through two lines of newly planted trees. "Bega and her helpers from the farms planted these last year," the boy told them. The school was almost as large as the scriptorium at Lindisfarne. Children and adults had been put to work in imaginative ways. One was carving wood, another worked with clay; several copied psalms. Wool carding and knitting went on. In yet another building a group practiced singing.

A bell rang. They all went to the chapel. Psalms were chanted. A young man spoke a line, and everyone repeated it after him. Bega read from a Gospel. She read a line from the Latin, repeated it in the Britons' language, and everyone repeated that again. The prayers were said, then some children spoke prayers they had made themselves. Never had Aidan heard the like.

It felt as if this "monastery" really belonged to those dear people. After vespers the children returned to their homes and Bega talked with Aidan alone. "I expected to find a tiny hermitage tucked away somewhere," he told her, "how on earth did you get all this land?" "It's simple," she laughed. "I went to the farmer and begged a place where I could build a hermit's cell. When he agreed to this, I said he would be blessed, and that if he gave me more land I could develop things that would bless his family, his neighbors, and his fields. I suspect he did not want to give me more land. However, since he did not like to say this directly, he said—and remember this was in the middle of summer—"I will give you as much land as is covered in snow by this time tomorrow." The next day the weather took a sudden turn for the worse, and there was a snow storm. For about thirty minutes three miles of land was covered in snow. Perhaps my farmer friend was too proud to break the promise he had made in front of his family, but I like to think that the awe of God came upon him through this miracle, and that is why he kept his word."

During days that followed Aidan got to know local people. The condition of some of the serfs was appalling. But Bega had set up a team who took clean clothes and food to their homes. They washed children and old people, and they taught them a story from the Gospel each time they visited.

When Aidan met the farmer and his wife, he realized why they had such genuine affection for Bega. The wife had been taken ill, and they could find no cure. Bega prayed with her, and as she sat beside her the farmer's wife took hold of Bega's ring and clasped it to her. From that time she began to heal. Others, too had been healed when they took hold of the ring. A little girl who was dumb began to speak after holding it. He was concerned lest superstition should take hold of these good people and he spoke to Bega about it. "I know that it is Christ who heals," she said, "but sometimes some physical sign gives people assurance of this, and the healing Spirit delights to flow through things God has created, whether they are human hands or precious metals."

Over the next few evenings Bega told Aidan her story—a story of the rape and the voyage alone across the wave-tossed seas, of encounters with poor and rich people upon whom her life had depended, of the ups and downs of the court at Rheged, of her often disappointed explorations along the shore, and of her arrival, at last, in that place. Most women who had been raped would seek a refuge where they could nurse their wounds. They would be bitter or broken, or at least bruised. How could this woman be so radiant, so out-going, so vital? Aidan asked her. "This," she said, and raised her right arm. The golden ring which the children call a bracelet dazzled him as it glinted in the sun. A cross was engraved upon it.

When Bega was raped she had, indeed, she explained, felt violated, unprotected, hopeless. She had cried out to God and as she cried she ran as fast and as far as possible. She stumbled upon a hermitage which three sisters of Christ had made their home. They fed her and listened to her story. Recognizing that she must hasten on lest she be caught they urged her to take the ring. "We live in simplicity, and this is the only sacred object that costs much in this world's eyes. We are brides of Christ and we are vowed to the Trinity. We decided that instead of us each having a ring to signify we are a bride of Christ, we would share one large ring, through which each of us could place one finger, as daughters of the Trinity. We call ourselves "The Fellowship of the Ring—Three in One and One in Three, now and in eternity." May this be to you a sign that you are a bride of Christ, a sign of Christ's beauty that will replace the ugliness with which you have been marked. May this be to you a sign of the protection of your Lord. May it be a sign of the Trinity, that wherever God leads you, there you will have a fellowship so loving, so alive, that it will be a fellowship of gold." With those words ringing in her ears Bega had fled on, on to her voyage across the sea, to her endless voyage with God.

There was silence when Bega had finished telling her story, a silence so precious that words would have been unwelcome intruders. A tear fell from Aidan's eye. He stood, and bowed, and went to the guest's cell for the night. He asked her to share what she could with the brothers on the morrow. Together they prayed for her as Aidan received her vows.

THE BRITONS

The faith-sharing team planned to move on to Brennecatum, a hill-bound enclave of Britons twenty miles inland from Bega's hermitage. This was a new kind of test for Aidan. Until now he had worked with allies or ben-eficiaries of Oswald: these people resented both their Saxon overlords and their religious emissaries.

Aidan had taken care to learn all he could about these Britons. The Britons thought of the mission team, since they were agents of the Saxons, as outsiders. The Britons had been forced to learn some Saxon, of course, in order to exchange and trade, but they would have more in common with the brothers' Irish tongue.

At their first attempt they were rebuffed, so they gathered to pray and discuss what they might do. The varied personalities of Aidan's team were as vivid as a butterfly's wings. Tonbert felt Brennecatum was in thrall to demons, and that they should walk round its boundaries commanding the demons to depart. One brother said they should hold vigils, and another that they should find a Briton who worshipped at the Carlisle church, ask him to join their team, and then make another attempt to visit Brennecatum. Aidan suggested that before they did anything they should gain an understanding of why those Britons felt as they did. He pointed out that whereas the Saxons called those Britons the Welsh, they called themselves the Cymru, meaning land of comrades. He suggested that they should speak and think of them as comrades. The next question was, how could they gain understanding without first finding a resident who was willing to tell them what these people felt? Aidan wrestled in his thoughts as to how they could disarm the fortress in the mind of that people. To them, Oswald and his collaborators were the Great Satan. Before Oswald, they had entertained hopes that they might win back their lands from the oppressor: after Oswald's wholesale successes, every such hope had been extinguished.

A single thought came to him in the night—"Saint Patrick." Patrick was a Briton. He was brought up at the Fort of Bann at the western end of the Roman Wall. He went to school in Carlisle. His father was a deacon in the church, and his grandfather a priest. Suppose they could trace any of his descendants? Suppose the Carlisle monastery and local churches organized a summer festival to celebrate the feats of this holy man? This would be talked about. Patrick had been kidnapped by the Irish pirates. Suppose they, as Irishmen, made confession of their forefathers' sins in forcing young Britons to be slave laborers in a foreign land? Patrick was still a lad when this happened. Suppose they invited the young people of the area to re-enact the drama of the capture of Patrick and other local youngsters? There were young people in Brennecatum—would they be drawn to participate? They could be sure of nothing, but at least their aim would be to capture the imagination of some.

After much hard work the summer festival took place. Colorfully dressed people re-enacted the story of Patrick: his kidnapping and work as a farm slave, his conversion, escape, call to return, daring feats, and colorful encounters as he turned Ireland into a land of saints and scholars. They were astonished by the response. A young woman named Nia became a keen supporter. Her boyfriend took part in the hill races with a friend from Brennecatum named David. Nia, her boy friend, and David became so interested in the project that they agreed to take part in a "listening day" at Carlisle. The idea was that, having listened to the story of Patrick in a previous century, the brothers would now listen to the experience of Patrick's unhappy heirs today.

That is how the brothers grasped more clearly the Britons' suspicion of the English colonizers who had trodden down their land, their language, and their history, of the Irish who raided their coastlands, and even of other Britons, for in olden days they killed and fought one another. David, the Brennecatum runner, said that although his people no longer had priests or Gospels, they still celebrated the Paschal festival as a holiday, and were suspicious of Christians who thought they knew better than them.

David was quite competitive. He challenged one of the young brothers, Lamhfhada, who was a runner himself, to stay with Nia and her boyfriend in his family's large house, and compete in the forthcoming hill race. Aidan agreed to this, little knowing what it would lead to. David urged Lamhflada to run with him up the mountain. Lamhfhada was used only to the flat sands around Lindisfarne, and did not run up hills as did David. In his eagerness to keep up with David he lost his foothold as they leapt down the rock-strewn slopes and he fell badly. He cried out in pain, and could not move. His leg was broken. David ran down to get help. An hour later three men from Brennecatum arrived, placed Lamhfada on a stretcher, and took him to David's home. David's parents agreed he could stay there until he could walk again. During this time neighbors and friends of David called. They said they had come to help, but they often sat and talked. Lamhfada said he was sorry for causing them trouble and confessed that his pride had caused him to fall. Because Lamhfhada was in need of help, and hid behind no pride, the locals found him no threat, and warmed to him. He became a talking point—even a friend. The invisible barrier that had made this settlement seem like an impregnable fortress was wearing thin.

Aidan decided that they should leave several brothers at Carlisle when the rest of the the team returned to Lindisfarne. Months later he learned that Lamhfada had become a regular guest at David's home, and that other brothers were now also welcomed. Before they returned the brothers blessed the homes, the infants and the cattle of those dear folk.

chapter 17

OSWALD, OH OSWALD!

Another winter gave way to spring. Through Oswald, yet another door opened. That was his gift. A man of such vision, such zeal, such generosity of spirit. This time he opened a door for Aidan to meet Princess Hilda. She was among certain relatives of King Edwin who had fled the kingdom when he was killed but she, at least, now felt it safe to return. Oswald had made the kingdom secure, and had turned former enemies into friends. In fact he had invited them to the mid-summer festivities. This said much for Oswald—he harbored no grudges. It also said much for Hilda. She, too, held no grudges, and had taken risks in returning.

Aidan sat opposite her at the feast. She was the second daughter of King Edwin's nephew, Hereric. Her mother, Breguswith, came from a noble family of the Britons at Elmet. Aidan learned that she was born in Deira, which Oswald's father Ethelfrith had cruelly occupied for eleven years before Edwin. She was brought up a pagan, but at the age of eleven had been baptized by Paulinus, the Roman monk whom Edwin's Queen had brought as her chaplain from Kent. Thousands were baptized with Hilda on Easter Day at York. When Edwin was killed they returned to their pagan gods, but Hilda did not. "Why did you not?" Aidan asked her. "Because," she told him, "I knew Christ's religion was true, and truth is more important even than life itself."

She spoke of the bloodshed, the conflict, the unbelief in Northumbria, and doubted if it would ever cease for long. She had thoughts of making her future elsewhere. "You Irish are gentler," she said, "and you see God where others see only a hostile world." "We Irish have a saying," Aidan told Hilda, "that when the Son of God rose from the dead he leapt across the world like the sun, and every spot of land on which his shadow fell became sacred—and his shadow fell on many places in our lands on the edge of the world." "That," said Hilda, "is beautiful and I will treasure it."

Aidan and Hilda became friends under Oswald's protection. She visited Lindisfarne. She was shown the school, the scriptorium, the guest quarters, the fishing and milling places, and the manaig—the married quarters. She took a keen interest in the monastery and asked many questions. For example, one of their promising Gospel illuminators was working on the eagle that graces the opening page of John's Gospel. "That doesn't look quite like a golden eagle to me" she commented. "It is not," the scribe informed her, "it is the white tailed sea eagle that I saw in the Cheviot Hills last year."

Hilda told Aidan about her father's warring English forebears. Aelle first conquered Northumbria's southern kingdom of Deira and ruled from the old Roman garrison at York. Oswald's father, King Ethelfrith of Bernicia, grasping to rule Aelle's kingdom too, married his daughter Acha, assassinated Aelle, and forced Aelle's son Edwin, his own brother-in-law, into exile. Hilda's father, Prince Hereric fled and was killed since he like Edwin, posed a threat to Ethelfrith.

Aidan drew out of Hilda how those three poor women, Breguswith, her infant Hereswith and the unborn Hilda, clung to an unhappy existence without a man to protect them, and without knowledge of God to sustain them. Yet, Hilda said, God can give solace to his children, even if they do not know him, by means of signs. Her mother had a vision. After searching in vain for her husband she lay exhausted. Among the folds of her garments she felt something hard, heavy and cold. It was a jewel, greater than she had seen at any royal court, whose brilliance shed beams across other lands.

Hilda described how she took advantage of Bishop Paulinus's residence at York and the Latin books and tutors in order to embrace Christian learning, and how almost all those who were baptized with her returned to pagan gods after Edwin was slain. "I fear we here have little to offer you in such learning," Aidan said, "for we are a mission monastery, not a university." "I hear that you Irish have fallen in love with the desert fathers and mothers," Hilda said, "tell me how they have changed you." Aidan told her about their vigils in wild places and their penitential disciplines. He told her how most bishops in Ireland lived vows of poverty and obedience, under a spiritual father, and had neither their own property nor the power to command the community of which they were a member. "At York" Hilda said, "the church buildings were very grand. Your buildings are so simple, but then you find glory in God's good creation I think. And I understand," she continued, "that your missionaries go among the people and listen to them." After Hilda's return Aidan reflected on so many doors Oswald had opened which had led to significant breakthroughs of God's kingdom.

Oswald turned his attention to trouble makers on his northern borders. He had earlier laid siege to Dun Eidyn and occupied the region of the Britons north of the Forth river. Now he asked Aidan to join him there, where leaders of four once hostile races gathered to confer. It dawned upon Aidan what a work of mercy the Lord had wrought in those lands. The ongoing mission of blessed Columba's churches, strengthened by Oswald's alliances, had created a common Christian way among the indigenous peoples north of the river Tweed. They conferred with Britons whose forebears had been fostered in the Faith by the likes of Serf, Modwenna, and Kentigern. They renewed contact with fellow Irish from Dalriada. Even representatives of the lowland Picts joined the Saxons for this conference—sent by their King Nectan. The Britons required priests in their settlements at Culross, Dun Bar, Inverest Hill, and the place the Saxons call Whittinghame. The Irish hermits along the Forth were linked more closely with the Northumbrian church. Anticipating that there would be an increase in trade and movement of peoples in this region, Aidan expressed a hope that they might establish a series of new churches north of Lindisfarne, including, in due time, a church in the shadow of the Great Rock at Dun Eidyn and a hermitage on Bass Isle.

Oswald rode long distances in order to create friendships with the rulers of other kingdoms. He would race ahead with his elite warriors, to be followed by the carriages stocked with provisions. His links with the West Saxons were growing. In his first year he and Cynegils, the West Saxons' king, made a strategic alliance to prevent Mercia's tyrant, Penda, from attacking them. Oswald spent time with Ebbe and Aelfride at Ox Ford. He persuaded Cynegils to let the missionary Birinus preach to his pagan people. Birinus came from the Franks to the Britons on the advice of Pope Honorius. However, on his arrival he found the West Saxons so pagan that he decided to devote his ministry to them. At Oswald's urging King Cynegils gave Birinus hospitality and agreed to be baptized by him. Oswald was his godfather. Later Cynegil's son Cwichelm and his daughter Cyneburga were baptized along with Cwichelm's son Cuthred.

Oswald asked for Cyneburga's hand in marriage. Birinus conducted the wedding. Oswald's presence helped Birinus in his spiritual work, and immediately after the wedding Oswald and Cynegils gave him Dorchester, the capital of Wessex, for his diocesan see. He built many churches and by his labors called many to the Lord. Although Aidan was not at the wedding, he conducted a service of prayer and blessing on the royal couple upon their return to Bamburgh.

Oswald also made links with the East Saxons and East Angles. He asked Aidan to meet a fellow monk from Ireland named Fursey, who sought safe passage to the East Angles, among whom he hoped to start a mission. Oswald granted him his protection and asked him to speak on his behalf in negotiations with King Sigebert of the East Angles, and later with his successors Ecgric and Anna. Fursey was an intense and visionary man. Aidan liked to tell how he sweated when he recalled his out of the body experience of four fires that threatened to devour the earth. These fires were Falsehood, Covetousness, Discord, and Injustice. Fursey pleaded with everyone to turn to God in order to spare the land from those imminent fires. Sigebert had inherited his rule from King Redwald. Oswald and Fursey encouraged Sigebert to join one of Bishop Felix's monasteries, and helped to put the most Christ-like King Anna in his place.

Oswald never forgot his old allies, the Dalriadan Kings, who had helped him gain his throne. In 637 two rival branches of the Ui Neills in northern Ireland fought a fierce battle at Mag Rath. Oswald sent warriors to fight with the Dalriada branch. Warriors from the Picts and the Britons joined them, though they lost that battle. Oswald secured an agreement between the Dalriadans and the Picts: in return for their loyalty to him, he offered a degree of warrior support and hospitality. When Oswald's nephew Alfrith, son of his younger brother Oswy, was born in Ireland to a woman of high blood, Aidan felt that the bonds between the Irish and the English were inviolable, though later he became less sure. In a stroke of diplomatic genius, Oswald arranged for his brother, Prince Oswy to marry Princess Rhiainfelt, the last remaining heiress of North Rheged. This old Celtic and Christian kingdom became part of Northumbria without even a skirmish.

Once Oswald had extended and secured his borders he focused his energy on building up Deira, the southern part of his kingdom. He completed the work begun by King Edwin on St. Peter's church at York, and adorned it with lavish decorations. This pleased both the remnant of Christians of the Roman persuasion who lived in those parts, and those in kingdoms further south who would need symbols of power and wealth if they were to respond to the further initiatives Oswald had in mind. Oswald reminded people publicly that, as Bishop of all Northumbrians, Aidan was Bishop of York. The buildings were not to Aidan's taste (he resisted all pressure to "improve" his simple wooden church at Lindisfarne), but he performed his duties at York with a dignity that out-shone these adornments. Much more to Aidan's taste was the decision to invite Princess Heui to establish a monastery on the coastal headland at Harts Pool.

Princess Hilda married Ererld, one of Oswald's most loyal young thanes, and a true Christian, at the royal center at Holystone, and asked Aidan to conduct the ceremony. Oswald, and many relatives, were present; so, too, were the poorest workers from Ererld's estate not many miles distant. Aidan prayed that Hilda and Ererld would be fruitful with children, and was overjoyed to receive a message some months later that Hilda had conceived a child. Joy turned to sadness, however, for this dear woman, who had already suffered so many trials, lost the child.

Sometimes on a winter's night Oswald and Aidan would sit with a few staff and plot possibilities for new churches. They wished to encourage monastic settlements on land endowed by the king that would be led by a team of monks appointed by Aidan—thus retaining a purity and hospitality of heart that so easily fled in other endowments. They began at Melrose. Aidan desired to promote English brothers as leaders as soon as possible, yet he also wanted them to be steeped in the values of the Gospels and in a spirituality that had so formed the Irish. So he made two canny appointments. He made Eata, one of the most promising of Lindisfarne's English students, abbot, and placed the older, learned and spiritual Boisil under him as prior. This required much trust from them both, and it brought rich rewards. A monastery at Gates Head followed, and then others. Then they planned for places where they hoped to appoint a local priest, such as Marske, Kildale, and Billingham.

How was it possible for Oswald's worldly power and Aidan's monastic humility to walk hand in hand? Their differing roles did at times seem as difficult to blend as oil and water. Yet both were genuine servants of Christ, and both grew to like and honor each other. If Aidan was asked who was the greatest man he had met, he would reply that without a doubt it was Oswald. Even in Ireland, Aidan used to say, good Christians who gained power sometimes misused it. Oswald gained greater influence over English, Irish and other kingdoms, and in a shorter time, than any other ruler, yet always he loved the poor, devoutly served Christ, and won the affection of many without resort to deception. He was a great warrior, but, apart from securing defensive positions with the least violence possible, he never fought except when he was under threat. He was magnanimous in victory. He had a gift for friendship and for building alliances.

Aidan admired Oswald for fully using his opportunities to develop as a warrior prince while shunning his father's cruel streak. Aidan thought this was due to his mother Acha, who was a kind, steady woman of insight and who employed good people to assist in the children's upbringing. Oswald was ruddy and physically alive, but not restless. He was at peace with himself. Often Aidan saw him silent, deep in prayer. So they weaved in and out of each others' lives as brothers in Christ. A bond formed between them. They became soul friends. And they shared a satisfaction that the flame of Christ was spreading far and wide. Never had Aidan imagined that he could be part of something so amazing, so divine as this mission to bring Christ's ways to so many of the English kingdoms. Were there ever two leaders, before or since, one of the church and the other an earthly ruler, who worked so closely and with such effect to bring God's kingdom on earth as it is in heaven?

In his wildest dreams at the outset of his mission Aidan could not have envisaged such fruit. With one exception (Penda, the pagan ruler of the large midland kingdom of Mercia—the only major English kingdom to remain outside Oswald's grand alliance) the English lands looked set to become lands of Christ.

* * *

In early August in the year of our Lord 642 Mercia's pagan tyrant, with venomous intent, massed his warriors at Maserfield, in the west near the regions of the Welsh. Oswald raced there to lead his allies into battle.

Bamburgh was deserted but for the women, their children and the servants. Aidan hesitated. Should he be with his brothers at Lindisfarne, with the fearful remnant at Bamburgh, or with the warriors? At Lindisfarne they held a vigil through the night. In the morning he broke his walking-only rule and rode to the royal town. He listened to the fears of the warriors' families. He encouraged them to place their trust in God, and they discussed what might be done if the worst were to happen. He stayed with them that night, for they were like sheep without a shepherd.

If Oswald's forces had won, they would expect to hear the distant noise of returning hoofs. One day and then another passed, and nothing was heard. On the third night a solitary rider came, breathless and distressed. Oswald and his men had been massacred. Oswald's limbs had been dismembered and hung from trees, his head placed on a pole to warn any one from ever again daring to confront Penda in battle. Aidan decided to stay another day with those grieving folk. They held prayers and lit candles in the church, and he tried to comfort them as best he could. Later, alone, he wept.

Oh Oswald
Oak among briars
Ruddy and swift
True and valiant heart
Man of God
Mighty warrior, friend of the poor
You bound peoples together under the laws of Christ
How are the mighty fallen.

The following day many gathered at Lindisfarne to honor this great leader and man of God and to pray for his soul. Aidan delivered this eulogy:

> Oswald's great grandfather, Ida, captured Bamburgh in 547, but it remained little more than a bridgehead, a base for raiding into the Britons' lands. Northumbria was the creation of Oswald's father, Ethelfrith. When Oswald's grandfather, Ethelric died, Ethelfrith made himself ruler of Deira, too. Ethlefrith conquered armies and ruled much of the lands of the Britons: so did his son. But Ethelfrith knew not God, nor the gentle ways of Christ: Oswald knew them, and because of this he became the friend of his peoples, and of the poor, as well as of his God. Under him killing fields were transformed into fields of high endeavor, material provision, and love of God, and the English peoples were given a banner of faith under which to unite.
>
> Oswald had stature, both physical and spiritual. His head, round and radiant, his forehead broad and prominent, his long face revealing nobility, his nobility of spirit outshining them all. How many of his subjects knew that often he would remain at his prayers from matins until daybreak? He sat with his hands on his knees, his palms facing upward, open to heaven.
>
> What may we learn from our beloved king's example? He was decisive. "Time and tide wait for no man"—he seized the opportunity. In Saxon law he had gained the right to the throne upon the death of his elder brother—and he was prepared. In Dalriada he was part of a fighting-fit force of warriors, but also of a dynasty bound to each in bonds of friendship, and he had forged a life-giving relationship with Segene, our abbot at Iona. They shared their thinking and their praying. Oswald's enterprise had a strong spiritual under girding.
>
> He was open to God and to his people. That is why he was able to receive a vision the night before his battle against Cadwallon, and tell his colleagues about it, and invite them all, even those who were as yet unbelievers, to kneel and pray.
>
> He was strong and manly, and yet he was tender and childlike—a winning combination. He exhibited flair—a capacity to think big and do the unexpected thing that made other things possible. Hence his dash to Lindsey at the start of his reign. Lesser men would have feared that while he was away others would have undermined him at Bamburgh. But he earned people's confidence, communicated well, and delegated. Trust and friendship replaced the bullying and deceits that preceded his rule. . .

Aidan recounted the story of the two kings of Israel, Saul and David. He concluded: "If Ethelfrith was Saul, then Oswald was David—the king after God's own heart." Silence reigned among the mourners.

During the uncertain days that followed they heard that when Oswald saw that they were surrounded by enemy forces and that he was about to be slain he prayed for the souls of his warriors. His last words became a proverb among the people for many generations: "God have mercy on their souls," said Oswald falling to the ground. Aidan did not know that one day Oswald would be a model of a great ruler throughout Europe; churches would be named after him and fables written about him. One thing he did know: never again on this earth would he meet such a man.

Terrible fighting ensued. For many weeks they did not know whose warriors would take over Bamburgh. The slain warriors' families fled to relatives. Oswald's widow fled to his estates in the west, in the dale of Knuz. The serfs and a few attendants remained. Aidan brought one or two of Oswald's closest aides in to the monastery, for he sensed they would be a threat to a new ruler, though they proved a blessing to the brothers. Ererld was one of those slain. Hilda fled to the East Anglian court, where her nephew, Eadwulf, was now king.

Oswald's death broke Aidan's heart. The sense of loss gnawed at him day and night. Would he, bereft and broken, hold on to the truth of the many mysteries at the core of things or would he retreat into bitter refuge from the outrages that life inflicts?

chapter 18

TROUBLED WATERS

Dark night cast its shadow over Northumbria. Fear gripped its people. The tyrant Penda of Mercia strode from the killing ground at Maserfied to become the unchallenged power in Britain. However, he made it his first priority to secure his newly extended border territories. Only after that would he pounce on Bamburgh.

Lindisfarne made emergency plans in the event of an invasion. Some brothers would return by boat to Iona. Certain English students would return to their family estates and join in guerilla warfare. The poorest would stay and offer their services to their new lord. A few older brothers volunteered to remain in their monasteries and plead for peaceful co-existence with their new rulers. Aidan would remain Bishop in name to all Northumbrians from a base in Dalriada.

In the event a combination of a Dalriada offensive and an act of God kept Penda at bay. Dalriada excelled itself. Its fosterling, Oswald's younger half brother Oswy, had once been fourth in line to Bernicia's throne. Now that his father and both his brothers had been slain he was the rightful heir. His Dalriadan protectors, horrified at the prospect of a pagan take-over of their former Christian neighbor, rose up to provide Oswy with an army that secured him Bamburgh and Bernicia. The Deirans, to the south, asked Oswin, last in the line of Aelle, to rule them. Once again Northumbria was divided into two kingdoms, uneasily eyeing the other, both in fear of their Mercian foe.

Oswy and Oswin shared a common great grandfather, but they had little else in common. Oswin was a devout Christian. Oswy—who knew what really motivated him? Both, however, wanted Aidan as their bishop. Oswin said to Aidan: "The Northumbrians may be divided again into two kingdoms, but let not the church be so divided. You are the bishop of all Northumbrians, a sign of unity that can strengthen our faith in hard times and give us hope for the future." Even if the Christian mission was safe from pagan destruction in the immediate future, could Aidan, stripped of his most sustaining friendship, bear the weight that would now be put upon him? And was Northumbria in fact safe?

Penda moved towards Bamburgh. Oswy retreated to the northern borders. He called a new generation of Saxon warriors to join his Dalriadan allies. Among these was Cuthbert, an outstanding youth whose family were devout Christians. This combined army caused Penda to turn back, but for how long?

Battles were fought in the months of greatest light. Oswy rode off to secure his inland territory. Aidan decided to make his Farne Isle retreat before the dark nights set in. On his second morning there he espied clouds of dust on the distant mainland. These clouds drew nearer. His curiosity turned to concern, and then to horror as he saw their cause: hundreds of men dressed for battle were driving their horses ever nearer to the king's stronghold. By the time they entered the town he knew they were Penda's warriors. Mercifully, he thought, Oswy's fort was well nigh impregnable, high on the great Rock, but he was mystified by their busy coming and going. That night they lay in siege around the garrison. The following day they broke down the wooden fences and the huts of the poor, and built great piles of wood. They were preparing to burn down the town, smoke out the fort, and in due course to occupy it.

The invaders lit the piles of wood and smoke billowed towards the fort. For a moment Aidan thought of escape but his meditations had prepared him for this hour. He simply faced the town, raised his arms, and prayed "See, Lord, what Penda is doing." He kept first one, and then the other arm raised. As he stood like this in prayer the wind changed direction; the smoke and flames blew in the faces of the horses and their riders. They panicked, turned, and fled, never to return.

Many people had seen Aidan thus. They sent a boat to fetch him back. He called the people to the church. He led them in prayers of thanksgiving and psalms of praise. "Some trust in chariots, some trust in horses, but we will trust in the Lord our God. They will collapse and fall, but we shall rise and stand upright" they chanted (Ps 20: 7, 8). AAidan learned from such experiences that it is sometimes necessary to take authority in the name of Christ, and that this authority is of a different order from that imposed by human wills.

Oswy's passion was to build up his power base. The methods he used were not always compatible with the values Aidan taught. Aidan's meetings with Oswy were businesslike, but not of the heart as were the meetings with Oswald. They sometimes dined at the same table, but Aidan and his chaplain determined to eat sparingly and leave the table before carousing took over. Oswy continued the practice of endowing land for a monastery, usually to gain credence on earth or in heaven, or in an attempt to induce heaven to grant him a victory in battle, but he had little interest in the spiritual life that should animate it. Aidan had to plough that field alone.

Oswy had no great love for Northumbria. He fled it when only four years old, and during much of Oswald's reign he fought only in the regions north of the river Tweed. In alliance with Domnall Brec he engaged in the siege of Dun Eidyn, and fought several battles against hostile Britons. He had at least two sons out of wedlock. His wife Reinmelth, grand-daughter of the great Urien of the now almost defunct royal house of Rheged, came with him to Bamburgh. Aidan sensed that she, like so many women in arranged marriages suffered loveless indignities. She disappeared in the first year of his reign. There was no further explanation. Their son, Alchfrith, proved to be a mixed blessing—at times he seemed in rebellion against his father.

Before the year was out Oswy, with Saxon and Dalriadan warriors undertook a daring raid into the Mercian heartland and retrieved his brother Oswald's severed arm and other relics from Maserfield. Aidan agreed that Oswald's head should be enshrined at Lindisfarne, and his arm be placed in a shrine of silver in the church of St. Peter at Bamburgh. As word traveled that Bishop Aidan had once prophesied that Oswald's right arm would not perish, and this was living proof that his prophecy had come true, people supported him for reasons that he himself discouraged. Then Oswy annexed Rheged. Those two actions—the enshrinement and the annexation—seem to have given Oswy sufficient standing as a king to ask for Kent's Princess Eanfled to be his queen. This marriage was doubly convenient, for Eanfled had Deirian blood in her, so the marriage helped to cement his bonds with both Kent and Deira.

Oswy had ambitions to restore the large hall at the royal center at Yeavering which Edwin had built, and where Paulinus baptized thousands in the river Glen. This was eighty two feet in length and rose high above the river. Since this hall could hold over three hundred people, Oswy decided he would promulgate his new laws there and dazzle the people with feasts, entertainers and revels into the night. He loved to gather and reward his warriors there, flanked each side by his finely dressed thanes. Aidan was concerned lest the only things Oswy treasured were this world's possessions which moth and rust soon decay. Several things happened during Oswy's unhappy reign, however, that pointed those with eyes to see to the higher authority of the King of kings.

On hearing that Kent's king granted his daughter in marriage Oswy asked Utta, the abbot at Gates Head, to lead an escort party to fetch the Princess. The first Aidan heard of this was when Utta came to talk with him about this fraught mission. That was not the first time Oswy acted as if the church was his possession. True, he could, if he wished, have sent all the Irish monks back to Iona, but then he would have lost Dalriadan support. Aidan bided his time until Oswy was in a frame of mind to discuss good procedures in such matters.

Utta, a sincere man of stature, proposed to travel to Kent by land, gift the horses to the king, and return with the Princess by boat to Bamburgh, since the sea route was safe from bandits. Nevertheless, Utta was fearful lest storms capsize their boat laden with royal goods and the princess. He asked Aidan's advice and his prayers of protection. Aidan blessed a phial of oil and gave it to Utta. He prophesied "You will meet storms and winds. When they hit you, remember to pour this oil on the sea; the winds will drop at once, the sea will become calm, and will bring you home in serenity." That royal escort was, indeed, caught in a life-endangering storm. At first they panicked but as soon as Utta remembered he poured the oil on the troubled waters. All became still. That incident was the origin of a phrase that passed into the English language: "to pour oil on troubled waters." It taught the English that Christ's authority can be exercised in all circumstances.

Aidan conducted the royal wedding and got to know the queen. She was fine in her looks, with long black hair and a determined face, off-set by expensive robes. She had strong affections and a strong faith. It never occurred to her to adapt her Roman expressions of the faith to her new situation; that wasn't the English way as she knew it. So she kept to the Roman calendar and ways. Her coming changed the atmosphere at Bamburgh.

Over the ensuing years it also changed the atmosphere at Lindisfarne. In 648 the school and monastery were rapidly becoming the focus of Christianity in Anglo Saxon England. They had even achieved international fame as a center of learning and culture. Aidan came to preside at a festive Holy Communion to mark a new term and a new season. The entire monastery—students, workers, new arrivals, and guests—assembled to celebrate the Saving Sacrifice. A delicious smell of freshly baked bread filled the air. A brother from the kitchen placed a loaf upon the simple wooden altar. Like their brothers in eastern lands the Irish monks savored this bread as they savored God. They knew that those in the Roman tradition used hard, dry wafers in imitation of the Jews who used bread made without yeast at their Passover meal, but the tradition in all the churches of Columba, following the Gospel of John, was that Jesus' Last Supper was the day before the Passover, when bread with yeast was used. In any case, they liked to say, the yeast was all used up as it transformed the dough into bread, so they were using bread that was both unleavened and transforming.

Aidan, dressed in his usual simple attire, re-enacted the words and actions of Christ: "Christ, determined to give Himself up to death for the life of the world, gave us this great Mystery. He took bread, this sign of his presence in creation, into his holy and life-giving hands and blessed it." He took a piece of bread in each hand and stretched out his hands in the shape of the cross. He looked towards heaven and blessed the bread again. "Jesus gave this to his disciples," Aidan continued, "saying: Take, eat of it, all of you. For this is my Body, which is broken for you and for many, to be given for the forgiveness of sins. Do this in remembrance of me." Aidan took the cup of red wine, gently moved it towards the west, east, north and south in the form of a cross and continued: "Take, drink of it, all of you. For this is my Blood of the new covenant which is shed for you and for many, to be given for the remission of sins. Do this in remembrance of me. For every time you eat of this Bread and drink of this cup, you proclaim My death, confess My resurrection and remember Me until I come." Aidan asked that the Holy Spirit, like dew from heaven, might fall upon the bread. The congregation sang, held out their hands, palms open, to receive the food of heaven, and confessed their faith. Aidan made the sign of the cross three times over the bread and wine and knelt in silence. Tears welled up. The tears were for the Saving Victim himself, and for the people He came to save, especially the English, who had so many hungers yet to be satisfied.

When the liturgy was over, the youngest pupils took baskets of fresh, blessed bread and distributed chunks to everyone. They walked across fields to the huts of workers who were still unbelievers and these too received the bread.

Queen Eanfled was present. This was unusual, for she seldom worshipped outside a royal center where she could command customs that suited her Roman tastes. She was there because she had sponsored a nobleman, who sought healing at the monastery, and his attendant, an outstanding young nobleman who would study there. The attendant was named Wilfred. His ability and energy was matched only by his restless and tempestuous nature.

The queen's presence, the arrival of a monk who had the right to an attendant, and of a student who took more notice of the queen and her views than of those of the simple Irish brothers and their bishop, posed some critical questions about the nature of authority. Wilfred was itching to go to Rome. He had heard of its glories. Since the Emperor Constantine had made Christianity the empire's official religion, many had envisaged the church as an imperial court. God was the supreme Emperor, the bishops were his regents on earth who should be dressed in imperial purple and placed on thrones when they were consecrated. A bishop should dress, reside in a house and be served by staff as befitted one of high status. They thought of the Irish, who came from a country that had never been in the Roman empire, as a rather pathetic anachronism, to be tolerated, perhaps humored, in the hope that they would soon be superseded. That was the way Wilfred thought, and Aidan doubted whether their humble ways would ever satisfy him.

Success brings clashes of expectation and tests of ethos. Lindisfarne would now be tested. Aidan never believed that all bishops should be like himself, he believed in variety of calling and culture. He was, however, as were many Irish and Britons, more attracted to the model of Bishop Martin of Tours than to the imperial model. Martin had sat on a cow stool instead of a throne when he had been made Bishop, he had exchanged a palatial residence for a hermit's cell and as a result had inspired Christians to live as one community—there was no "us and them." That kind of community could be thought of as a colony of heaven, which had more lasting value than had a colony of a temporal empire, however splendid its buildings and bishops. Aidan was quietly convinced that his own call to eschew a horse, to dress simply, to walk everywhere, to worship in a bare, wooden church, and to have no favoritism was from God and according to the Gospel. He was convinced that the various roles in the church were a description of a function, they were nothing to do with power or prestige. A bishop was a shepherd and overseer and in his pioneer situation he was also a missionary, but every believer had their calling, each calling had its own dignity—they were all in it together.

A challenge confronted Aidan. He had to model how to relate in Christ-like ways to fellow Christians at the court who were contemptuous of his ways. The queen celebrated Easter according to the dates they followed in Kent and Rome. This came to a head when Aidan celebrated the resurrection one Easter at Bamburgh and she refused to attend because she was still in Lent. Aidan celebrated a second Easter with her and her attendants the following Sunday. He always remained warm and interested in the Queen and her courtiers, he accepted differences without judgment, and calmly got on with what was required.

Aidan was by no means against outward symbols of the splendor of God, but he preferred these symbols to be sited among the people and to express the power of the cross—transformation through brokenness—rather than the power of prestige and wealth. He wanted a spiritual home, a village monastery, not a mere building, however impressive, to be the center of the Christian life of Northumbrians. Queen Eanfled, supported by her biggest fan, Wilfred, wanted grand physical signs of Christianity to be built. This prompted Aidan to discuss with Oswy what further visible signs of the Faith they could establish in Bernicia.

Some months after that new term celebration Barr asked to see Aidan. He reported that Wilfred was a disruptive influence who constantly interrupted a teacher in order to give his opinions. He would say such things as "We need great buildings and artifacts here such as they have in Rome." Aidan was not against glories of art and poetry, but he believed these should grow naturally from the soil of inspiration. He said to Barr "It's nakedness that is important. If these things he speaks of are gifts they will be a blessing; if they are contrived—like the tower of Babel—they will hinder the Gospel."

Aidan never thought that the ways of simplicity and integrity could be imposed, but he prayed they would be embraced by English students as the Irish brothers shared their lives with them in sacred trust. Chad and his brothers were living proof that this was possible.

A certain spontaneity and sparkle disappeared from the daily round of work and prayer. Aidan sensed the danger that Christianity could become stiff. He did something about this. He recounted to the Lindisfarne brothers that time in Lent when Columba urged everyone to lighten up, to enjoy life, and God. Aidan encouraged the brothers to do the same and spent some time with them. They took food in their satchels and wandered to the loch where the migrating birds land. Some linnets, the birds of heaven, flew over and their eyes soared beyond the kingdom's pretentious ways.

Aidan was delighted when Baldwine, one of the students, sat beside him and spoke words like these:

Delightful it is to stand on the rock gazing into the face of the sea.
To hear the heaving waves chanting a tune to God in heaven.
To see the stones sparkling in the sunlight
To hear the joyous shrieks of the swooping gulls
To hear the seals singing on the sand banks
To hear the crashing of the breakers like thunder in heaven
To watch the ebb and flow of the ocean tide
To let sorrow fill our hearts for the blood shed in this land
To let hope flow in afresh with the incoming tide.
Let us bless almighty God, whose power extends over sea and earth.
Let us study sacred books to calm our souls
Let us do our daily work, giving to the poor.
Let us make our daily prayers, sometimes chanting, sometimes quiet
Always thanking God.
Delightful it is to live on a sacred isle
Serving the King of Kings.

On another day Caelin, who had the touch of a poet, brought Aidan a prayer he had written in English. Was this a first fruits of a common prayer of an English church, Aidan wondered?

> Here be the peace of those who do your sacred will
> Here be the praise of God by night and day.
> Here be the place where strong ones serve the weakest
> Here be a sight of Christ's most gentle way.
> Here be the strength of prophets righting greed and wrong
> Here be the green of land that's tilled with love
> Here be the soil of holy lives maturing
> Here be a people one with all the saints above.

The travelling mission teams were in abeyance following Oswald's death, but they got back on the roads. Aidan always aimed to bequeath to the English their own indigenous church, with its own leadership, within one generation. With Oswald on the throne, he took for granted that he, Oswald and the Iona elders would reach common discernment as to when all church appointments would be made by the church in Northumbria itself rather than from Iona. Oswald's death strengthened his determination to train and delegate to an English leadership. He took aside Chad, Cedd and other brothers, and they explored for a day what to do in a crisis. "When all around you is falling apart," Aidan said, "the one thing you can do is to convert people and train them up as disciples of Christ and as future leaders."

In the year 650 Aidan again sat long on the Farne Isle rocks in retreat. He watched the tide flow in and ebb away again. "Is God's work to be like this?" he asked himself. He reflected how the tide of Christ's Gospel had flowed fast across this, the largest of the English kingdoms. Villagers had flocked to receive their mission brothers, and some villages already had their own priest. Lindisfarne flourished, its school and guest rooms were overflowing. Daughter monasteries had been established in other parts of the kingdom, and the Faith had been embraced by leading families. It was due to God—and Oswald. Perhaps, too, it was because the failure of Corman's mission had caused them to re-think how they should express the Gospel. He had recalled the Lord's words "the pagans lord it over one another but you must be as servants." They had renounced human power and prestige as ways of advancing God's kingdom. This had endeared them to the English people—they had taken both them and the Gospel to their hearts.

When he saw the tide ebb, however, he worried lest that, too, would be their experience. Were there already signs? People criticized the very simplicity that they had embraced as their calling. They said that Aidan's simple dress did not befit the "high dignity of a bishop." They said their thread-bare communities could be swept away, as in a flood, if a hostile ruler came to the throne, and that they should build grand churches, estates and institutions that would give the church an equal footing with the powerful in the land. Aidan wondered also if the tide within himself was beginning to ebb: his energy was less than it used to be. He thought, too, of the sudden storms that seem to come from nowhere and wreak their havoc. Could a sudden storm blow them off course, or blow away the entire mission without trace? Then he recalled the Gospel story of Jesus asleep on a boat during a storm, of his terrified disciples who awoke him, and of Jesus raising his arm and rebuking the wind and the storm, which obeyed him. He was reminded that there is an authority which is greater than all the thrones and threats of this world.

After his return to Bamburgh a visitor brought news of something good that was growing up far from the intrigues of rulers. Brothers were establishing a fledgling community in the mouth of the river Tyne. The Tyne, sixty miles south of Lindisfarne, was a key traffic route in the middle of the kingdom. Aidan had recruited four Irish monks and eight of their former English students to build a little "village of God" where the ships came in. This was in keeping with Aidan's plan to produce an indigenous church within one generation. They now had more than a hundred English mission priests who had trained at Lindisfarne or a daughter community. It was the brother of one of these English priests, Cynnyd, who told Aidan the following story.

The brothers at the Tyne were transporting large logs on their boats with which to build the monastery dwellings. Fierce winds changed direction, and blew them out to sea. Their small boats tossed up and down; they were in danger of losing their cargo and even their lives. A crowd of peasants gathered on the shore and mouthed obscenities at them. "Good riddance. We don't want your religion" they shouted. But a youth named Cuthbert, he who had responded to Oswy's appeal for the young to join his warriors in defense of their kingdom, was relaxing on that shore. Cuthbert, who had embraced the new religion with all his heart rebuked them, and explained that the monks were good people. They turned on him and tried to shut him up. Whereupon he knelt on the sand, with arms raised, and prayed that God would keep the brothers safe. As he prayed the winds changed sharply, and the insults ceased. Those ignorant people began to sense the power of God and to respect the new religion. "We can be thankful to God," Aidan told Cynydd "that we now have communities of Christ in twenty seven places, and we can be thankful that we have Christians like that youth."

Cuthbert was a fruit of Aidan's mission. His parents had passed on its Christ-like qualities of faith to him, and had been among Oswald's most trusted thanes. Not for him the viciousness, fears, withdrawals, or betrayals born of insecurity. Here was a lad who was sure of himself and sure of his faith, who was capable of feeling compassion for the endangered monks, responsible enough to challenge his peers and, when they ridiculed him, to stand up and be counted in the name of Christ. One day, though no one could then have guessed it, he would become the foremost leader of the English church. "I would like to meet that young man" said Aidan, but he never did.

Troubled waters of many kinds would engulf the mission to the English, but one thing all now knew: As Jesus once stilled winds and waves, and Aidan's oil calmed stormy seas, so now the prayers even of an English youth could save a monastery and turn a hostile crowd.

chapter 19

SPIRITUAL FOSTER MOTHERS FOR THE ENGLISH

Aidan had always been dimly aware that some element in the Irish mission to the English was missing. This missing element came into sharper focus in the days after Oswald's death when he feared lest their mission should become side-lined by the power lusts of Saxon men. He realized that the English lacked spiritual foster mothers.

The Irish could not imagine how there could be a Christian people without its spiritual foster mothers. Ita of Killeedy was one of many holy women whom they called "a foster mother of the saints of Ireland." She excelled in the Six Gifts of Womanhood which Christian Ireland looked for in the well educated girl: wisdom, purity, beauty, music, sweet speech, and embroidery. People like Ita, and Samthann, and Darerca of Killeevy, and of course, Brigid, were as essential to their spiritual formation as were the Twelve Apostles of Ireland.

Aidan's mind often went back to holy Brigid and his childhood visits to Kildare. Brigid was known as the mid-wife of Jesus. They understood by this that she brought Jesus to birth in their land. "Mary's Son, my Friend, come and bless our kitchens; may we have fullness through you" she prayed as her mother worked as a slave in a kitchen. Aidan found himself praying this for the kitchens of the English. Brigid ruled both women and men in her monastery at Kildare, which replaced the forts as the seat of influence. In Aidan's thinking, each people and each generation needed these spiritual foster mothers—most of all the English. There were parts of the English make-up that only spiritual foster mothers could reach.

It was true that Columba had no female monks at Iona and, of necessity, Aidan had begun his mission with only male monks. But even Columba had brought his mother, Eithne to Hinba Island, and she became as much a mother to the brothers as she was to him; and then, of course, they created Women's Island. Saxon men spent their lives in battle and in bruising behavior: the English needed women who would nurture tenderness and insight in their homes and in their faith communities.

From his early years in Northumbria Aidan kept his eyes open for godly widows whom they could teach and bring into vows, among both the English and the Irish who had come among them. He encouraged them to be anamcharas to young people. That is why he received Kenswith and Hieu, as well as Bega into vows. And that is why he had asked Princess Hieu, who came from Ireland with other members of her family, to start the community of women at the Isle of the Hart, ninety miles south of Lindisfarne. He had heard that the East Angles, further south, were producing a first crop of spiritual foster mothers. Two of King Redwald's nephews fathered daughters who showed outstanding spiritual promise, Seaxburga and Etheldreda, whom Hilda helped to mentor. Such things encouraged Aidan to build on slender beginnings.

Princess Ebbe returned to Bernicia after her husband Aelfride was slain in battle. She discussed with Aidan the possibility of taking vows, and he suggested she test this by gathering a group of women who would follow a simple rule. King Oswy gave his sister the Roman camp near the river Derwent, at Indomora, as a place where she could gather some dedicated women. They drew up a list of noble women whose husbands had been slain in battle whom they felt should be invited to test a vocation with her. That place, however, was unsuitable as a spiritual nursery. It was typical of Oswy; he thought only in terms of power and prestige. If his military fortunes were to change, warriors would rush there and Ebbe and her sisters would have to move elsewhere.

Then there were developments with Hilda. Her sister Hereswith and her husband Aethilric raised their son Ealdwulf in the East Anglian court, but when both these were slain Hereswith joined a growing number of East Anglian women who took the veil in one of the Irish monasteries of Gaul. When Ererld was slain with Oswald at Maserfield, Hilda joined her sister at the East Anglian court and, unknown to Aidan, accompanied her sister on her journey to this monastery, at Chelles. In 647 Aidan heard that Hilda was intent on taking vows there, too.

On hearing this news he felt numb. His feelings from childhood that he was a Number Two person came flooding back. Surely that was why Hilda had chosen Chelles? This feeling was quite illogical. He knew well that Chelles had been founded by Balthild, the Christian East Angle who had been captured in a raid. She was sold as a slave to an official of Clovis 11, the young, long-haired Frankish king of Burgundy. When this Christian king saw her he was so captivated that he took her as his queen. He knew that Bathild was of a similar spirit to the Irish brothers in Northumbria. Aidan knew well that Chelles, like the growing number of monasteries in the northern Frankish kingdoms, was influenced by his countryman Columbanus. On his arrival in that land Columbanus had sensed a movement of God among the Frankish nobles, and he became the friend and mentor of many. Aidan sensed that the Irish passion to serve God and the poor in the simplicity of nature shone through many of those monasteries. Inspired by these, Balthild used her money to free slaves, and in fact ended slavery in that kingdom. She also used her money to found Chelles, and was regarded as its abbess. Chelles's Rule drew much from Columbanus, as well as from Benedict, the monk from Monte Cassino. Hereswith's family, including Hilda, had natural links and spiritual affinity with Balthild. What was more natural than for Hereswith to join Chelles, and for its abbess to invite Hild also to join them? And after all the upheavals and tragedies Hilda had suffered in the land of her birth, who could blame her for seeking a better life elsewhere?

In fact, Aidan felt nothing but despair. Longings that until then he had hardly dare name rushed into his mind: the longing that the English should have as many spiritual foster mothers as the Irish; that the English kingdoms should have their great double monasteries for men and women as did the Frankish kingdoms and Kildare in his own land. He became angry. How could the English ever know what God's Kingdom on earth is meant to be without women as well as men being in leadership?

Compared to Chelles, he had nothing to offer Hilda. A spiritual struggle raged inside him. Was the Christian thing to meekly accept that they should not expect someone of Hilda's caliber to be content with their undeveloped mission? As was his practice, Aidan meditated on Jesus' actions in the Gospels. As he meditated he knew that he was there among the English, not on his own behalf, but on behalf of the church of Christ, and of Christ himself. He rebuked the "Number Two" demon, he sensed it was Christ who wished to draw Hilda and others to become the spiritual foster mothers of the English. He asked Oswy to send a royal horse rider to the East Anglian court with an urgent message to Hilda. The message was this: "Do not go to Chelles. Your country needs you to establish its first community of women in vows. I want this to be the first of many. Do not worry that we have no existing monastery where we can train you. We will train you. Do not under estimate this call. I ask your obedience."

Hilda's decision to say yes meant more to him than anything since his arrival in Northumbria. Without her coming back, their mission would have remained only half a mission.

Aidan arranged to meet Hilda at the royal center at Holystone. There he poured out his vision for spiritual foster mothers of the English—and in time, for double monasteries for men and women led by an abbess. He spoke of his forebear, Brigid, whom some called The Mary of the Irish. As Jesus gave his mother to nurture the first church in the Roman Empire, so God called Brigid to this role among the first church of the Irish. He then looked at Hilda: "You could be the Mary of the English" he said.

Hilda reminded him that she had no training in the monastic life, that she had spent thirty six years engrossed in the changing fortunes of her family. She felt she needed an ordered program of study and spiritual formation, and that is why she had agreed to go to Chelles. They talked of her education. Truth to tell, Aidan felt that she had read more books and met more teachers than he. However, their monastic libraries were increasing, and he promised he would get copies of books to Hilda. They now also had several brothers who had completed advanced studies in Ireland, and he would send one of these to her. It was not all one way. Hilda yearned that English Christians should weave their faith in to all of life, and she knew that the Irish Christians had learned to do just that. This she could learn best, not in Gaul, but in Northumbria.

They talked about the role of the soul friend, the anamchara. Aidan told Hilda about Dara the Wise, and that he hoped many such women would emerge among the English. Hilda pointed out that in a proper monastery she would have been under the daily guidance of a senior nun. Aidan shared many things that had passed between Micah and Tomas and himself. He told her: we will visit you often and you will be under guidance."

Then they talked about The Rule. When Hilda and Aidan first met, he had said that the abba or amma *is* the Rule. Their life, their habits, their attitude, their teaching, were the foundation, and any brother or sister could ask questions about how these applied in a particular situation. Hilda pointed out that though this might work well in the first years of a founder, as monastic churches grew, and became school and farm and guest house as well as prayer house, a more detailed and written Rule was essential. She spoke of Columbanus's Rule, which Chelles had incorporated. Even that, she said, did not cover matters that she foresaw would need attention. Columbanus founded missionary monasteries—the English were a different kind of people and needed rules for a settled situation.

Hilda was often a step ahead of Aidan, but he tried not to hold her back. She had made a big sacrifice in heeding his call, and he would honor her. She would have her own space, her own authority. She would begin with a small group in a hermitage by the mouth of the river Wear. They would reflect on this experience—then she would be given larger responsibilities. Aidan asked her to establish a small community of widows in that place. Hilda gathered some friends, and Aidan suggested one or two others. He had a shock in store. Each woman chose a new monastic name. What characters they were!

THOSE AMAZING WOMEN BY THE RIVER WEAR

The locals hardly knew what hit them! Each woman lived up to her name. "Gentle Strength" Mildryth organized the building of huts for themselves and visitors, a refectory, a spinning workshop, a little scriptorium. Nothing would deter her, though she conserved her energy well. She worked for long hours, but steadily and without fuss. "Bold Battle Bathilde" decided to visit the serfs in the area. She was horrified at what she found. Some had untended wounds, others were embittered by feuds. One day she brought back a woman who was heavy with child. Her husband beat her and took all but the bad food for himself and their son. Bathilde brought this poor woman and bathed her; she fed her well, and was wet nurse at the birth. "We can't leave it at this" she said to her sisters, "that husband of hers will deny all but the rotten food to mother, and she and the baby might die." So a little hospice was built, and always there were some poor woman there. Those battered women expressed such gratitude—far more so than wealthy people. Some brought back their children and listened to the Gospel stories, and went home and repeated these to their neighbors.

"These people need education" said Bright Counsel Bertrude. So a wooden hall was built. Great log fires were lit and once every week their growing number of acquaintances came for storytelling, singing, warm drinks, and freshly baked bread. In the middle of these evenings Bertrude would get up and ask people what in their dreams they would like to do. "We will help you to fulfill your dreams" she told them. First one, and then another, were enlisted in some way. One person learned to cook and another to sew. One learned to script and another to card wool from the sheep until it could be used to knit garments. Others learned to speak well for the first time. A sewing group was formed, then a spinning group.

Noble Aetheln started the herb garden. She built a protecting wall of rocks and stones and planted herbs for use as medicines in the hospice and herbs for flavorings in the cooking. Eventually they had twenty beds, one for each herb. They grew cumin, fennel, comfrey, feverfew, yarrow, pimpernel, rosemary, sage, rue, lavender, mint, and lovage. Aetheln boasted that chamomile could help heal three score diseases. Once she brought in a man whose spleen caused him much pain. She mixed chamomile with water to ease his pain. She used chamomile for many purposes: to prevent premature birth in women, as a compound mixed with oil to relieve fevers, chewed into a compress for swollen eyelids, mixed with vinegar to cure scalp disease, and blended with wine to protect against poisonous bites.

That was just the start. Soon those ladies had a kitchen garden where they grew food for their ever increasing number of meals: turnips, parsnips, legumes, onions, leeks, mint, nettle, rocket, wormwood, basil, melons to name only a few. Then they developed the orchard. Those women planted more trees in two years than an entire thane's estate might plant in a life time.

Little Elf Elvina may have been small in stature, but she was a bundle of energy, and her eyes never ceased to twinkle. She had ten new ideas every day. Prayer mats was one of them. She organized a group to stitch these. They looked very like the prayer mat that Ameer used in the monastery in Syria. Indeed, she said she had learned of these from traders who had come from eastern parts. Soon each sister and a number of locals had their prayer mats, and each guest had one too. They would place them in front of the Cross and kneel. Sometimes, like Ameer, they faced east to greet Christ, who rises as does the sun, in the east.

Hilda had a good memory. During one of Aidan's visits she recalled a story he once told her of Columba's visit to Durrow, when he was told that the apples were too sour to eat. He blessed them, and people swore that from then on the apples became sweet. The women's first crop of apples was none too sweet, either, and after Hild had recounted this story she suggested Aidan bless their orchard. Some said their apples tasted better from that time on.

Aetheln was not content with three gardens. "Human beings need beauty" she would say, "so we shall have bright and scented flowers." Aidan noticed these were situated in front of the latrines—a very good idea, but one that he had never thought of. Some of the dyes used in the scriptorium were extracted from these flowers. He chuckled when he heard the locals were calling that place Women's Village, but he rejoiced that perhaps at last the English, had their spiritual foster mothers.

On one of his visits to Women's Village Aidan asked Hilda to say more about her statement that "the English are different." "Other people" (she politely did not mention the Irish) "do one thing at a time. The English are like jugglers who keep several balls in the air at the same time. They are practical. If some practical need arises they stop what they are doing and attend to it. To help them be like this, and yet live in community, they will need routines and rotas." There is nothing wrong with that, Aidan thought to himself, so long as the fire within is kindled each day.

Once word got round that women could take vows not just as hermits, but as those who live in community, Aidan received an increasing number of requests. . Heui asked permission to become a hermit, so Aidan asked Hilda to take some of her women from Stowe, and others who now needed training, to the larger rath at Hart's Pool. Further dwellings were erected there. They stood out like silhouettes on the headland, and so did the sisters as they strode across the fields in the wind.

Queen Enfleda made Oswin promise he would give lands for new monasteries if God gave him victory in a battle. Before one potentially calamitous battle she persuaded him to offer their new infant, Elfelda, to God if victory was granted. As a result of the ensuing victory the royal couple handed over their one year old to Hilda to be her spiritual foster mother Until she became a nun. Elfleda imbibed Irish milk as well as Roman ceremony. Though Aidan never knew, she became one of the strongest spiritual foster mothers in the land.

Aidan talked to Hilda about Bega, and suggested that she should come under her tutelage at Hart's Pool. "I have three thoughts" Hilda said. "My first thought is that, if this is God's will, Bega herself, who has mystical gifts, will be shown in her spirit that this is God's calling before we contact her. My second thought is that one of Ererld's widowed cousins, who lives only fifty miles from Bega, might become a kind of anamchara to the children and their families there, when Bega leaves, so that they can enjoy the fruits of what Bega has sown among them. We should encourage their pursuits, their education and their desire to be a neighborhood inspired by God. You never know, we may one day have vocations to the religious life from that place. My third thought is that, before her life is over, Bega will start a daughter monastery of ours."

As Aidan reflected upon these emerging foster mothers of the English, he at first thought how far they lagged behind Ireland. But on further reflection, admiration grew in him for the qualities these women were putting into the soul of the English. In contrast to the brutal strength of the so recently pagan warriors, these women poured in the milk of human kindness, along with a supple strength that could bend with the winds and survive calamity. The picture was certainly patchy, but something new and essential was coming into place. It had to be, for the growth of the church could not for long depend upon the support of a single king.

chapter 20

DEIRA'S BRIGHT SUN AND THE ECLIPSE

642–651

To cross the boundary from Bernicia into Deira was like passing from night into day. If Aidan's relations with Oswy were formal, those with Oswin were like the rising sun. Oswin was much more than a king, he was a magnificent human being. After Edwin was slain at the battle of Hatfield Chase, Oswin's father, Osric had secured the throne of Deira, but within a year both he and Bernicia's King Eanfrith had been massacred by the combined forces of the Welsh and the Mercians. Young Oswin fled for safety to the West Saxons. There he grew into outstanding physical and spiritual stature. Oswald, who was accepted as king by both Bernicia and Deira, and married the West Saxons' princess, might have felt threatened by Oswin's presence, but in fact their bonds as brothers in Christ proved stronger than their potential as dynastic rivals.

Aidan was not surprised when, following Oswald's death, the Deirians made Oswin their king by popular demand. The people admired him as a hunter and sportsman, and they thought of him as a friend. He took an interest in them whether they were of high or low birth. He had no chance of becoming a Bretwalda, of course—his kingdom was much smaller than Oswy's, and his only significant centers were Catterick and York. Nevertheless he attracted good men from almost every province to serve as his warriors and his court was like a large family.

Oswin could easily have appointed someone else to be bishop of York, but, as his message to Aidan made clear, he saw the church as a fellowship that embraced both the sub-kingdoms of Northumbria. He hoped that, as Bishop of York as well as of Lindisfarne, Aidan would reside in Deira for a season each year, and he did everything in his power to make Aidan feel he had a spiritual home there.

During Oswald's reign Aidan visited York only twice. His priority was to build up mission teams and monasteries nearer to Lindisfarne. Now, Aidan argued with himself, it was time to give equal attention to the church's mission south of the river Wear. Truth to tell, he was drawn to Oswin and wished to be often in his company.

Aidan was at first somewhat in awe of Oswin. Irish monks are thin and poor. Oswin had great strength, fine looks, many possessions, and much finery. Aidan found himself in the presence of someone who had everything of this world, and yet was uncorrupted by it. Despite his attractiveness to others, Oswin had deep humility and love of God. His big heart and easy converse soon thawed Aidan's diffidence.

At their first meeting Aidan told him of his life in Ireland, of his pilgrimage to northern Africa, and of his heartbreak that the Gospel had been lost to the people there, and then he gave a brief outline of the growth of God's work under Oswald. They began to confide in each other their hopes and fears. This was not easy for either of them, for Oswin's cousin was Oswy's queen and the anxiety they both shared was, in truth, Oswy. Tensions simmered between the two kingdoms throughout his reign. Oswin sensed that Oswy coveted his kingdom. He sensed that Oswy wanted to use Aidan and the church to further his ambitions. If ever Aidan's famed discretion was tested, it was in those conferences with Oswin

Someone called Oswin "the Bright Sun of Deira." From the point of view of the church this was an apt description. Oswin was concerned to advance the education of the clergy. Through his thoughtfulness Deira became well supplied with Gospels and other books, altars, and church adornments. He and Aidan planned how to strengthen existing churches and establish new churches, monasteries, and hermitages. They placed priests in the larger villages.

They erected preaching crosses like that at the Roman wall, and built cells where people could rest and pray. Fresh beams of Christ's light shone in the ancient settlements of Verteris, Derventio, Calcaria, Lagentium, Begelocum, Mamucium, Racum Veteranorum, Olenacum, and Verbia. They aspired eventually to have a place of prayer on every high place, and a Christian community in every valley and port where there was a settlement. They made plans for a Prayer Walk through the heart of the kingdom in two years time. Oswin would launch it by the river Humber, and ride, with his retinue carrying banners, the full length of the route. Aidan would follow on foot with a faith sharing team, and stop to pray with the folk in each place. They expected that many people, Christians and pagan well-wishers alike, would walk with them. Oswin had his own ideas for spreading the Faith. He proposed that the following autumn he gather his youngest thanes at York and create a temporary school, when brothers from the monasteries would teach the thanes about prayer, scripture, the desert athletes of the Spirit, forgiveness, the work of the anamchara, and spiritual warfare.

Despite his twin love of hunting and of the church, Oswin never lost touch with the poor and uneducated. These came to love their king. He and Aidan planned for the church, over seven years, to create a net that ensured food and care for the poor throughout the kingdom. Oswin, however, saw the poor as recipients: Aidan saw them as royal souls. This difference of approach was brought to light in a dramatic incident.

Although Oswin knew that Aidan liked to walk among the people, he was concerned that Aidan was getting older, and now had to travel further. He publicly gave Aidan his best royal horse, with its priceless royal trappings. "Just use it when you have to cross rivers or go on a long journey," he said, perhaps humoring him. Aidan felt unable to refuse this magnanimous gift.

Some days later he was walking with his team, the horse in tow behind them, when a beggar asked for alms. He only wanted a few coins to buy himself some food. Aidan did not carry money and he was finding the horse an unwanted complication, which conflicted with his vow of simplicity. So he instructed one of the brothers to give the beggar the horse, along with its silver harness and trappings.

On their return to the court, when the king came back from hunting before the evening meal, someone told him what Aidan had done. For the first time in his life Aidan witnessed Oswin erupt in fury. "How dare you give to a beggar a priceless gift I chose specifically for you as bishop" he shouted. "We have many less valuable horses and items you are welcome to give to the poor, without letting that beggar have the one thing I had chosen just for you." Aidan found himself replying, calmly and without hesitation: "What are you saying? Surely this son of a mare is not more precious to you than that son of God?"

The king stormed his way to the fire to warm himself, saying nothing for a considerable time. Suddenly, he gave his sword to his thanes, knelt at Aidan's feet, asked his forgiveness and said "Never again will I speak of this or form any opinion as to what money of mine or how much of it you should give to God's children."

Those words of Aidan and of Oswin were repeated so often down the generations that they seeped into the English mind. They reflected the statement in the Gospel of John the loved disciple that Christ is the light within every human being. If a beggar is a child of God, every human life is sacred and worthy of respect.

Aidan quickly lifted the king up and assured him he would be satisfied if he would banish his sorrow and join in the feast. The king did recover himself, but Aidan was seized with a fateful intuition. His sadness was so great that his chaplain noticed tears in his eyes. He asked him in their Irish tongue, so no one else would know what was said, why he was weeping. "Because," Aidan said, "I never before saw so humble a king, and I know that no Saxon king so humble will for long survive." To survive a Saxon king had always to be macho, and have his hand near the hilt of his sword.

As Aidan went to sleep that night he thought of their bright hopes for Deira and of the next day's long return to Bernicia. He slept, but not for long. He was woken by a vivid image. A bright sun dawned on the day of longest light; before its end, however, there was an eclipse. Brightest day had turned to blackest night.

* * *

Foreboding gnawed at Aidan throughout the long journey back to Bamburgh. Those who traveled with him could not understand it; they were in the afterglow of a wonderful time. A lifetime of images flitted through Aidan's mind: The Kildare bard's account of betrayal and blood at Medcaut; Oswald's bloody victory by the Roman Wall; his merciless dismemberment at Maserfield; the self-serving reign of Oswy. Should Aidan emulate John, the forerunner of Jesus, who rebuked a king for his wrongful deeds, and confront Osway? John lost his head for his courage in doing that. And now this awful intuition, though it ran contrary to evidence, about Oswin.

Aidan remembered his rule, to practice giving thanks to God in all circumstances. He thanked God for those four dear English brothers who did so well at school—Cynebil, Caelin, Chad, and Cedd—and who looked set to become much loved wandering scholars. He did not doubt that they would be used to instruct new converts in their own and probably other kingdoms. He could be thankful that at least in a few places new churches were still being established in Bernicia, and groups were discussing future possibilities. There was talk of taking stones from the Roman fort at Binchester to build a church at a crossing place by the river Wear where ancient tracks each side of the river connect. Already a group prayed there. They had named it Escombe. That place could become an oasis in the desolate no-man's land that lay between the rivers Tees and Tyne. He tried to give thanks, but verses from psalms blanketed his thanksgivings out like dark clouds: "as sheep are dumb before the slaughterer, so are your people, O Lord."

Many matters awaited his attention. He dealt with these. He tried to bear with dignity burdens that sometimes felt crippling, but still anxiety gnawed at his very bones. The atmosphere at Bamburgh seemed grim; Oswy was not there. Then the news came, second hand as usual these days. Oswy, keen to re-unite the two kingdoms under his rule, had declared war on Oswin.

Aidan felt numb, and stranded. News was so hard to come by. He heard that Oswin at first raised an army near Catterick, but once he realized that he could never win against Oswy's far superior numbers, he disbanded his army, wishing to save their lives. He heard that Oswin had negotiated with Oswy that he would retire. He went with his aide Tondgere to Gilling, where his friend Hunwold offered him a home not far from King Edwin's former house. There, in that supposedly safe place, Oswin was killed by an unknown assailant.

Aidan was in his little cell by the church just outside the bounds of the garrison when the news of Oswin's assassination was brought to him. Sharp pains seized him. He staggered towards the church. He stopped outside it, holding on to the buttress for support. If he was going to die he wished to die with the breath and beauty of God's creation around him: earth his bed, heaven his home. He clutched his heart in pain, unable to speak. Aides rushed to him. They laid him down. Doctors came. Since they could not move him, they built a little shelter around him, and strapped makeshift bedding to the buttress.

A multitude of thoughts flashed through Aidan's mind. Who would replace him? He had wanted to hand on an indigenous church to his successor; they were nearly, but not quite ready for that. His chaplain would send word to Iona. They would propose someone to come as bishop, someone Oswy would not object to. Who might it be? Finan, he wondered?

He recalled praying at the bed side of dying villagers, he recalled his tears of admiration and grief for Oswald, who died so nobly with forgiveness in his heart. Was it his turn now to die? He thought about what the Irish call their place of resurrection. For them it is important to die, or at least to be buried, in the place into which God has called them to pour out their life, the place from which they will intercede in the next world, the place from which they will rise again at the general resurrection—but he did not belong to a place, he belonged to a people.

He thought about the future of the church. Rome was far away. Yet he had heard about changes in the church. He knew that the Paschal Festival was kept on different dates, and the disputes about this were growing shrill. He had been told that no one wanted to raise this issue while he was bishop. No doubt it would come to a head when he was gone. He believed in unity. If wolves were devouring the sheep in one part of the church, true shepherds must come from another part.

Boisil came to see him. He read quietly from that Sunday's Gospel: "I have a baptism of fire to undergo. What stress I am under until it is completed. Do you think that I have come to bring peace on earth? No, I tell you, but rather division! From now on five in one household will be divided. . . father against son . . . daughter-in-law against mother-in-law" (Luke 12: 49–53). He laid his hands on Aidan's head and prayed. "Think of Jesus, think of Jesus" he said.

Depression sat heavy upon him. The flame that had impelled him throughout his life began to flicker out. A gentle lady in the court named Kemi bathed him. She crooned a song: "Into the arms of Jesus, into the arms of Jesus, into the arms of Jesus, angels and Mary beside. . ." He rallied a little. "He may survive" she said, "it is too early to say."

Another visitor came. He spoke to Aidan alone, in a whisper. It was Oswy himself who had paid the assassin to take Oswin's life, like Judas who betrayed Christ for thirty pieces of silver. A shock of pain tore through Aidan's body. He ceased to breathe and lay rigid. They fetched a senior brother. "He is dead" he said.

chapter 21

FIRE FROM HEAVEN

As his soul left his body Aidan's life flashed before him—his infancy and childhood, Durrow and Iona, Dunadd and Northumbria. Glimpses of future happenings came to him, whether soon or far into the future he did not know. Was he, like the apostle Paul, caught up in the third heaven? He witnessed countless scenes, smelt scents, heard sounds of indescribable beauty. He felt that he was in a garden of paradise. All thought of returning to earth left him and he wondered if he would be led into the eternal heaven.

A man ablaze with shining face led him towards a green hill where the sun was rising as on a most glorious summer day. They walked towards the hill, only to discover a deep, broad valley that had no end. This came between them and the sun-lit hill. Myriads of wretched souls writhed in this valley. They cried out, without hope, and there was no one to hear their cries. They were misshapen, and Aidan longed that they should be made whole. "Do not be misled," his guide said, "this is not hell as you think." The guide then departed, and darkness enveloped Aidan.

He stood in terror, uncertain what he should do. A foul stench arose, followed by long, hollow laughter. Evil spirits appeared, dragging human souls and throwing them down into the valley. One of these was dressed like a priest, another like a princess, and another like a lad from one of the farms. Aidan was filled with dread. He could not distinguish between the human laughter and that of the devils. The devils threatened to take him, too. He turned round. In the far distance he saw a tongue of flame, no larger than the smallest finger of a hand. Gradually this flame drew nearer, and the devils fled. He never saw the valley of tormented souls again.

As the flame came alongside him he realized that it was in fact the guide who had led him to that place, but now he was even more radiant than before. "At last," Aidan thought, "we can go to the rising sun." However, a high, gray wall blocked their path. It seemed to come from nowhere and to be endlessly long and high. Aidan could see no gate, no window, no steps. He was much surprised, therefore, that they suddenly found themselves on top of this wall, how, he did not know. From this high viewpoint they could see before them a meadow so full of sweet flowers that their scents erased from his mind the stench that had been so shortly before. Beyond the meadow, reaching far into the distance were glorious mountains and waterfalls. In our earth we have the seven colors of the rainbow. In this earth there were seven hundred colors. In our earth there are a limited range of sounds. In this earth each creature, each rock and stone, each plant, indeed, each petal, had its own sound. There were deep, echoing sounds like many waterfalls. There were a range of notes far greater in number than those in the music people play on harps. Each note had its own resonance, tone, and pattern of vibrations. Then it was that Aidan knew that this was the real earth, the new earth that the scriptures speak of, and he knew that the earth mortals briefly inhabit is but the shadow.

An innumerable company of men, women, and children came into view, gaily dressed while they ate a picnic. Further along he saw a vast amphitheatre. People of all colors sang, and danced and played music of so many styles he could not take it all in, though everything about this was delightful. "Is this the kingdom of heaven?" he asked his guide. "No," he said, "not as you imagine it." Before Aidan could see into it further the guide took him back the way they had come.

"Do you know what all these things are which you have seen?" the guide asked Aidan. "No, I do not," he said "The valley that you saw with the tormented souls, and the devils who took pleasure in entrapping them is the place where those souls have to be tested before they can face the Court of Light. The Son of God never ceases to pray that they will see themselves as they really are, and He prays that they and the devils will be converted. But He has ordained that his Body, the church, should pray night and day for the conversion of the devils and of the humans in their power." "Does that mean that these mortals and these devils will one day come to heaven?" Aidan asked. "The answer to that cannot be told," his guide said.

"Even if that is not certain," Aidan said to the guide, "surely that happy crowd and those who sang in the meadow are the souls in heaven?" "Not so," said his guide. "That is the garden where those who depart earthly life in love of the King of life, and practice good works, spend time. They are not yet ready to pass straight into the presence of the King. Nevertheless, at the day of accounting they will see the King himself."

"Shortly," Aidan heard his guide say, "you will return briefly into your body. This is so that you may tell the story of how God has formed you and used you to bring a people to spiritual birth. You are to summon your devoted young English scribes, Oisin and his brother. They are to write down everything that you recount. Before you return to earth you will be given glimpses of things that have been and will be. Some of these cannot be described in human words, but you must share what you can of these, too, with your faithful scribes."

Before Aidan returned into his body a myriad scenes flashed before him. He saw his saw dear mother, father, and brother. He saw Fionnula, Rianh, Donnacha, and Dara under the divine canopy. He saw that Eanfleda, wife of Oswy, persuaded her husband, as a penance for some misdeed, to give land where monasteries were to be founded. He saw a time when holy souls would make Ingethlingum and many such places dwellings of God. He saw dear Hilda in a large monastery on a headland high above the shore. She shone like a jewel whose rays reached beyond the western shores to other lands. He saw her spiritual children with a myriad callings streaming from her. He saw also Bega in a small monastery not many miles from Hilda's. A pathway went from one to the other and angels of God walked to and fro. He saw a peasant race through a field of cows and past human dwellings; he played a harp and sang to the world the stories of Christ in the English tongue.

Aidan saw Oswald sitting on a marvelous throne of light, his foot treading down the sword he had laid aside. He spied numerous churches among the Saxon peoples across the sea, even as far as Constantinople, which were dedicated to this man of God. And he saw many courts of kings where children were taught the deeds and manner of this servant of Christ, and where those who aspired to be rulers sought to follow his example. Oswald was not alone. Arthur was with him, and Oswin and other noble warriors. They were finely arrayed and metal glinted, yet there was no pride or violent intent among them—courage, valor, and forgiveness reigned. Aelfride, too, was among them.

He saw Sorley the former Druid, seated with many similar men and women. The spirit of wisdom hovered over them.

Long, dark shapes crossed the sea to Lindisfarne, and this beloved isle lay waste for centuries, with nothing but the lowing of cows. Yet before the end of the world he saw it again burst with life, and pilgrims, hungry for God, flocked to it from the four corners of the earth. He saw pilgrims the world over who cried "We are the children of Aidan and Hilda."

He saw Ireland and the lands of the English at war, and smoke and fields of blood and bodies strewn and untended, and he heard shouting and insults hurled. Then people of peace came, Irish and English, and washed the dead, and healed the land, and joined in a fellowship of forgiving hearts.

Into his vision came uncountable followers of the Prophet Moham-med. They had found the Lost Gospel. A partial rainbow appeared. Beneath it were assembled Britannia's four warring peoples singing "Shine, Britan-nia, Britannia light the waves." This was replaced by a rainbow of a thousand people of many races who all chorused in the English tongue "Now we never, never, never shall be slaves." Each glowed and carried a torch of flame.

He saw the entire world as if it was a vast clay writing tablet. Around it all the bishops of Christ's holy church sat in a single circle. Above each of them hovered a flame, like the flames that hovered above the disciples on the Day of Pentecost. The tablet fragmented into pieces; the bishops were separated on its different parts, and the flames grew dim. Yet he saw also that, before the end of the world, a large flame was held out, from which the ebbing flame of each bishop could be re-kindled. In order for this to happen each of them had to move from the place where they were, and go to the place where this new flame was. In this way, by some miracle, the bishops became a circle again, and the clay tablet became one, but still with the cracks showing where once it had been in fragments.

Aidan looked down upon his own bones, decaying in the burial ground at Lindisfarne. The bones were divided and taken to many places: to Bamburgh and to a large church near the river Wear; to Iona and on from there to Innisboffin and Mayo in Ireland. They were taken to the church at Glaston founded by the noble centurion Joseph of Arimathea. They were taken to other places too—and all these bones disappeared. Not one of them could be found. He asked his guide why this should be. "Because," he said, "your place of resurrection is not a place, it is the world."

Aidan's spirit began to come back into his body. He felt as if he was travelling through eons, then into a tunnel of light. This tunnel became somewhat darker, as if it was made of clouds; and then he found himself back on the bed in the little awning they had made within the church. He was still lucid.

He summoned Oisin and his brother, these young novices with hearts of gold whom he loved dearly. Their presence was balm to his soul. They had talent as scribes, but also that most important quality—discretion. Aidan told them that God had sent him back to earth in order to accomplish a task, and that he needed them in order to fulfill it. The task was to recount to them the story of his life as it had been lit up in the third heaven. He knew that it would be hard for them to write it all down. Indeed that proved to be so. But they gave all they had to give and they were inspired by God.

As Aidan haltingly recounted all this, even in his weakness, the pattern and meaning of his life became clearer. He realized that he was born under the sky-fired mantle of holy Columba, who lit Christ's flame within him. It was Columba who prophesied that his namesake, Aidan, must ascend the throne of Dunadd. From noble Aidan came Arthur, who rallied the forces of Christ across the kingdoms. From King Aidan's family the loving hand of fosterage was extended to the English exiles, who formed bonds with his Irish people that not all the wars of history would ever destroy. From this came the mission to the English. Aidan prophesied to his beloved scribes with gasping breaths that one day the English speaking peoples, with the Gospel blazing at their heart, would cover the earth as the waters cover the sea.

As Oisin and his brother wrote down all they were told their souls within them were kindled into heavenly flame. After they had finished they checked with each other and filled in gaps. Aidan lay beside them, silent, unconscious, until in a last burst he shouted "It is finished." There was a long silence. "Hold my hands" he then whispered to the brothers. As each held one of his hands he looked into their faces, his eyes full of light. "Pass on the flame" he smiled. Oisin's younger twin brother, although he was English, had chosen an Irish name when he took his vows. His name was Aodhna. It means "Born of Fire."

* * *

Aidan was taken in solemn procession to Lindisfarne for his burial, preceded by royal pipers. Two brothers were flame-bearers. He had insisted that his coffin be as simple as that of a poor peasant. By the end he no longer cared what happened to his body—the fire, that's what he cared about. Crowds flocked to that small island—some for the first time—to pay their last respects. The Queen read these words from the prophet Isaiah: "I will give you as a light to the nations, that my salvation may reach to the ends of the earth." Some thought she had received some kind of vision on the night that Aidan died, and had requested to read that Holy Scripture. Mother Hilda read these words:

> Wisdom entered the soul of a servant of God
> and withstood dread kings with wonders and signs.
> She gave to holy people the reward of their labors
> and guided them along a marvelous way.
> She became a shelter to them by day

and a starry flame through the night.
Wisdom 10:16–17

Seven brothers, talented in chanting, escorted Aidan into the Eternal
Glory with these words:

Holy Aidan, Flame of Christ
Chosen by God to be the shepherd of the English
You were ascetic in the line of the desert fathers
Shepherd-like in the line of faithful pastors
Missionary in the line of evangelists of the Gospel
Intercessor
Memorizer of Scripture
Defender of truth and right
Champion of the poor
Builder of community.
Rejoice and enter into the joy of your Lord.

You who poured oil on troubled waters
Teach us to bring your peace to a troubled world.
You who established our first school for English boys
Teach us to learn true wisdom.
You whose raised hand caused the invading tyrant to withdraw
Raise our hands to be as Christ's.

Illumined by the rays of the True Sun
You brought light into the darkest corners of this kingdom.
Forsaking the vain glory of earthly battles,
you entered into the spiritual battle against evil and ignorance.
Fasting from food and fastidious company
you taught us how to subject the flesh to the spirit.
Learning stillness, you put to death the rampant noise of human strife.

Rejoice, pillar of the church
Who entered into joy through many sorrows.
Rejoice, bearer of the holy flame
May you shine for ever in the presence of the Three-who-are One
To whom be glory through the ages of ages. Amen.

EPILOGUE

On the night of Aidan's death, 31 August in the year of our Lord 651, the young English warrior Cuthbert was guarding sheep on the Lammermuir Hills, some forty miles north of the church where Aidan died. As a result of what he was about to witness he would offer himself for life service at one of Aidan's monasteries, and become one of the English church's greatest leaders.

Looking up he saw a pillar of fire stab awake the night. Never before, nor ever again, would he see its like. The fiery cloud divided into two. The larger part zoomed off towards the coast, taking what seemed some awesome presence with it. The smaller part became the shape of a finger. The finger moved towards him, pointing, he swore it, at the very heart of his being. A bird flew overhead.

A PERSONAL REFLECTION
FROM THE AUTHOR

The identity of every country is shaped by multiple experiences, memories, myths and iconic figures. In the Bible, the Hebrew people were shaped by evil as well as good impulses, but their truest calling was rooted in God-guided archetypal figures: they were "children of Abraham" and they were named after the man who wrestled with God and was given a new name—Israel. Over the last few centuries of the second millennium many of the non-indigenous settlers in North America and other continents were dispersed from Celtic lands whose "sins of empire" are well-known. However, the truest, most Christ-like archetypal figures in these and other Celtic lands were not the oppressive or schismatic or slave-owning Christians of later centuries, but the formative saints: Patrick and Brigid in Ireland, Columba in Scotland, David in Wales, Cuthbert in England. Embracing all these lands was Aidan, born in Ireland, maturing in Scotland, then Bishop of an area that included Welsh-speaking Britons in the West, Scots and Pictish Britons in the north, and Anglo Saxon English in the south. The story of Aidan can surely help those in the lands of this dispersion to connect with an overlooked part of their spiritual DNA.

When USA pilgrims visit Lindisfarne I joke that the original WASPS were converted here. The WASPS were not white anglo-saxon protestants, they were white anglo-saxon pagans. This always gets a laugh. I wonder why? Is there a part of our lives that still needs to be converted? Can Aidan re-convert a dying Christendom as well as inspire fresh, indigenous expressions of Christianity

My connection with Aidan began in 1988. I had exercised Christian ministry in urban and rural areas, with new cultures through the Bible Society, and in a new area where all the mainstream churches commissioned me to establish "one family of Christians in one neighborhood." A conviction grew in me that a whole dimension was missing in the way churches operated—that competing with a consumer society on its own terms led to numerical decline (because business entrepreneurs do things bigger and quicker) and the death of community. I sensed that western Christianity had become disconnected from the poor, nature, and the unseen world. In order to reflect on these things I took a sabbatical journey to pilgrim sites in diverse countries which ended on England's Holy Island of Lindisfarne on New Year's Eve in the depths of winter.

Fifteen minutes past midnight I stumbled through deep darkness into a stable that had been turned into a prayer cell. I had been led into a Bethlehem place, not a top-down Jerusalem place—to a bare pilgrim island that was called the Cradle of Christianity, which symbolized for me, the gentle, authentic, organic, holistic approach modeled by Aidan who based his seventh century Irish Mission to the English here. I knelt on the hard ground. I felt as if the earth shook violently and my inside spun round at high speed. I heard an unmistakable, though inaudible voice say: "I want a new cradling. I want my people to live close to me in creation, in the people of all backgrounds, in the unseen world of the Spirit, saints, and angels. I want my people to discard excess baggage accumulated through the centuries, to live simply and travel with me, with space in their hearts for hospitality." I knew I could never be the same again.

I have expanded on this experience more fully in two books: Exploring Celtic Spirituality (Kevin Mayhew 2004) and New Celtic Monasticism for everyday people (Kevin Mayhew 2014). This experience led me to intensive study of Aidan and the Irish Christianity from which he came, and to regular, intentional meetings with three couples whose thinking and experiences resonated with mine. After two years of meeting we became convinced that God wanted a movement among His people that reflected these insights. We drew up a Way of Life that calls us to a rhythm of prayer and work, study and re-creation, creation-care and healing, simplicity and outreach, and which draws inspiration from Celtic as well as biblical and later Christians. Part of this Way of Life was given in prophetic words jotted down in a rain-soaked notebook as two of the founders traversed Lindisfarne in a gale. We publicly launched the Way of Life and invited anyone in the world to follow it with the guidance of a soul friend—the English word for the Irish anamchara. The USA, Ireland, and Britain were represented at the launch—now there are followers of the Way of Life in four continents.

We wondered what name we should give to this new movement. Perhaps in anticipation of Ancient Faith: Future Mission thinking, we decided to name it after two Celtic pioneer Christians of different race and gender who were in some ways ordinary Christians rather than superstars: Aidan and Hilda. In some countries the movement is known as Anam Cara—but we all draw inspiration from Aidan and his protégé Hilda. We committed to set up a Celtic Christian Studies program. I have been its principal tutor and the founder of our Celtic Christian Studies Library on Lindisfarne. I was commissioned to be the Community's founding guardian. For many years I have "lived" with Aidan on his island, and have spent extended periods on the Isle of Iona, whose seventh century monastery in what is now Scotland sent him to evangelize the English. I have also spent "time with Aidan" in the Ireland from which he came, where half my family lives. I have visited sites linked with him, and pondered about their history, lay-out, writings, and influence. I have trodden in Aidan's steps, asked myself questions about what, why, and how he went about his life and mission, and what were the hidden dynamics of his "hero's journey".

HISTORICAL NOTES

Information that claims to be historical may be placed into these categories: a) certain b) probable c) possible d) unlikely e) impossible. None of the settings and dates in the book are impossible, though the chapter on Aidan's pilgrimage to Alexandria is unlikely.

We know much about Aidan's legacy, and some seminal episodes and character sketches of Aidan's time in the English kingdom of Northumbria described by the monk historian Bede. The Ecclesiastical History of the English People, completed by Bede in 731 was re-issued with extensive notes by Oxford University Press in 1999. Nothing certain about Aidan is known before his commissioning in Iona. We know about the Iona monastery, founded in 563 by Columba, one of Ireland's foremost saints, from sources such as Adomnan's Life of Columba (Life of St. Columba by Adomnan of Iona edited and with extensive notes by Richard Sharpe—Penguin Classics). Although we know nothing certain about Aidan's boyhood, we know much about the Ireland in which he most likely grew up. A mass of information about Aidan's Ireland is contained in Early Christian Ireland by T.M. Charles-Edwards (Cambridge University Press 2000) and in Early Medieval Ireland 400–1200 by Daibhi O Croinin (Longman 1995). The Sources for the Early Christian History of Ireland: Ecclesiastical by James F Kenney (Four Courts Press 1997) gives details of 659 source documents. Irish Monasticism: origins and early development by John Ryan SJ (Four Courts Press 1992) provides information about the monasteries. The place of women, including spiritual foster mothers, is explored in Women in a Celtic Church: Ireland 450–1150 by Christina Harrington (Oxford University Press 2002).

Information about the life and kings of seventh century Northumbria comes from primary sources such as Annales Cambriae (Castle Studies Research, 2007), Bede, Ecclesiastical History of the English People (Oxford University Press 2005), Swanton, M.J. (ed) Anglo-Saxon Chronicle (University of Exeter Press 1996) and

Nennius, The History of the Britons (Kessinger Publishing 2004). Secondary sources include Anglo-Saxon England Volume 36 (Cambridge University Press 2007), Blair, Hunter, Learning and Literature in Anglo-Saxon England, Marsden, John Northymbre Saga: the History of the Anglo-Saxon Kings of Northumbria (Llanerch), The English Settlements (Oxford University Press 1986), Thornbury, Emily, Anglo-Saxon England Volume 36 (Cambridge University Press 2007 published online at www.journals.cambridge.org/ase and Wormald, Patrick The Times of Bede: Studies in Early English Christian Society and its Historian (Blackwell Publishing 2006).

PART ONE — KINDLING FIRES: IRELAND AND THE EARLY YEARS

Chapter 1: The Boy

The historical background recounted in this chapter is drawn from sources such as Early Christian Ireland by T.M. Charles-Edwards (Cambridge University Press 2000) and Early Medieval Ireland 400–1200 by Daibhi O Croinin (Longman 1995). For an online outline history of Irish kingdoms with maps see Ireland's History in Maps (500 AD) www.rootsweb.ancestry.com/~irlkik/ihm/ire500.htm The general patterns of tribal positioning are known, but exact boundaries and dates are not certain.

Canon O'Hanlon, in his multi-volume Lives of the Irish Saints assumes that the Bishop Aidan who had oversight of the monastery on Scattery Island in the mouth of the river Shannon, whose father, Lugar was related to Saint Brigid of Kildare, and who was brought up near the river Shannon, was our Aidan. This is not impossible, and I reflect these assumptions in the stories.

Bede observes that Aidan was noted for qualities such as gentleness, discretion, authenticity, love of the poor, justice, and spiritual discipline— "he lived as he taught." I visualize boyhood experiences and issues he had to face which were the forge upon which such qualities were formed. Typically, his soul friend, or spiritual mother would have been a key person in his formation, as well as his parents.

We learn, particularly from the many Lives of Irish saints, that as Christianity had spread through Ireland in the aftermath of role models such as Patrick, Brigid, and Brendan the love of all-out ascetic commitment took root, but not in a judgmental or grim way. The Irish were friendly, hospitable, and flexible. Those who took vows were part of a much wider monastic village where everyone belonged and felt at home. They loved both learning and the poor, prayer and poetry. They thought of themselves as on the edge of the world, and they delighted to explore fresh horizons both physically and spiritually. They had vivid imaginations. If Jesus had twelve men and women as his core mission team for Judea, they naturally expected that He wanted Ireland to have its twelve apostles and spiritual foster mothers. These terms feature in various annuls and hagiographies. If all-out Christians had fled into Egypt's deserts in the previous century to become Athletes of Christ, then they would seek out deserted places in Irish bogs and woods, make vigils, and observe three seasons of Lent, so that they, too, might be Desert Christians. They loved nature, and it never occurred to them that many centuries later "Christian" societies would disconnect nature from Christ, or the material from the spiritual. They were at home in their bodies—they saw God in mundane chores but also in visions of angels and heaven, which was always near, and they believed in the resurrection of the body. Their faith communities multiplied, often in response to some prophetic word to the founder, and were known as monastic families. These enjoyed a close relationship with their tribe. In such a milieu Aidan may well have been formed.

We may ask ourselves why Aidan was named "Little Flame"? We do not know whether he was given this name at birth or as his monastic name, whether it reflects the fact that he had flame coloured hair, a fiery temperament or some experience that influenced his parents. I imagine the latter, and that he was born on the night Saint Columba died. Columba died at Iona on the night of June 9th 597. His hagiographer, Adomnan, records that on that night friends of Columba were fishing in the river Find, in Donegal, across the sea in northern Ireland, when "they saw in the eastern sky an immense pillar of fire shining as the sun at noon," which they took to be a sign of Columba's entry to heaven. I imagine that Aidan's mother saw this further south in Ireland. The date of his birth is imaginary but feasible. We know that Aidan arrived in Northumbria in 635. A senior but still energetic monk was required to lead the mission, so it is likely he was born a little before 600.

The suggestion that Aidan was born near the river Shannon is feasible. Many settlements were beside rivers, and the Shannon or its tributaries nourish more than eleven counties of Ireland. Since Aidan was a monk in one of Columba's family of monasteries (at Iona) it is reasonable to assume that he was educated in one of Columba's monasteries in Ireland before being transferred. These were on the northern side of the Shannon. I searched for a suitable location for his home on the northern side. If he was associated with Scattery Island it seemed sensible to site his home within a day or two's boat journey from that place. I then had to scour hill forts where a sixth century chieftain most likely had lived, with fertile land below for a farm settlement. That is how I lighted upon Liath Crag, near Killaloe. Killaloe is named after the hermit Molua, or Lua, who established his community (cill) there in the sixth century. St Flanna's Church of Ireland Cathedral houses Ogham and Runic inscriptions. The Heritage Centre by the bridge at Killaloe provides useful information.

In the early seventh century, Luccreth moccu Chiara, wrote poems recording the legendary origins of Munster dynasties, including Conailla Medb michuru ("Medb enjoined illegal contracts"), which contains the oldest surviving reference to characters and events from the Ulster Cycle. In Ireland, the prose epic or saga developed, and kept on developing, for well over a thousand years. In the Book of Leinster, a manuscript of the middle twelfth century, we find a list of the names of 187 epic sagas. It is believed that ollam, or arch-poet, who was the highest dignitary among the poets, and whose training lasted for some twelve years, was obliged to learn two hundred and fifty of these prime sagas and one hundred secondary ones. The manuscripts themselves divide these prime sagas into the following categories, from the very names of which we may get a glance of the genius of the early Gael, and form some conception of the tragic nature of his epic: Destruction of Fortified Places, Cow Spoils (i.e., cattle-raids), Courtships or Wooings, Battles, Stories of Caves, Navigations, Tragical Deaths, Feasts, Sieges, Adventures of Travel, Elopements, Slaughters, Water-eruptions, Expeditions, Progresses, and Visions. "He is no poet," says the Book of Leinster, "who does not synchronize and harmonize all these stories." My inclusion of bards and their sagas during Aidan's childhood reflects this background.

There is insufficient data to make generalizations about Celtic views on physical strength, sexuality, and war. The Celtic Revolution: how Europe was turned upside down from the early Romans to King Arthur by the Cambridge historian Simon Young depicts the Celts in Europe before the Romans established their dominance as furious warriors, sometimes running naked with long hair flowing behind them, covered in war paint and shouting in such blood curdling ways that they instilled terror in their enemies. Young argues that Celts played crucial roles in three revolutions: making the Roman Empire, saving Dark Age Christianity, and creating the modern mind. It was their lack of organisation that enabled the Romans to defeat them in the end, but for many years it was by no means clear that the Romans would succeed.

The coming of Christianity brought a new set of values. This did not end tribal battles but it created new heroes, who were Christ's warriors fighting with spiritual weapons, going all out for God. Manhood lay in being like Christ, strong, faithful, daring, as the epics about Brendan's voyages and the writings of Columbanus make clear. So men were not emasculated by the new faith, but in modern terms we might surmise that they became in touch with their anima as well as with their animus.

The place of women probably varied in different tribes and changed over the course of time. Graves from pre-Roman times indicate that it was possible for some women to occupy a high place in society. Roman writers: such as Plutarch, mention the place of women as mediators in disputes. In the first century Tacitus thought that "the Celts made no distinction between male and female rulers." Legally, men had power over women. Women could have land rights during their life-time, but upon their death, unlike with men, the land reverted to the previous owner. Some women were war leaders, such as Boudicca in Britain. In Christian times certain daughters of chiefs founded large communities and became acknowledged leaders. According to the legends Ita, renowned as a spiritual leader, nevertheless had bodyguards and led her tribe to victory against attackers. Brigid appointed Bishop Conleth to rule the men's section of her monastery—but she governed it overall. The impression one gets from the Lives of saints is that Irish Christians were much more relaxed about men and women intermingling than were either the desert fathers or Christians on the continent, who were taught to shun women. This was no doubt in part because the Irish were part of large extended families and local communities, and perhaps also because of their sense of God's Presence in all.

The Spiritual Foster Mother and the Wise Woman

The historical model for Dara's role lay in the ancient custom of fosterage. Fosterage by a well educated person was the rule in families related to the local king, poets or artisans or who owned land or stock. Fosterage normally ended for the boy at fifteen or seventeen and for the girl at fourteen (Ryan p209). Also, now that monasteries were established, orphans and others were being accepted.

In early churches in Britain and Ireland a person who acted as a mentor, confessor, or spiritual guide was called by the Welsh a periglour, and by the Irish and the Scots an anamchara, meaning "friend of the soul." Later the Roman Catholic Church limited this role to male priests, and Reformers neglected it, but, in the earliest days of Celtic Christianity such relationships were open to lay and ordained people, women and men. A story about Saint Brigid, found in the early ninth century Martyrology of Oengus the Culdee, attests to the importance of the anamchara:

"A young cleric of the community of Ferns, a foster-son of Brigit's, used to come to her with dainties. He was often with her in the refectory to partake of food. Once after going to communion she strikes a clapper. "Well, young cleric there," says Brigit, "do you have a soul friend?" "I have," replied the young man. "Let us sing his requiem," says Brigit. "Why so?" asks the young cleric. "For he has died," says Brigit. "When you had finished half your ration I saw that he was dead." "How did you know that?" "Easy to say, (Brigit replies) from the time that your soul friend was dead, I saw that your food was put (directly) in the trunk of your body, since you were without any head. Go forth and eat nothing until you get a soul friend, for anyone without a soul friend is like a body without a head: is like the water of a polluted lake, neither good for drinking nor for washing. That is the person without a soul friend." "

Dara reflects something of a Celtic Wise Woman. Some modern Celtic enthusiasts make much of the concept of the Celtic Wise Woman. For example, blogger Brigid Geegan Blanton www.desertrosebooks.com/wise-woman3.html writes: "The celtic focus on a connection with nature and the rejuvenating quality of the hearth is combined and expressed in the life of the wise woman. She is more than a repository of herbal lore and orator of beloved stories; she is strength and intuition. The wise woman advises us to look into our hearts for answers instead of solely reasoning with our mind. She stokes the fire of spirituality within and prompts us to tend to our longing for a relationship with God."

Manhood, Bards and Poetry

We can learn how people understood manhood and womanhood from the myths they handed down. Fionn mac Cumhaill, known in English as Finn McCool, was a mythical hunter-warrior of Irish mythology. The stories of Fionn and his followers the Fianna, form the Fenian Cycle (or Fiannaid-heacht), much of it purported to be narrated by Fionn's son, the poet Oisín. The Fenian Cycle is one of the four major cycles of Irish mythology along with the Mythological Cycle, the Ulster Cycle, and the Historical Cycle. These stories and poems were written at different times between the seventh and twelfth centuries and were later collated. The reference to hurling in the following extract indicates a late compilation, but it captures popular perceptions of both the manly youngster and the wise woman: "Cumhal's wife was named Murna, and she bore him two sons. The younger was born after Cumhal's death, and his name was called Demna. And because his mother feared that the sons of Morna would find him out and kill him, she gave him to a Druidess and another wise woman of Cumhal's household, and bade them take him away and rear him as best they could. So they took him into the wild woods on the Slieve Bloom Mountains, and there they trained him to hunt and fish and to throw the spear, and he grew strong, and as beautiful as a child of the Fairy Folk. If he were in the same field with a hare he could run so that the hare could never leave the field, for Demna was always before it. He could run down and slay a stag with no dogs to help him, and he could kill a wild duck on the wing with a stone from his sling. And the Druidess taught him the learning of the time, and also the story of his race and nation, and told him of his right to be captain of the Fianna of Erinn when his day of destiny should come."

Chapter 2: Durrow

The site of this monastery, which Columba founded about 585, is located as Durrow Abbey, Co Offaly eight kilometers to the north of Tullamore on the N52 to Kilbeggan. The Irish name for the site, Dermaig, is translated as "the Plain of the Oaks." The Eiscir Riada and the Slí Mhór, which run approximately 600 meters north of the site, may have played an important role in the foundation of the monastery in this location. Little now remains, but St. Columba's well, and the ninth century High Cross are preserved.

The story assumes that since we know Aidan joined the Columba family of monasteries he would have started in a Columban monastery nearer home. There were smaller Columban monasteries nearer to Killaloe than was Durrow, but since Durrow was the nearest large monastery, about which we have most information, I placed Aidan there. We do not possess a detailed description of the school at Durrow, but fragmentary information from written and archeological sources allows scholars to build up a picture of typical education in seventh century Irish monasteries. Some of this material is assembled in Early Irish Monastic Schools: A Study of Ireland's Contribution to Early Medieval Culture by Hugh Graham, formerly Professor of Education, College of St. Teresa, Winona, Minnesota (Talbot Press Dublin 1923—now available online at www.archive.org/stream/. . ./ earlyirishmonastoograhuoft_djvu.txt). Irish Monasticism: origins and early development by John Ryan SJ (Four Courts Press 1992) collates information about monastic manual, intellectual, and spiritual practices.

The curriculum books we imagine Aidan being introduced to in the story are known to have circulated in some monasteries in both Ireland and Britain. Adomnan, for example, mentions Basil and Cassian as authors of books in the Iona library. Books were precious—it required a considerable number of calves' skins to copy one Gospel—but the passion to set up scriptoria where copying went on daily indicates that books multiplied. The descriptions of activities and tools are factual. The Springmount Bog Tablets which were unearthed recently are wooden tablets covered in wax dated to about 600 A.D.

Christianity brought a written language to Ireland for the first time. It was Latin, the living language then used in most of the Roman Empire and in church liturgy and Bible manuscripts. The writing system before that was Ogam, which distinguished between a mere twenty different sounds by means of points and strokes placed on a straight line. The Irish soon learned to create an alphabet and write in their own language, too. A poem in praise of Columba, probably commissioned by Columba's kinsman, the king of the Ui Neill clan, was almost certainly written within three or four years of Columba's death in 597 and is the earliest vernacular poem in western Europe. It was Christianity, too, that introduced schools on a wide basis. Before that there were just a few select schools for druids and bards, who had to memorise everything and who trained for up to twenty years. Most monasteries of any size established a school for boys, who were accepted from the age of seven.

The Bible was, in a sense, Ireland's first book. Saint Patrick quoted from about forty books of the Bible in his short Declaration, or Confession. The Bible held a central place in monastic education. Once a boy had mastered the alphabet, a book of psalms was placed in his hands, and he committed many of them to memory. After that came the Gospels and the Acts of the Apostles. Columbanus, who was alive during Aidan's boyhood, composed a commentary on the psalms while he was still a young man in Ireland. We know that Columba, like many others, had a passion to transcribe Psalms and Gospels for both learning and evangelism purposes. Young people had an enthusiasm for the Scriptures. There are stories of Christians in Britain and Ireland chanting psalms while standing in the sea, and there is the famous story of a group of keen young monks who petitioned their abbot to be allowed to recite all one hundred and fifty psalms each day!

The Book of Durrow is a decorated manuscript of the Four Gospels now at Trinity College Dublin. It is traditionally associated with Durrow monastery, though some scholars have argued for an origin in Iona or Northumbria. Flann mac Máel Sechnaill (high king 879—916) encased it in a shrine. It probably dates from the late seventh century—making it the earliest surviving fully decorated Gospel book in Britain or Ireland—though conflicting views place it in the early eighth century.

The monastery proper was the space enclosed by the earth ditch or mound, the vallum. Within this were the church or churches, oratories, refectory, kitchen, school, armarium—a chamber for the preservation of books and literary apparatus, sometimes a special scriptorium, the hospice or guest house, cells for the monks, and the workshops for the smith and the carpenter. Outside of the vallum were the various other indispensable buildings connected with the monastery of which the storehouse and the mill are the most important. There was usually a byre for the cows situated in convenient pasture land. If the monastery was located inland there was a fish pond, or a convenient harbour, if near the sea.

The structure of these early monasteries was of a simple and inexpensive character. They were built at first of earth, wattles, or wood. It was not until the eighth century that stone buildings began to be substituted for wooden ones, as a protection against the ravages of the Danes. The simplicity and temporary character of these early foundations would account for the quickness with which monastic cities sprang up as well as for the fact that comparatively few material remains of these monastic settlements are now to be seen. They are now remembered chiefly for the great spiritual and literary heritage which they were the means of transmitting.

The scheme of education was carefully graduated and probably extended from 7 to 26 years in the case of monastic students and from 7 to 30 years for lay students. The lay or bardic studies were limited originally to native "secular" learning. The monastic course included both "secular" (to use a modern word that would be alien to Aidan's people) and religious studies, both Latin and Irish were used as a medium of instruction, and the study of native literature was not neglected. In the monastic school special attention was given to the study of the Sacred Scriptures—both the Old and the New Testament. There was frequent questioning and explanation. The degree of Ollamh or Doctor was reserved for those whose learning was profound. This great scholar was entitled to the privilege of sitting in the banqueting-house with the king.

What made the pagan Irish open and ready to receive the Word? Irish monks wrote down stories from their pre-Christian culture, which they valued. We learn from these (whether we take them as historical records or the reading back of later perceptions) that druids intuited that a religion with greater light was to come and to be welcomed. There is the story in the Fenian Cycle of Conor mac Nessa, King of Ulster, who asked his druid what was the meaning of the sun's eclipse. The druid explained that far away the son of the High King of the world was being put to death. Knowledge of Christ, it was said, was granted to King Cormac, son of Art by divine illumination, and thenceforth he refused to consult the druids or to worship the images which they made as emblems of the Immortal Ones. No doubt the open heart of missionaries such as Patrick towards the people of his adopted land (as a former slave he had no "colonial" pretensions) helped to keep Irish hearts open. There were, of course, power contests between ego-centered druids and Christian missionaries, but there are as many stories of good druids and chiefs who recognized and responded to goodness in the faces of people like Patrick and Columba.

The curriculum in monastic schools was broad, including not only the study of Scripture with the commentaries of the Greek and Latin Fathers, but also the study of the pagan authors of Greece and Rome, and Irish language and literature. Science in the modem sense of the word was unknown, but as regards Geography, Computation, and Astronomy the Irish Monastic Schools were as advanced as any in Europe. At least in the ninth century, philosophy and dialectic were eagerly studied. Art too flourished, especially the illumination of manuscripts, various ornamental forms of metal work and stone-carving.

Just as Christianity itself did not mean the abolition but rather the fulfillment of Hebrew ideals and traditions, so when Christianity was introduced into Ireland where an ancient native culture was flourishing, the new culture did not displace the old but rather combined with it to form a new type of culture which in course of time became at once both Irish and Christian. In the schools everything that was not absolutely opposed to the ideals of Christianity was utilized to enrich the course of study. Thus the native laws, literature, music, and art became the handmaid of Christianity. The same liberal and enlightened conception of education would explain the success with which the Irish monks pursued the study of the pagan classics. The Christianity of the Irish monk was sufficiently robust to prevent any of those scruples of conscience which were said to have haunted the continental monk who loved his Virgil.

It was a maxim in the early monasteries that the monks support themselves by the labour of their own hands. There was no privileged class—all who were physically fit had to take part in the manual labour, including the scribes and abbot.

What of the connections in the Celtic view between word and image and our creative powers to reflect back the world's beauty? To the Irish, the incarnation of God's Son in one far off part of the earth, which they read about in the Gospels, meant that the kind of things he did there he could also do in Ireland. He was the True Sun, whose rays shone in their land as much as in Jerusalem or Rome. He had twelve apostles, so Ireland had its twelve apostles. Their Saint Brigid would be Christ's midwife. Biblical characters were depicted visually on stone pillars. These were fashioned after Aidan's time. Perhaps in his lifetime such figures were carved on wood, none of which survives. They used fire and water and wind as images of divine actions. In their illuminated Gospel manuscripts they painted the symbol of each Gospel writer: the man, the lion, the ox, and the eagle. The Durrow Gospels are the earliest example of this.

Morgan, whose Latin name was Pelagius, was a British theologian who had a wrestler's frame, lived like a monk, taught in Rome and was accused by Augustine of denying "original sin." The possibility is more widely accepted today that Augustine and others misunderstood Pelagius. They thought he taught that we can deserve grace. He did not. He taught that we are capable of either opening or closing ourselves to grace. God has given us responsibility. Thus when the apostle Paul urges Christians not to fall into grumbling or fornication, he was not wasting his time. Those he wrote to were capable of responding to his advice. In this sense every person has free moral choice. The Latin words used such as "merit" can be interpreted in two ways. Pelagius did not mean that when we respond positively we merit grace or salvation in the sense that it is based on our own merit, he meant that we qualify, i.e. it becomes possible, for us to receive grace or salvation. For a full treatment of this issue see Rees, B.R.Pelagius: A Reluctant Heretic, (The Boydell Press 1991).

It is likely that the Rule of a first generation community consisted of the founder's verbal guidelines and actions, though Columbanus wrote a Rule for his dispersed monks, and Bangor and Clonfert were said to have Rules, which are now lost. Otherwise the first written Rules that have come down to us date from the eighth century. These typically include hospitality and the injunction to treat visitors as if they were Christ. The inquisitive politician Sir Roger Twisden assumed The Rule of Saint Columba was chiefly borrowed from the ancient oriental monastic institutes. Both Celtic Rules and the Benedictine Rule certainly reflect the earlier Rules of the Egyptian desert in regard to such matters as hospitality. See The Celtic Monk: Rules & Writings of Early Irish Monks by Uinseann O Maidin (Cistercian Studies).

The Document known as The Rule of St Columba was written down in Irish perhaps several centuries after Columba and is not to be confused with the Rule which his namesake Columbanus wrote. I cannot trace any attempt by scholars to put a date on its composition, but it presumably reflects the spirit of Columba and his monasteries as they were perceived by its anonymous writer. This is the text:

- Be alone in a separate place near a chief city, if thy conscience is not prepared to be in common with the crowd.

- Be always naked in imitation of Christ and the Evangelists.

- Whatsoever little or much thou possesseth of anything, whether clothing, or food, or drink, let it be at the command of the senior and at his disposal, for it is not befitting a religious to have any distinction of property with his own free brother.

- Let a fast place, with one door, enclose thee.

- A few religious men to converse with thee of God and his Testament; to visit thee on days of solemnity; to strengthen thee in the Testaments of God, and the narratives of the Scriptures.

- A person too who would talk with thee in idle words, or of the world; or who murmurs at what he cannot remedy or prevent, but who would distress thee more should he be a tattler between friends and foes, thou shalt not admit him to thee, but at once give him thy benediction should he deserve it.

- Let thy servant be a discreet, religious, not tale-telling man, who is to attend continually on thee, with moderate labour of course, but always ready.

- Yield submission to every rule that is of devotion.

- A mind prepared for red martyrdom [that is death for the faith].

- A mind fortified and steadfast for white martyrdom. [That is ascetic practices] Forgiveness from the heart of every one.

- Constant prayers for those who trouble thee.

- Fervour in singing the office for the dead, as if every faithful dead was a particular friend of thine.

- Hymns for souls to be sung standing.

- Let thy vigils be constant from eve to eve, under the direction of another person.

- Three labors in the day, viz., prayers, work, and reading.

- The work to be divided into three parts, viz., thine own work, and the work of thy place, as regards its real wants; secondly, thy share of the brethren's [work]; lastly, to help the neighbours, viz., by instruction or writing, or sewing garments, or whatever labour they may be in want of, ut Dominus ait, "Non apparebis ante Me vacuus" [as the Lord says, "You shall not appear before me empty."].

- Everything in its proper order; Nemo enim coronabitur nisi qui legitime certaverit. [For no one is crowned except he who has striven lawfully.]

- Follow alms-giving before all things.

- Take not of food till thou art hungry.
- Sleep not till thou feelest desire.
- Speak not except on business.
- Every increase which comes to thee in lawful meals, or in wearing apparel, give it for pity to the brethren that want it, or to the poor in like manner.
- The love of God with all thy heart and all thy strength.
- The love of thy neighbour as thyself.
- Abide in the Testament of God throughout all times.
- Thy measure of prayer shall be until thy tears come;
- Or thy measure of work of labor till thy tears come.
- Or thy measure of thy work of labor, or of thy genuflections, until thy perspiration often comes, if thy tears are not free.

From A. W. Haddan and W. Stubbs, Councils and Ecclesiastical Documents Relating to Great Britain and Ireland II, i (Oxford: Oxford University Press, 1873), pp. 119–121.

The stories about the spilt milk and Laisren lightening up come from Adomnan.

A book written by a brother at Glenstall Abbey, Ireland, explores the connection between the Irish monasteries and the bardic tradition: Celtic Threads: exploring the wisdom of our heritage by Padraigín Clancy (Veritas, 1999).

Chapter 3: Egypt

This fictional pilgrimage is set in the historical circumstances of the Marseilles bishopric and the ransack in 619 of Alexandria, the capital city of Egypt and of that part of the Christian world, with its great port and patriarchate.

The idea of pilgrimaging beyond familiar territory within Ireland and Britain was in the DNA of Columba's monasteries at Durrow and Iona, as these verses from an ancient Irish Dialogue Between Columba and Cormac suggest:

> Cormac, offspring of Liatham, of aspect bright,
> The champion of heaven and earth,
> Came out of his southern, warm country
> Upon a visit, upon a pilgrimage.

Two wild oxen of noble appearance
Conveyed the devout cleric
From the south, from the broad rapid Lai (river Lee)
To Cormac's Cross at Cairndruim (Durrow).

That was about pilgrimage within Ireland. But pilgrimage to Bible sites had developed in previous centuries. Helena, the mother of the Roman Emperor Constantine, made a pilgrimage to the Holy Land in 326 and believed she retrieved a part of the cross on which Jesus died. Knowledge of this spread throughout the Roman Empire; it became the subject of the finest poem of Cynewulf, Bishop of Lindisfarne from 740 to 780. Egeria, who is thought to have lived in Galicia, in modern Spain, made a pilgrimage to the Holy Land about 381—384. She wrote an account of her journey in a long letter to women at home which survives in fragmentary form in a later copy. John Wilkinson's Egeria's Travels: Newly Translated (Aris & Phillips 1999) includes supporting documents and notes.

Before the Muslim conquest of the seventh century, pilgrims came to the Bible lands from Byzantium and the West in search of sacred relics for their churches. Around the year 680 Bishop Arculf, of Gaul, went on pilgrimage to holy places in the Holy Land, Syria, Constantinople, and Alexandria. During his return he was blown off course and stayed a while on Iona. Adomnan, then its Abbot, wrote down every description by Arculf of the important things he had seen and produced his own treatise On the Holy Places. Before or during the time that Arculf visited Iona, Adomnan read other works on the Holy Land as is obvious from some of the questions he puts to Arculf. It is also clear from the composition that Adomnan used a number of books, as well as classical sources, which are echoed in his work, such as Eucherius and Jerome.

Pilgrimages were made from Britain and Ireland to Rome and Jerusalem from at least the fifth century. St Jerome (d. 420) wrote from his retreat at Bethlehem that Judea overflowed with pilgrims, and that, round about the Holy Sepulcher were heard sung, in divers tongues, the praises of the Lord. Albeit he wrote to his friend Paulinus as if to discourage too many thoughtless or dangerous pilgrimages: "The court of heaven is as open in Britain as at Jerusalem." The subsequent barbarian occupations of mainland Europe seem to have halted overland pilgrimages to places like Rome during Aidan's early years, though Columbanus managed to get to Italy in 612.

However, trade by sea routes to and from places such as Alexandria continued. There exists evidence of a Mediterranean trade in a single passage in the Life of John the Almsgiver, Patriarch of Alexandria between 610–621, in which reference is made to a vessel sailing to Alexandria from

Britain with a cargo of tin, doubtless come from Cornwall or Somerset. The Coptic Orthodox Church traces its origin to the apostolic mission of Saint Mark, who arrived in Alexandria in around 60 AD and stayed for about seven years. During this time Mark converted many to Christianity and performed miracles. His body was still honored as the founder of the Christian Church at Alexandria until the ninth century.

What about links in the reverse direction, between Egypt and Ireland? The influences are certainly there—the debate is about how much these sprang from art and writings which inspired the Irish imagination, and how many direct links there were, if any. Scholars interpret an Ogham inscription on a stone near St. Olan's Well in the parish of Aghabulloge, County Cork as reading: "Pray for Olan the Egyptian." There are learned articles by Monique Blanc-Ortolan of the Musee des Arts Decoratifs, Paris, and Pierre du Bourguet of the Louvre on "Coptic and Irish Art" and by Joseph F.T. Kelly of John Carroll University, Cleveland, Ohio, on "Coptic Influences in the British Isles" in the Coptic Encyclopedia. Archdale King, who wrote books on the ancient rites of many middle eastern churches, explored the links between Celtic Ireland and Coptic Egypt. He suggests that much of the contact took place before the Muslim Conquest of 640. Professor Stokes tells us about the Irish monk Dicuil, who around 825 wrote his Liber de Mensure orbis terre describing the pyramids. It would seem that Egypt was often visited by pilgrims to the Holy Land. Stokes instances the Saltair Na Rann, an anthology of biblical poems attributed to Oengus the Culdee, but containing the sixth or seventh century Book of Adam and Eve, composed in Egypt and known in no other European country except Ireland.

The Martyrology of Oengus the Culdee, an early ninth century monastic bishop of Clonenagh (Co. Offaly) and later of Tallaght, has a litany invoking "Seven monks of Egypt in Disert Uilaig, I invoke unto my aid, through Jesus Christ." [Morfesseor do manchaib Egipr(e) in disiurt Uilaig. Dr. Cahal Dallat, Genealogist and Historical Consultant, of Ballycastle, County Antrim, identified Disert Ilidh or Uilaigh with Dundesert, near Crumlin, County Antrim.

The Irish Independent of 6 September 2010 carried the following report: A 1,200-year-old manuscript has revealed remarkable evidence of a connection between the early Christian Church in Ireland and the Middle Eastern Coptic Church. The Faddan More Psalter was found in a north Tipperary bog four years ago in the townland of Faddan More, near Birr. The fragmented illuminated vellum manuscript is a book of psalms and dates back to the late eighth century. Its origins remain a mystery. The manuscript was found upright in the bog for over 1,000 years suggesting it was hidden that way by someone on the run. The painstaking four-year conservation process, led by Irish book conservator John Gillis, has revealed tiny fragments of papyrus in the lining of the Egyptian-style leather binding of the manuscript, the first tangible link between early Christianity in Ireland and the Middle-Eastern Coptic Church. The discovery has confounded many accepted theories of early Irish Christianity.

Read more: http://www.irishcentral.com/news/Bog-manuscript—most-important-find-since-Ardagh-Chalice-102283079.html#ixzz1qawQidUb

Marseilles, Cassian and Gregory

The Mediterranean coast of France and the Rhone valley were early centers of Christianity. For most of the long history of Marseilles, France's oldest city and a major natural port, the town occupied the same fortified 70 hectares on the north side of the Old Port from its founding until 1660. Christianity came to Marseilles near the end of the Roman era, as shown by catacombs on Garde Hill. The Church represented the only real authority during this period, and a bishopric was installed in the beginning of the fourth century.

Cassian was a monk and ascetic writer of Southern Gaul, and the first to introduce the rules of Eastern monasticism into the West. While yet a youth he visited the holy places in Palestine, accompanied by an older friend, Germanus. In Bethlehem they took monastic vows, but, desiring to acquire the science of sanctity they visited significant spiritual fathers in the Egyptian desert. There Cassian collected the materials for his two principal works, the "Institutes" and "Conferences." They went to Constantinople, where Cassian became a deacon. He was then sent to Rome. About 415 he was at Marseilles where he wrote up his two books, and he founded two monasteries, one for men, over the tomb of St. Victor, a martyr of the last Christian persecution under Maximian (286–305), and the other for women. These were among the first monasteries in the western world after that founded by Martin at Tours. The remainder of Cassian's days were passed at or near Marseilles. His personal influence and his writings contributed greatly to the diffusion of monasticism in the West.

Following the attack on Rome in 410, and subsequent invasions of western Europe by people known to Romans as barbarians (because the great Roman language, laws and literature were foreign to them), Marseilles became the object of rivalry between different barbarian factions. It suffered repeated lootings and even near destruction at their hands. Attacks and pillaging increased, and by the seventh century, Marseilles was reduced to the fortified position of the bishopric on St Laurent Hill, above where

Fort Saint Jean is now located at the mouth of the Old Port. Yet it survived and remained an active port city, with Far-Eastern trade.

www.beyond.fr/villages/marseille-history-provence-france.html

Pilgrims may still visit the crypt of the Abbey of St. Victor (the site of Cassian's monastery) and the Old Port fort (by the site of the bishopric).

Gregory was the Bishop of Tours who died there about 594. He was a much-traveled historian, and we derive much information from books such as his Life of the (Gallic) Fathers and History of the Franks.

Alexandria and the Patriarch

A horizontal division had appeared in the Roman Empire. In much of Europe barbarian kings now ruled. Egypt, Syria, Greece, and parts of North Africa remained under imperial rule which had transferred its headquarters to Constantinople. The emperor of this Christian Empire ruled through Greek-speaking civil servants in the great cities such as Alexandria and Antioch.

Alexandria's library was a world center of learning, with an estimated 400,000 to 500,000 works along with priceless treasures of art and antiquity. Scholars flocked there to study a blend of Greek, Hebrew, Egyptian, Chaldean, and Persian subjects. Alexandria (founded by Alexander the Great) had become a major centre of the Christian world, and this was in part attributed to the missionary efforts of Mark, the Evangelist and Gospel writer. Its patriarch at this time was John the Fifth. John was born in Cyprus into a wealthy family. He married and had several children, but they and his wife died. At the age of 50 he was chosen as Patriarch of Alexandria by Nicetas, his adopted brother, who had helped the Roman emperor Heraclius come to power.

When he became patriarch he is said to have handed out 80,000 pieces of gold to hospitals and monasteries, and he also founded new ones. As patriarch, John became known for his generosity, even giving away his own bedding to the poor. He lived in the greatest austerity as to diet, apparel, and furniture. He worked hard to improve their lot, ordering the use of exact weights and measures, forbidding his officials to take bribes and by making himself available to anyone for consultations. In 614, after 21 days of relentless siege warfare, Jerusalem was captured. The Byzantine chronicles relate that the Sassanid army and the Jews slaughtered tens of thousands of Christians in the city. John came to the rescue by providing large amounts of money, food, clothing, and also transport to take it to those people most in need. Prisoners, particularly nuns, were rescued with his money, but his generosity was directed to any group or person in need, irrespective of creed or race. A certain merchant, who had been three times ruined by shipwrecks, had as often found relief from the patriarch, who the third time gave him a ship belonging to the church, laden with twenty thousand measures of corn. This vessel was driven by a storm to the British Islands, and a famine raging there, the owners sold their cargo to great advantage, and brought back a considerable value in exchange, one half in money, the other in pewter. The patriarch was forced to flee Alexandria by the Persian invasion of Egypt in 619. Returning to Cyprus, he died soon thereafter. The main source for his biography is a Life written by Leontius of Neapolis in Cyprus. Merchant ships continued to sail from Alexandria to Britain and Ireland.

Between 618 and 621 AD, the Sassanid Persian army defeated the East Roman (Byzantine) forces in Egypt and occupied the province. The fall of Alexandria, the capital of Roman Egypt, marked the first and most important stage in the Sassanid campaign to conquer this rich province, which fell completely under Persian rule within two years. Ten years later the Muslim Rashidun army occupied Alexandria. The Muslim Arabs journeyed north and west via Gaza in the coastal north or via Suez and Babylon. The Christian Byzantines had already lost the Levant and its Arab ally, the Ghassanid Kingdom, to the Muslims. All this left the Byzantine Empire dangerously exposed and vulnerable to the invaders.

There are diverse versions of the burning of Alexandria's library, in part or whole, at various times, ranging from Julius Caesar (by mistake) to Patriarch Theophilus (who destroyed pagan documents) to the Muslim Caliph Omar in 640. It is not certain that the invasion of 619 involved a library burning, or that Patriarch John would have been aware of followers of the Prophet Muhammad quite that early.

In most military conquests of cities the invading force captures the headquarters, the governing group flee or are killed, and the poor, indigenous population remain as servants of the new regime. That is doubtless what happened in Alexandria in 619. We know that the port, as well as the patriarch's headquarters was taken over. So for Aidan to find his way to the poor Coptic Christians' quarter is realistic.

The Coptic Cross

Egyptians were known as Copts, as are Egypt's Christians to this day. The Coptic Cross often incorporates a circle and the four "arms" are usually the same length. The end of each arm may have a slight enlargement, or "bud." For the Coptic Church the circle represents the everlasting love of God, as

shown through Christ's crucifixion. It also symbolizes Christ's halo and resurrection. Christ's resurrection is central to Coptic doctrine and perhaps for
this reason, Coptic Crosses are more usually seen without the figure of the
dead Christ. The bud resonates with the Celtic idea of the cross being a tree
that bears fruit.

Barbarians

The term "barbarian" was used to refer to people outside the Roman Empire. These peoples lacked the laws, the language, and the education that
Roman civilisation brought. It was common among Christians to believe
that only people within the empire could be evangelised: others were too
violent to listen to a new message.

Although this pilgrimage and Aidan's welcome by poor Coptic
Christians is fictitious, the existence of a bond between the Irish and the
Egyptians is, as we have seen, more certain. In a letter to Charlemagne, the
Northumbrian scholar Alcuin of York described the Irish monks as "pueri
Egyptiaci" ("children of Egypt"). The proudest boast of Celtic monasticism
was that, in the words of the Antiphonary of Bangor:

> This house full of delight
> Is built on the rock
> And indeed the true vine
> Transplanted out of Egypt.

The early monks of Britain and Ireland consciously regarded Saint
Antony of Egypt as their ideal and their prototype, an inspiration that was
acknowledged by contemporaries.

A growing body of evidence suggests that contact between the Mediterranean and early Christian Britain was surprisingly frequent. Egyptian
pottery—perhaps originally containing wine or olive oil—has been found
during excavations at Tintagel Castle in Cornwall, the supposed birthplace
of King Arthur, while the Irish Litany of Saints remembers "the seven
monks of Egypt [who lived] in Disert Uilaig" on the west coast of Ireland.
Travel guides in circulation in early Christian Britain gave accounts of the
Egyptian monasteries. One of the earliest known Insular gospel books,
the Cuthbert Gospels, is bound and sewn in a specifically Coptic manner,
which Michelle Brown believes indicates "an actual learning/teaching process" linking Egypt and Northumbria.

William Dalrymple's article The Egyptian Connection in The New York
Review (October 2008) observes that "The Irish wheel cross, the symbol of

Celtic Christianity, has recently been shown to have been a Coptic invention, depicted on a Coptic burial pall of the fifth century, three centuries before the design first appears in Scotland and Ireland."

So common did pilgrimages around the Mediterranean become a generation or two after Aidan that Saint Boniface wrote to the Archbishop of Canterbury asking that he "forbid matrons and nuns from making" such journeys as "a great part of them perish and few keep their virtue." There was also traffic in the opposite direction: one of the earliest leaders of the Anglo-Saxon church was the Byzantine Theodore of Tarsus, sent to be archbishop of Canterbury from his home in what is now southern Turkey.

The Silk Route

The Silk Route was part of wider network of interlinking trade routes across the Afro-Eurasian landmass that connected East, South, and Western Asia with the Mediterranean and European world, as well as parts of North and East Africa. From the Arab countries the route went north to Alexandria and east into Asia, and vice versa. The land routes were supplemented by sea routes, which extended from the Red Sea to coastal India, China and Southeast Asia. Extending 4,000 miles (6,500 km), the Silk Road gets its name from the lucrative Chinese silk trade along it. Trade on the Silk Road was a significant factor in the development of the great civilizations of China, India, Ancient Egypt, Persia, Arabia, and Ancient Rome, and in several respects helped lay the foundations for the modern world. Many other goods, technologies, religions, and philosophies also traveled along the Silk Routes. Goods included silk, satin, hemp and other fine fabrics, musk, other perfumes, spices, medicines, jewels, glassware, and even rhubarb, as well as slaves. Very few traversed the route from end to end; for the most part, goods were transported by a series of agents on varying routes and were traded in the bustling markets of the oasis towns.

The main traders from the 5th to the 8th centuries after Christ were Persian and Arab. Tribal societies previously living in isolation along the Silk Road or pastoralists who were of barbarian cultural development were drawn to the riches and opportunities of the civilizations connected by the Silk Road, taking on the trades of marauders or mercenaries. Many barbarian tribes became skilled warriors able to conquer rich cities and fertile lands, and forge strong military empires. In the west, the Silk Road reached its peak during the time of the (Christian) Byzantine Empire

The Prophet Mohammed

Born in 570 CE in the Arabian city of Mecca, he was orphaned at an early age and brought up under the care of his uncle Abu Talib. He later worked as a merchant, and as a shepherd, and was first married by age 25. Discontented with life in Mecca, he retreated to a cave in the surrounding mountains for meditation and reflection. According to Islamic beliefs it was here, at age 40, in the month of Ramadan, that he received his first revelation from God. Three years after this event Muhammad started preaching these revelations publicly, proclaiming that "God is One," that complete "surrender" to Him (lit. islām) is the only acceptable way to God, and that he himself was a prophet and messenger of God, in the same vein as other prophets such as Moses and Jesus.

Muhammad gained few followers early on, and was met with hostility from some Meccan tribes. To escape persecution, Muhammad sent some of his followers to Abyssinia, where the Christian ruler befriended them, before he and his remaining followers in Mecca migrated to Medina (then known as Yathrib) in the year 622. After eight years in Medina of fighting with the tribes, his followers, who by then had grown to 10,000, conquered Mecca. Muhammad destroyed the symbols of paganism there and then sent his followers out to destroy all of the remaining pagan temples throughout Eastern Arabia.

The Durrow Abbot

Apart from Durrow's founding abbot, Laisren, the names of other abbots in the seventh century seem not to be known, although Cummian, who wrote a letter about the date of Easter to Segene, abbot of Iona, and Beccan, a hermit, in 632/3 may well have been an abbot. Bechan is a fictional abbot.

Chapter 4: Visitors Rekindle the Flame

Adomnan gives the impression of a constant stream of visitors to Iona, and no doubt this also applied to Durrow. Many were brothers from other monasteries and some were distinguished members of ruling families. These stayed for fairly short periods. Penitents might include ordinary lay Christians, and they would stay for a longer period during which they did penance.

The story of Libran is told in chapter 40 of Adomnan's Life of Columba. In the Irish laws of that time a fine in lieu of the death penalty for murder was permitted. These were known as the Brehon law. It was a civil, not a criminal law and was based upon the principle that a crime against a person, be it theft, assault, battery, or murder was an affront to his "honor" or dignity. Every person in the Ireland of that day was assigned an "honor price" and if you committed a crime against that person you were responsible to pay all or part of the person's "honor price" to restore his honor or dignity. It was a barter and an agrarian society and money was scarce so honor price was normally expressed in terms of cattle or other livestock. A common craftsman such as a carpenter or a stone mason might well have an honor price of "twelve young red heifers." Slaves and servants would have a much lower honor price while physicians, proprietors, merchants, lawyers would have a much higher honor price. Each Brehon Court had at least one "Dalaigh" who was responsible for gathering evidence and prosecuting the culprit in court. The Sister Fidelma murder mysteries, written by historian Peter Tremaine, feature a dalaigh who is a nun and sister to the king.

Soon after Columba sailed from Ireland and built his main monastery on Iona in 563, he established a smaller monastery on the island of Tiree called Mag Luinge. This is thought to have been at the site of today's Soroby graveyard. The island was known even then for its fertility and has been described as Iona's granary. St. Columba once ordered the Tiree monastery to send a fat beast and six measures of grain to a dying man on Coll after he had been caught trying to kill some seals that belonged to Iona.

Columba was credited with unusual powers of "seeing." Once two holy men wanted to leave Iona and sail in opposite directions. Each wanted a following wind. Columba said "Tomorrow, first thing in the morning, Baithéne [the abbot of Tiree] will have a following wind for his journey. . ." The Lord granted this. . .and at the third hour of the same day Columba sent for Colmán the priest and said to him, "Baithéne has now arrived safely at the harbour [on Tiree]. . . Soon the Lord will bring the wind round to the north." Within an hour the south wind had obeyed St. Columba's word and had become a breeze blowing from the north [for the voyage to Ireland].

Tiree monastery also took men seeking to atone for past crimes. One of these penitents was Libran, who worked with reeds. Adomnan's account ends with these words: "This truthful prophecy of the saint regarding the same man was afterwards fulfilled; for when he had faithfully served the Lord for many revolving years of holy obedience in the monastery of the Plain of Lunge (Tiree), after the departure of St. Columba from the world, he was sent, in extreme old age, on a mission to Scotia (Ireland) regarding the interests of the monastery, and proceeded as soon as he landed through the Plain of Breg (Maghbreg, in Meath), till he reached the monastery of the Oakwood Plain. Being there received as a stranger in the guest-chamber, and suffering from a certain disease, he passed to the Lord in peace on the seventh day of his illness, and was buried with the chosen monks of St. Columba, according to his prophecy, to await the resurrection unto eternal life."

I have used poetic license to locate the monastery of The Oakwood Plain at Durrow rather than Derry.

The Alphabet of Devotion

Few scholars dispute that Colman's Alphabet of Devotion was influential, but there is disagreement as to which Colman was its author. According to the early Latin Life of Colman, Columba requested at an assembly of the leading nobles and clergy of Ireland that a site be granted for a monastery to Colmán. In response to this the king of Mide (Meath) granted him a site at Lynally. One record says he died in 611, but I am imagining that he lived another decade.

I give the benefit of doubt to those scholars who like Thomas Owen Clancy & Gilbert Markus in Iona: The Earliest Poetry of a Celtic Monastery (Edinburgh: Edinburgh University Press, 1997) think that this Colman was the author of The Alphabet. They include it in a bibliography of the likely texts which made up the library at the Iona monastery. In Celtic Cultural Studies—an Online Journal, Steve Sweeney-Turner writes that "due to certain somewhat infamous Norse excesses one millennium ago, we have no material proof of exactly what the original Iona community was reading, but from a thorough-going textual analysis of their surviving writings, Clancy and Markus have deduced the likely contents of that famous library, and supplied us with a useful reading-list. Moreover, Colmán's text—written outwith Iona, but very much within its pedagogical and epistemological criteria—provides us with direct clues through allusion to canonic monastic texts in the tradition following St. Martin of Tours, so beloved of the early Goidelic Christian communities." So, although Colman's visit to Durrow is imaginary, it is likely that Aidan would have known his Alphabet of Devotion sooner or later.

John Carey has made a translation of this wonderful text in his anthology King of Mysteries—Early Irish Religious Writings (Four Courts Press, Dublin, 231–2). In his introduction he describes it as "a collection of precepts and maxims, arranged in sequences of varying length, which reflect a keen perception of the ethics and psychology of the contemplative life. Drawing on the monastic treatises of John Cassian (died 435), on the sapiential books of the Old Testament, and probably on native wisdom literature as well, the author distils his teachings into phrases of two or three words each—statements whose crystalline economy of expression demands slow and meditative reading. . ... Although much of his teaching is applicable to any Christian, or indeed to anyone seeking to live a spiritual life, its audience was evidently a monastic one: the text speaks of rising at the summons of the bell, obedience to the prior, and communal life with the brethren. It is conceived, like much Irish didactic literature, as a series of instructions given by a master to his disciple. . . It was clearly intended to sink deep within the memories of those who heard it and, once absorbed, to guide them from within."

The celebrations of the life of Saint Kevin, founder of the "monastic city" of Glendalough, are imaginary, but most of the other features in the story reflect historical background. There are conflicting dates in various annuls for the death of Kevin, but all agree that he lived to a very old age.

We do not know how long a novitiate was in Aidan's time; in the medieval period the length of a novitiate varied between monasteries. We know from Bede that a person could be made a deacon from the age of nineteen, and could not be priested until they were thirty and we assume that custom was uniform in Ireland and Northumbria.

Chapter 5: Senan's Isle

Inis Cathaigh or Scattery Island

This small island lies in the Shannon Estuary, 5 km south of Kilrush, County Clare. It was inhabited from its foundation by Saint Senan about 534 until the last inhabitants left in 1978. It is now in the care of Ireland's Office of Public Works. There is no electricity on the island, but in the summer a boat sometimes takes visitors from Kilrush to the monastic remains, which consist of an oratory, a house, seven chapels, a round tower, and a well. The Irish name Inis Cathaigh was formerly anglicized Iniscathy, and finally became Scattery. The story of Innis Cathaig by Daniel Mescot provides information about this monastic island over the centuries. This has recently been republished by and is available online. Until 1111, when the Synod of Rath brought in the Diocesan structure, parishes were under the jurisdiction of this island. I have befriended local pilgrimage networks who accept the tradition that there were ancient links between the three islands of Scattery, Iona and Lindisfarne, through Aidan, and who wish to revitalize these links today.

Senan

St Senan, who has appeared in some lists of "The Twelve Apostles of Ireland," established a series of monastic communities on islands in the mouths of rivers, from Slaney in Wexford, in Clare, and finally on Scattery island. He was patron of the Corcu Baiscinn, and of the Ui Fidgente, the ruling kindreds of the territory on the southern side of the estuary of the Shannon. As a farming youth his herd was stranded south of the Shannon after the tide had risen to make it impassable. The owner of a fort refused him shelter. Perhaps he recalled the Bible story of Moses people who were led across the sea to safety though their pursuers were drowned. At any rate God led him and his herd safely across the Shannon. Then and there he stuck his spear into the ground and dedicated the island to God.

The metrical Latin version of Senan's Life is the oldest, but has little connection with Inis Cathaig. The Irish Life, which includes fanciful material, reflects tenth century legends of the lower Shannon and may have been written within the community at Inis Cathaig. The Book of Lismore, compiled in the fifteenth century from earlier, lost sources, also contains a Life of Senan. Dates in these documents appear to be unchecked conjectures and are widely conflicting. Odran's late Life, no doubt projecting back, says Senan had 60 friars, 30 priests and 7 bishops. A story in the prose Life portrays Senan as a senior holy man. Saints Brendan of Birr and Kieran of Clonmacnois came with brothers to visit him for spiritual direction. This caused upset in the guest house, but a boat with provisions arrived.

The memory of Senan is alive and cherished locally. I have visited the site of his birth, and a well associated with him on the mainland. Mary Hamilton, pastor of the West Clare Christian Fellowship, has taken me to the route locals believe Senan took when he led his cattle across the low water to safe grazing.

Aidan

A person named Aidan is cited as its Bishop several times in Inis Cathaig's history. This may indicate that Aidan was a popular name, or that an early overseer of that name had such stature that others named themselves after him. There is no proof that the first Inis Cathaig Aidan was the Aidan of Lindisfarne, but Canon O'Hanlon assumes that he was in his monumental Lives of the Irish Saints. In view of the loose way dates were recorded the slight incongruity of dates is not significant, nor is the argument that Aidan only became a bishop when he was appointed to Lindisfarne. The term was used in early Irish writings in a general sense to refer to the person in oversight.

Canera

We know nothing of Canera (variously spelt Cannera, Kinnera, Conaire, and Cainder) other than through the Lives of Senan and local tradition, but various Catholic parishes in USA are dedicated to her and portray her as an early Irish feminist! She is believed to have been native to Beanntraighe (Bantry or Bantry Bay) in western County Cork and to have lived much of her life there as an anchorite. An anchorite's withdrawal from society and the world is more extreme than a simple hermit so Canera's life must have been both spiritual and solitary. She was a virgin and although she lived as an anchorite, it is likely that she would have been brought food by relatives or friends. Although she may have never seen most of those who provided her basic needs, Canera must have been supported by a community.

Hermits and Women

Irish monastic villages were on the whole much more open and relaxed, and men and women mixed freely as part of their extended families. However, there was also the hermit tradition, inspired by the desert fathers, and small islands of celibate hermits could develop a rule that forbade women visitors for similar reasons. It seems that Inis Cathaig was such an island. The local tradition is that there were good relations between the brothers on Innis Cathaig and the women hermits on the mainland, but I have used the story of Senan and Canera to provide a rationale for the body on the shore.

The hermit tradition is an honoured part of most religions. In the Old Testament, prophets such as Elijah and Elisha fostered prophetic hermit schools, and Jesus built his work upon the movement led by John the Forerunner, who spent most of his life as a desert hermit. In Russia the staretz and the Sketes, in Celtic lands the hermitages have waxed and waned and are now reviving. The impulse behind the hermit calling is "to seek God alone." Hermits: the insights of solitude by Peter Francis (St. Martin's Press 1998) provides an overview of the eremitical life in different epochs and religions.

Water Clocks

Water clocks, along with sundials, are likely to be the oldest time-measuring instruments and were used in Asia thousand of years before Christ. Water clocks usually consisted of a vessel of water, having a small hole in the bottom, so that the liquid dripped out drop by drop. As the level within the jar was lowered, it showed the time upon a scale. Thus, if the hole was so small and the vessel was so large that it would require twenty-four hours for the water to drip away at an absolutely steady rate, it may be seen that the side of the vessel might easily have been marked with twenty-four divisions to indicate the hours. Other water clocks, or clepsydras, were cylindrical or bowl-shaped containers designed to slowly fill with water coming in at a constant rate. Markings on the inside surfaces measured the passage of "hours" as the water level reached them. These clocks were used to determine hours at night, but may have been used in daylight as well. The Roman senator Cassiodorus (c. 485–585) advocated the water clock in his rulebook for monastic life as a useful alarm for the "soldiers of Christ" (Cassiod. Inst. 30.4 f.).

Chapter 6: Fires of Controversy

The Easter Dispute and the transfer.

Although Aidan may not have been at Durrow, the letters of Cummian, Honorius, Segene, and the local synod are historical facts. The date and text of Pope Honorarius 1's Letter to Irish churches is lost. Scholars judge 628 to be the most likely year for it. Bede summarizes the letter. The fact that he omits the text may be because the Saxons (like the Romans after Honorius) had changed the computation used by Pope Victor to which Honorius appealed.

Kathleen Hughes explores the Easter question and the Irish renaissance in learning on pages 325–330 of A New History of Ireland: Prehistoric and Early Ireland (Oxford University Press 2008).

The Irish focus on the apostle John and his Gospel surfaces again in Bede's accounts of the Synod of Whitby and of Cuthbert's last week of study with his dying prior, Boisil, at Melrose.

Cummian

Cummian was born about 590, abandoned by his parents, and brought up in Saint Ita's community at Killeedy. Later he studied under Findbarr's school at Cork where he learned a love of poetry. James Kenney, in his The Sources for the Early History of Ireland: Ecclesiastical, quotes McArthy, editor of the Annuls of Ulster that Cummian was probably Abbot of Durrow, though others have suggested he was Abbot of Clonfert which was quite close.

He became Abbot some time after 621. His brother became King of Connaught, and between them they exercised great influence. Cummian took a leading part in the 630 Synod of Magh Lene, near Durrow. About a mile and a half from Shinrone, to the west of Roscrea, is Disert Chuimin, the remains of a cell where it is thought Cummian spent his year research- ing the Easter question. Cummian's letter is the only important controver- sial document on this issue which we possess. It was preserved by Ussher and is now available as Cummian's Letter: De Controversia Paschali edited by Maura Walsh and Daibhi O Croinin (Pontifical Institute of Mediaeval Studies, Toronto 1988)

It seems that Cummian and Segene, Abbot of Iona, were well known to each other. Segene's relative had been Abbot of Durrow before 600. Cum- mian's old tutor, Colman, wrote of him::

> Of Erin's priests, it were not meet
> That one should sit in Gregory's seat,
> Except that Cummian crossed the sea.
> For he Rome's ruler well might be.

The Easter Controversy

The issues re the dating of Easter, which has still not been resolved between the Eastern and Western Church, are so complex that I cannot claim to have every detail right. Various phases in this dispute came before or after Aidan's lifetime. It seems to me that four factors underlie this dispute. 1) Two principles: a) that Easter should be on a Sunday b) that it should be the Sunday following the first full moon after the Spring Equinox. 2) Sci- ence: how should churches compute the date of the equinox? 3) Hidden assumptions: on the continent was there a bias against the Jews and towards administrative convenience rather than nature? 4) Whatever decisions were made, were they implemented in a loving and respectful way?

First Phase

The original method of fixing the date of the Jewish Passover was the fourteenth day of Nisan in the Old Testament's Hebrew Calendar (for example Lev 23:5). According to the Gospel of John (for example John 19:14), this was the day that Jesus was crucified in Jerusalem. (The Synoptic Gospels place the day on 15 Nisan). A letter of Irenaeus (who was born in Smyrna and became Bishop of the church of Celts at Lyons, d. 202) states that Polycarp, the bishop of Smyrna, observed Easter on the fourteenth day of the moon, whatever day of the week that might be, following the tradition which he claimed to have derived from St. John the Apostle, whom he knew. At the time of Pope Victor I, about AD 190, the dioceses of the Roman Province of Asia (probably greater Anatolia) which then had a large Celtic population, followed this practice. The term for this is Quartodecimanism (because it was the fourteenth day). The churches elsewhere kept Easter on the Sunday following. Pope Victor I attempted to excommunicate the Quartodecimans, turning the divergence of practice into a full-blown ecclesiastical controversy. According to Eusebius, synods were convened and letters were exchanged, but in the end, having over-stepped his mark Pope Victor was rebuked and had to back down. This information comes from Eusebius. Irenaeus' letter advocates that Easter should be on a Sunday but pleads that diversity of practice be respected.

Second Phase

The 325 Council of Nicea decided that Easter shall be the first Sunday after the first full moon on or after the Spring Equinox, but if Sunday coincides with the Jewish Passover it shall be the first Sunday after that. On the continent Christians were distancing themselves from Jews, who were persecuted or unpopular. The Irish Christians had no quarrel with Jews (there were no Jews in Ireland) and they valued the Old Testament, so if occasionally Easter Sunday coincided with Passover, what did it matter?

Third Phase

The Council of Nicea made no ruling about the different ways of computing the date of the Passover. It might seem simple to wait until a day when the hours of dark and light are equal (the Spring Equinox) and wait until the first full moon after that. But to compute this in advance, in order to prepare for the festival, is a complicated process that involves calendars based on the movements of both the moon and the sun, and these calendars and computations diverged from one place (for example Antioch) to another (for example Alexandria). The Irish thought the equinox happened on 25 March, the continentals on 21st March. To the Irish, whose faith reflected God in creation, it was nonsense to celebrate the resurrection of Christ, the Light of the world, on a day when there was more darkness than light.

Various tables were produced that attempted to calculate Easter for a series of years. British and Irish churches used a calculation table (Celtic-84) that was similar to one approved by Saint Jerome, based on an eighty-four year cycle. However, by the sixth and seventh centuries it had become obsolete and had been replaced by those of Victorius of Aquitaine and, more accurately, those of Dionysius Exiguus. This 84-year cycle gave way to the Alexandrine computus in stages

As the Celtic world established renewed contact with the Continent it became aware of the divergence. The first clash over the matter came in Gaul in 602, when Columbanus resisted pressure from the local bishops to conform. Most groups, like the southern Irish, accepted the updated tables with relatively little difficulty, with the last significant objectors being the monks from Columba's monasteries. The southern Irish accepted the common Easter calculation at the Synod of Mag Léne around 630 (but not all monasteries conformed), as did the northern Irish at the Council of Birr around 697, and Northumbria with the Synod of Whitby in 664. In 716 Iona converted its practice.

Fourth Phase

After the promulgation of the Gregorian calendar in 1582, the Catholic and Protestant churches of the West came to follow a different method of computing the date of Easter from the one that had been previously accepted. Most Eastern Orthodox churches continued to follow the older practice and this difference has continued to the present time. In 1997 the World Council of Churches proposed a reform of the method of determining the date of Easter at a summit in Aleppo, Syria: Easter would be defined as the first Sunday following the first astronomical full moon following the astronomical vernal equinox, as determined from the meridian of Jerusalem. The reform would have been implemented starting in 2001, since in that year the Eastern and Western dates of Easter would coincide. This reform has not yet been implemented.

It was normal for transfers to take place between monasteries then as now.

PART TWO—TESTING FIRES:
IONA AND THE MIDDLE YEARS

Chapter 7:The Flame Fades

Adomnan's Life of St. Columba and the detailed historical notes of Richard Sharpe in the Penguin Classics edition is a key source of information. In their Iona: The Earliest Poetry of a Celtic Monastery (Edinburgh University Press 1995) Thomas Owen Clancy and Gilbert Markus provide two informative chapters on Iona's early history and on the life and work of the monastery. Columba by Tim Clarkson (Birlinn 2012) explores Iona, her neighbours, and King Aedan at Dunadd. Iona, Kells and Derry: The History and Hagiography of the Monastic Familia of Columba' by Maire Herbert (Four Courts Press 1996) touches on this period. Although Aidan's arrival and thoughts are imaginary, the descriptions are based on historical material.

Segene

Segene was the fifth abbot of Iona from 623 to 652 and of the same tribe, the Ui Neill, as Columba. He is said to have established or re-established a church on Rathlin Island, in the early 630s. He put his name to a letter to Pope Severinus in 638 vigorously defending the Irish dating of Easter. Adomnan informs us that Segene was a vital collector and transmitter of stories about Columba. The article on Iona, abbots of by T.M. Charles-Edwards in The Oxford Dictionary of National Biography (first published 2004) draws together the significant material about Segene, much of it from Adomnan.

Rule of Columba

As stated in the chapter on Durrow, we do not possess a Rule written by Columba. Most early Irish monastic founders were the Rule, through their life, practices, and verbal guidelines. Only after their death were their sayings and practices codified. The anonymous document, written centuries later, entitled The Rule of Columba is included in Councils and Ecclesiastical Documents Relating to Great Britain and Ireland II, I ed. by A. W. Haddan and W. Stubbs, (Oxford: Oxford University Press, 1873), pp. 119–121 and is available online from Fordham University, USA. It reflects something of early Irish monastic life and was presumably written by a member or sympathizer of the Columban monasteries. The quotations are from this document.

Hinba Island

The location of Hinba, the favourite island retreat of St Columba, described in Adomnán's Life, remains a topic of debate. Jura and the Garvellachs are front runners. The most southerly of the four Garvellach islands, Eileach an Naoimh, Scottish Gaelic for Isle of the Saints, has the remains of an ancient Celtic monastery believed to have been founded by St Brendan in 542. These, and the beehive cell where tradition says Columba's mother Eithne dwelt, can still be visited. Charismatic Christians assume that Columba was speaking in tongues, and that the light was similar to the auras that are depicted as halos in art.

Chapter 8: The Ebbe Affair

Bede gives the basic facts of the Saxon royal children, their flight to the Irish Christians, and their conversion to Christianity. The Anglo-Saxon Chronicle lists names and dates, and Adomnan has references to Oswald and his brother. Information about fosterage and treaties among Irish and other local rulers comes from various other sources. The Heroic Age Issue 4 Winter 2001: Oswald and the Irish by Michelle Ziegler (available online) provides detailed notes and bibliography on fosterage and "constructed kingship."

The father of the four royal children was Ethelfrith, the brutal Saxon king of Bernicia. He won major battles. He defeated his southern neighbour, the King of Deira, and so united the two kingdoms into one large and powerful kingdom of Northumbria. In 604 King Aidan, whom Columba had anointed as Christian king of the Irish Scots colony of Dalriada (roughly the area of today's Argyll) , rallied both his troops and Saxon warriors with whom he made a treaty after their defeat by Ethelfrith, and confronted Ethelfrith's forces at Degsastan. They suffered great loss of life, but in 616 Ethelfrith was slain, and his widow and children, knowing that the Dalriada people had proved to be faithful in their treaty obligations, sought refuge among them.

Ebbe

We know nothing of the first part of Ebbe's life, except the fact that she went into exile with her brothers. She emerges into history later when Bede records that she took vows and established a monastery in Northumbria (at today's St. Abbs Head). However, The Life of Saint Cuthbert by an anonymous monk of Lindisfarne describes her as a widow and I have assumed that she married while in exile in Dalriada. Almost the only church outside Northumbria dedicated to St. Ebbe is St. Ebbe's Oxford. For that reason, and because we know that Oswald later took great interest in the West Saxon royal family, and married the king's daughter Kyneburga, this imaginary story about Ebbe has her marry a West Saxon. The Miracles of Saint Aebbe of Coldingham and Saint Margaret of Scotland by Robert Bartlett (Oxford Medieval Texts) looks at some legends.

Women's Island

Before the Augustinian nunnery was established on Iona some time after the foundation of the Benedictine monastery in 1203, the monastic establishment was male only. It is assumed that there were no women resident on Iona during Aidan's time because Adomnan records that only monks attended Columba's funeral. Modern pilgrims to Iona who take the short ferry to it from Fionnphort on the Isle of Mull, pass a tiny islet on their right that is known as Women's Island. I have been unable to elicit an explanation for its name from local people. It seems likely to refer to a period before the nunnery was built on Iona. The eighth century Culdee reform movement allowed married people to make modified monastic vows. It has been speculated that this movement influenced Iona and that married monastics settled on Women's Island, but I know of no evidence for this. So I have used poetic license and imagined Ebbe's story to be the origin of its name.

References to herbs in monastic gardens occur in diverse sources.

Chapter 9: "King" Arthur

Arthurian literature is so vast that it fills whole sections of libraries. Most of it consists of fables written by people like Geoffrey of Monmouth in Britain and Chretien de Troyes in France that fed the twelfth century hunger for romantic chivalry. Endless commentaries linking these stories with those about the holy grail have proliferated and have become the stuff of Wagnerian music and Hollywood films.

Some question whether, centuries before the fables and hidden in the mists of history there might have been a real Arthur. Could he have been the war leader who temporarily rallied Celtic kingdoms against the invading Anglo-Saxons, and won a famous battle at an unknown place named Badon Hill around 500? Nennius gives this person the name Arthur in his ninth century History of Britain, which means that stories were circulating by then.

The only historical record of a leader named Arthur is in Adomnan's seventh century Life of Columba. The Annals of Tighernac, which were copied from earlier sources in the eleventh century by an Irish monk called Tigernac, also mention Arthur and his final battle. The case for King Aidan's son being the origin of the Arthur legends is argued by W. F. Skene in Arthur and the Britons in Wales and Scotland ed. Derek Bryce (Llanerch Enterprises. Lampeter, Dyfed. 1988). Adomnan records the first time that a senior church leader in Britain chose and anointed a king. Columba, who was related to the rulers of the Irish colony of Dalriada which included Iona, at first chose a more impressive relative to be King. But God told him to choose Aedan mac Gabrain. It became obvious why he was not Columba's first choice, for he became a monk, and before he did so he put his son Arthur (perhaps of a British mother) in charge of various areas and of battles. They were based at the Dunadd fort on the mainland, near to the present village of Kilmartin.

Arthuret Church, near Longtown, Cumbria, overlooks the site of the Battle of Arfderydd, which appears in the Annales Cambriae in the year 573. This mentions that the druid Merlin went mad after this battle and spent the rest of his life roaming the Forests of Celyddon , and that Bishop Kentigern tracked him down and baptized him. Skene suggests that the twelve famous battles of Arthur were fought between the two Roman walls of Hadrian and Anthony, and that Bishop Kentigern, after he fled to Wales, where he founded the community at today's St. Asaph, would have told the stories of Arthur and Merlin. These became the stories of the Welsh, who took them to their kinsmen who had emigrated to Armorica during the time of plague. Embroidered over the centuries, writers like Geoffrey of Monmouth in Britain and Chretien de Troyes used them for fiction with locations in the places where the stories circulated. For an on-line argument in favour of King Aidan's son being the origin of the later legends see www. legendofkingarthur.com/evidence.httm

Kings

The Irish were interested in the idea of the great and wise king. Cormac was thought to have been a High King of Ireland some time between second and fourth centuries who ruled from Tara for forty years. He was famous for his wise and generous judgments. The hero Fionn is supposed to have lived in Cormac's time, and most of the stories of the Fenian Cycle are set during his reign. Cormac's inspiring instructions for Kings are available online. Some scholars have dismissed such characters that appear as historical figures in Irish literature as no more than gods re-cast in human form. Myles Dillon argues against this approach in his The Cycles of the Kings (London 1946) and believes that "a fairly reliable historical tradition can be established from as early a time as the second century of the Christian era." We cannot know whether or not Cormac's Instructions were circulating in Aidan's time. Aidan's Ten Rules for Kings echo some of Cormac's rules,

Chapter 10: The Crisis

The story is imaginary. We know nothing of the inner life of Aidan. We may deduce, from what Bede tells us of the way he handled immense responsibilities as bishop of Northumbrians, that he arrived in Northumbria a mature man. Those who have areas of their life that remain unexamined, untested and undeveloped, are unable to sustain the weight put upon them by great practical and spiritual responsibilities. The weakest link in the chain of their life snaps. Whether Aidan matured seamlessly, or whether he had a mid-life crisis we cannot know. Aspects of this and the following story reflect elements of my own experience. I did not have one major mid-life crisis, I experienced several significant transitions when parts of my brittle shell were broken, and previously unrecognized angers, aspirations and aptitudes came to light. I was advised to go to a large tree in a remote shore and shout out my anger, and two people making love the other side of it did flee in shock!

We do not know who was Aidan's anamchara, but we may assume that he had one, since this was the custom in Irish monasteries of that time. Various legends of Odran have been passed down by word of mouth. The most gruesome to modern minds is that Odran wished to be the first martyr buried on Iona. When he was thought to be dead they placed him in the grave, but he moved. He asked them to continue to fill his grave with earth so that he could be the first martyr.

The Michaelmas custom of horse circling features in the Carmina Gadelica's accounts of much later practices: we cannot be sure whether Iona followed that custom, though we do know that Columba circled the island with his pack horse. We know that Iona had no women, and scholars think that in Columba's time only monks were resident on the island. Hereditary leadership was the norm in early Irish monasteries; this was reformed in the eighth century. The portrayal of stagnation at Iona reflects a common, though not a universal pattern in communities the second generation after the death of their founder.

The Mull of Kintyre is the southwestern most tip of the Kintyre Peninsula in southwest Scotland. On top of the rocks that overlook the present Saint Columba's chapel are two footprints carved into the rock. One dates from the nineteenth century, while the other is ancient and may have had some significance in the ceremony to inaugurate a new king, as there is a similar carving at Dunadd. From here, Ireland's Antrim coast and Rathlin Island are clearly visible and are less than fourteen miles distant. It is believed that Saint Columba landed here in AD 563, on his way to Iona. The walking distance from Columba's footprints to Dunadd is some 150 miles.

In Aidan's time there would have been occasional boats to and from Dunadd and Iona. Today people drive or walk north from Dunadd to Oban and take ferries from Oban to Mull and Iona.

Chapter 11: Killing field and angels

The story of Aidan now moves into a period for which there is brief but significant historical record.

Hill of Angels

The stories of Columba's all-day spiritual warfare which averted plague, and of the monks scenting his presence at the Hill of Angels years after his death are recorded by Adomnan. Pilgrims to Iona may still visit this little hill. This story of Aidan on the Hill of Angels is imaginary.

Eanfrith

Information about Eanfrith comes from Bede, Nennius, Adomnan and the Irish Annuls of Tigernach. Eanfrith's mother was Bebba, a Briton, the first wife of King Ethelfrith. When his father was slain he fled through the territory of the Britons at Strathclyde to the southern Picts, perhaps just north of the Firth of Forth. Bede thought that these Picts had been evangelized by Columba, and that they baptized Eanfrith as a Christian. Eanfrith's Pictish wife bore him not only a son, Talorcan, who became King of the Picts, but also a daughter, Beli, who married the King of Britons at Strathclyde.

According to Saxon laws Eanfrith, as the eldest son of King Ethelfrith, had the right to his throne. It is assumed that he would have raised an army of Britons and Picts as well as Saxon sympathizers. His renunciation of his faith once he assumed the throne must have been deeply upsetting to those Christians who had supported his life in exile. When he realized that the British King Cadwallon was continuing his relentless campaign to overrule Bernicia, it is likely that he was willing to negotiate and become a sort of sub-kingdom, especially since he was a half Briton himself, that may explain why he took only twelve people when he went to negotiate with Cadwallon—who promptly had him killed.

Oswald's Vision and Victory

Adomnan states: "I, Adomnan, had this narrative from the lips of my predecessor, the Abbot Failbe, who solemnly declared that he had himself heard King Oswald relating this same vision to Segene the abbot."

The words of Joshua that God addressed to Oswald through Columba were copied into the Anglo-Saxon forms for the coronation of kings, and form an anthem in the current coronation service for the monarch of the United Kingdom.

A Welsh bard records the death of Cadwallon in The Red Book of Hergest, (written between 1375–1425) and mentions that Oswald brought "iniquitous monks" with him. It seems that Cadwallon's supporters attributed his defeat in part to the moral and spiritual influence of the monks. Both Bede and Adomnan tell the story.

Chapter 12: The Call

The facts of Corman's mission, its failure and the decision to consecrate Aidan as bishop and send him on a second mission are from Bede. The gist of what Corman and Aidan say in the story comes from Bede but I have filled their words out. The time-table is unknown. I have assumed they would not travel as far as Lindisfarne in winter.

The other details, such as Aidan's illness and his soul work with Tomas are imaginary, and reflect certain elements of my own experience. Although we do not know in what ways Aidan was prepared for his great mission, I think we can take it that God usually prepares people and that Aidan was no exception.

In the universal church only bishops could consecrate a priest as a bishop. It seems that Abbot Segene, like his founder Columba, was not a bishop, but we know from Adomnan that bishops sometimes stayed at Iona. So I assume that bishops were present and that Easter was a most appropriate time for both a consecration and a commissioning of the thirteen missionaries.

Chapter 13: The journey of the twelve

The Names of the Twelve.

We cannot be certain we know the names of any of Aidan's first twelve monks, but two monks we do know about may well have been among them. Bede tells us about Boisil in his Life of Cuthbert and in his Ecclesiastical History. Boisil is an Irish name. We first hear about him as the Prior at Melrose, so we may presume that he was a monk at Lindisfarne before that. Bede thought of him as "a man of sublime virtues" as well as an eminent scholar. The holy names of the adorable Trinity were ever on his lips and he repeated the name Jesus Christ with tender affection. He frequently exclaimed, "How good a Jesus we have!" and wept so sincerely that onlookers were encouraged to join him. It was Boisil's evident sanctity which drew the young Cuthbert to Melrose, rather than the more famous Lindisfarne, in 651. Boisil prophesied his own death and Cuthbert's future, he mentored Cuthbert and they spent the last week of Boisil's life reflecting together on John's Gospel.

Bede mentions Diuma, whose name is Irish, as a monk of Lindisfarne, so we may presume he was either one of the original twelve or one of the reinforcements that followed. About 652 Lindisfarne's Irish Bishop Finan made Diuma a bishop and sent him with three other monks to convert the Middle Angles. Thus Diuma is the founder of Repton which became Lichfield diocese. Bede says that he and his companions "were listened to gladly," which perhaps suggests he had an attractive personality.

The Stopping Places

We do not know which route Aidan took, or whether his first stop was at Dunadd, but the three main routes between Iona and Lindisfarne are as in the story. For information about their stopping places I have drawn on local sources such as the Glen Lyon Archeological Society. HISTORIC ARGYLL 2009 Home to Glenorchy by Mhairi Ross, Ledaig collates useful facts and is available online.

Clachan an Dìseart, is the old name for Dalmally. The oldest Gaelic name for Glen Lyon is Glen Fasach—the desert or monastery glen. The 5,000 year old yew tree is propped up behind railings in Fortingall church-yard and the pagan stones stand in a nearby field. A recent archeological dig revealed the remains of a Celtic monastery there. The legend about Pontius Pilate is still talked about, though I suspect it emerged later than Aidan's time. Archeologists do however confirm that the Romans mined pearls in the area.

Aidan and his Twelve experienced Glen Lyon as a place of spiritual warfare. Some prophetic young Scots have a vision of a Highland Cathe-dral without walls that combines farming, medical care, daily prayer, guest accommodation, and training of teams who will re-evangelize the glens. I joined them for a spiritual mapping of the highlands which took us along the Glen Lyon route. We went to Eonan Mill. Eonan is the local name for Adomnan, who walked that route and established a mill and a church there. Local guide books claim that Lindisfarne brothers walked to Iona from Lindisfarne along that route. These pioneers sense that this is indeed a place of intense spiritual warfare.

Inchadney is on the outskirts of Kenmore. It is claimed that the deriva-tion of the word Inchadney is Aidan, the titular saint of Kenmore, which was sometimes spelt Inchaidin. A previous minister believed Aidan himself gathered people while on a missionary journey—perhaps even en route to Lindisfarne. See Famed Breadalbane: A local history written by the Rever-end William Gillies, Minister of Kenmore from 1912. According to tradi-tion Saint Cuthbert of Lindisfarne (died 687) established a church at Dull (which has recently been twinned with a place named Boring in the USA!). I have assumed that a cell already existed there. Conol, Fintan, Marnoc, Dunkeld, and Scone all feature in records. Cell Rígmonaid is now known as St. Andrews, famed for its university and golf. Thus there is a tradition, which circulates on the internet, that St. Cuthbert was the founder of the cell that became St. Andrew's University

The Picts lived as far south as the Firth of Forth. Following the conver-sion of their King Bruid by Columba in 587, near Loch Ness evangelization of Picts further south followed, and the royal centre would move to Perth. According to tradition Columba visited Perth, and St. John's Church marks the site of a Pictish monastery. In the centuries after Aidan Perth became a hub of Christianity. Dull church is on the site of an early Christian monastery founded by St Adomnán (Scottish Gaelic: N. Eònan), Abbot of Iona (died 704). Several early Christian cross-slabs dating to the seventh or eighth centuries are found there. I have assumed that Adomnan chose this site to found a monastery because some contacts with friendly Christians had already been made there and throughout the region by the likes of Aidan

Along the shore line from St. Andrews to Bamburgh are several caves associated with early Irish hermits, and several islands in the Firth of Forth contain ruins of early Celtic monastic cells. It cannot be ruled out that some of these existed at the time of Aidan's arrival.

Hermits on the Islands and Shores of the Firth of Forth

If the brothers had sailed south from St. Andrews they would have passed Pitterweem. Pitterweem, meaning "the place of the cave" refers to a sixth century Irish hermit named Saint Fillan. Visitors may pick up a key from the post office and visit this. In the distance they might have espied Culross further inland along the northern shore (towards today's Edinburgh). Here Saint Serf and a group of hermits brought up Mungo, who became the missionary founder of Glasgow and died about 612. According to some traditions Baldred was a hermit on Bass Rock before Aidan's arrival. In The Scotichronicon, Rev J.F.S. Gordon DD (1867) explores this. Inch is the Gaelic name for an island. Inchgarvie, Inchkeith, Incolm, and Inchmickery are thought to have had early Christian hermits but it is not certain when they came. The Isle of May is known to have had a ninth century Christian settlement, but radio carbon dating of bones in the cemetery date back to the seventh century.

Aberlady

In 1863 a fragment of an eighth century Christian Cross was found near the churchyard at Aberlady, a small town south of Edinburgh beside the Firth of Forth. The artwork on the Cross bears a striking resemblance to artwork in the Lindisfarne Gospels. This, together with other local finds and place names across the Lammermuir region suggest that a significant church foundation existed here in Anglo-Saxon times, and remained part of the pilgrimage route from Iona to Lindisfarne over succeeding centuries. It is believed that the Anglo-Saxons inherited the name Aberlady, and that there was at least a cell dedicated to the Virgin Mary in existence before Aidan's arrival. Local researchers assume that Aidan's monks stopped at Aberlady on their way to Bamburgh. They are inclined to think that they would have walked, because sea journeys were too dangerous. Whether they walked or came by boat, Aberlady was a natural stopping place. In 2012 local heritage enthusiasts launched the St. Aidan Way pilgrimage route from Aberlady to Lindisfarne.

In 750 King Eadbergh stopped at Aberlady on his journey to meet the Christian Pictish king from across the Forth. It is possible that Aidan a century earlier had the same idea.

The Picts

The Picts were a Celtic people living in ancient eastern and northern Scotland. They lived to the north of the rivers Forth and Clyde, and spoke the now-extinct Pictish language, which is thought to have been related to the Brythonic languages spoken by the Britons who lived to the south of them. Pictland, also called Pictavia by some sources, gradually merged with the Gaelic kingdom of Dalriada to form the Kingdom of Alba (Scotland).

Bede records that Ninian evangelised southern and Columba northern Picts. Recent archaeological work at Portmahomack places the foundation of the monastery there in the late sixth century. Among other major religious sites of eastern Pictland were Cennrígmonaid (later St Andrews), Dunkeld, Abernethy, and Rosemarkie. Pictland also had ties to churches in Northumbria, as seen in the reign of Nechtan mac Der Ilei. The evidence of place names suggests a wide area of Ionan influence in Pictland. Likewise, the Cáin Adomnáin (Law of Adomnán, Lex Innocentium) counts Nechtan's brother Bridei among its guarantors. It is feasible that Aidan took the northernmost route and that he sought to cement friendship with Christian Picts on the fringe of Northumbria.

Bernicia Bereft of a Christian Presence?

Bede observed in his History that until Oswald set up his cross at Heavenfield there had been no sign of Christian faith in all Bernicia—no church, no cross, no altar.

PART THREE—THE FLAME SPREADS: THE ENGLISH AND THE RIPE YEARS

Chapter 14: Building foundations

Max Adams suggests long hair at the back of his head and a moustache was Oswald's likely hair style, and cites descriptions of Bamburgh in chapter one of his *The King of the North: the life and times of Oswald of Northumbria* (Head of Zeus 2013).

Bede records that Farne Isle was uninhabited. Aidan is the first person on record as having made a retreat there. Inner Farne is now owned by Britain's National Trust. Visitors may go by boat from Seahouses in season.

The Origin of the Name Lindisfarne

Theories abound as to the origin of the name Lindisfarne. Both Welsh and Norwegian people point out that Lindis is the name of a native tree in their languages. An erudite research paper by Thomas Green of Exeter College, Oxford is available online. This explores the strengths and weaknesses of umpteen theories about the origin of the name. Green thinks the name is unlikely to be British/Celtic because the early Britons already had their name, Medcaut which, as he says, means "the island of healing."

One of the theories is that the name means "the people who migrated from Lindsey," the ancient name for Lincoln. Evidence from Anglian cemeteries shows that the Lincoln area was the heartland of the first Anglian (Anglo-Saxon/ English) occupation in the late fifth century. Archeology confirms that the area around Bamburgh, Yeavering, and Lindisfarne was the heartland of Bernicia, Northumbria's northern kingdom in the following century. Green thinks that the Lindisfaren might well have been Lindsay's ruling families who emigrated from Lindsey, settled in the Bamburgh/ Lindisfarne area, and became the founders of Bernicia. In 547 King Ida established his rule at Bamburgh: Green thinks he brought his elite people with him from Lindsey. And these Lindisfaren gave their name to the island nearby.

We have no detailed record of the building of the first monastery, but we do know they built simply and in wood, and we know about Anglo-Saxon monasteries a little later. Leicester University Archeological unit has excavated the Saxon village at Lindisfarne as it was in the century following Aidan. Publications include *Space silence and shortage on Lindisfarne: the* archaeology of asceticism in H Hamerow and A McGregor (eds.) Image and Power in the Archaeology of Early Medieval Britain. Essays in Honour of Rosemary Cramp Oxford: Oxbow (2001) 33–52. Marginality, multiple estates and environmental change: the case of Lindisfarne in G Coles et al (eds.) Archaeology on the Margin proceedings of the conference of the Association of Environmental Archaeologists, Edinburgh (1999).

Oswald's words "as the tide ebbs and flows" reproduce Bede's description of the island.

The Horse

Bede states Aidan "used to travel everywhere, in town and country, not on horseback but on foot, unless compelled by urgent necessity to do otherwise . . ." (Bede, Ecclesiastical History of the English People: 3:5)

Royal Centres

It is thought that the king would have traveled throughout his land dispensing justice and authority and collecting rents from his various estates. Such visits would be periodic and it is likely that he would visit each royal villa only once or twice a year. Bede refers to the royal centers of Bamburgh (which was always the royal centre of Bernicia) and of York (which was always the royal center of Deira). It is assumed that places where Bishop Paulinus had mass baptisms under King Edwin were linked to royal centers. These include Holystone, near Rothbury, where the large rectangular Lady's Well is still well preserved, and Yeavering, where major archeological work has recently been undertaken.

The collection of buildings discovered at Yeavering in the 1950s formed part of an Anglo-Saxon royal villa. This consisted of a series of buildings designed to provide short-term accommodation for the king and his household. Excavations at Yeavering by Brian Hope-Taylor uncovered a range of buildings, many associated with King Edwin. These included a great hall which he surmised was suitable for feasts and ceremonial occasions, and a wooden theatre, consisting of raised wooden benches facing a stage. The stage was designed to focus all attention on the person occupying it, with screens behind and to either side of it. For information and reconstruction images see www.pastperfect.org.uk/sites/yeavering/images/index.html

Local traditions associate the other places mentioned in the story as royal centers.

Coronation

Material on this is drawn from The Venerable Bede, His Life and Writings by George Forrest Browne (S.P.C.K. London 1905) reprinted by BiblioLife.

His information about the Dalriada coronations comes from Adomnan, but he does not cite which Anglo-Saxon document contains the words which were retained in the coronation service for British monarchs.

Bede tells us about the methods of Aidan and his brothers, but nothing as to their destinations: "Many came from the country of the Irish into Britain and to those English kingdoms over which Oswald reigned, preaching the word of faith with great devotion. Those of them who held the rank of priest administered the grace of baptism to those who believed. Churches were built in various places and the people flocked together with joy to hear the Word; lands and property of other kinds were given by royal bounty to establish monasteries, and English children, as well as their elders, were instructed by Irish teachers in advanced studies and in the observance of the discipline of a Rule. Indeed, they were mostly monks who came to preach. . ." (Bede, Ecclesiastical History of the English People 3:4).

Chapter 15: Villages of God

Lindisfarne was a monastery, school and diocesan see. All that we know of the school and its pupils comes from Bede. In spite of the fact that later Anglo-Saxon monasteries were often well-funded, we learn from Bede that, although the king endowed Lindisfarne, it had minimal buildings (Ecclesiastical History: 3:26) and frugal life-style. His Life of Cuthbert refers to dormitories. Other sources such as *Monastic Life in Anglo-Saxon England c.600–900* by Sarah Foot (Cambridge University Press, 2006) draw together general information about Anglo-Saxon schools and scriptoria. John Blair, in *The Early Churches at Lindisfarne*, chapter V11 in *The Wiley Blackwell Encyclopedia of Anglo-Saxon England: Second Edition* edited by Michael Lapidge, John Blair, Simon Keynes, and Donald Scragg states that "the architectural and topological evidence provides a strong suggestion that the early monastery contained two churches, roughly aligned on a west-east axis which also included a well and one or two standing crosses." The first fifty pages of Ian Bradley's Colonies of Heaven: Celtic Models for Today's Church (Darton Longman and Todd 2008) provides a summary of typical features of Irish monasteries. The information in the text is drawn from these sources and archeological articles.

Columba's monasteries had scriptoriums and Lindisfarne's scriptorium became famous, after Aidan's death, for the Lindisfarne Gospels, so we may assume that some sort of scriptorium was established during Aidan's life-time. Books played an important part in the monasteries of Columba.

It was widely acknowledged in Columban monasteries that some Scriptures were difficult to interpret. Adomnan wrote of Columba "everything that in the sacred scriptures is dark and most difficult became more plain" as a result of a mystical experience. (Oxford 1991 edition pages 208–9.)

Leicester University archeologists have delineated what they believe to be the bounds of the original monastic rath at Lindisfarne. On the Sunday nearest St. Aidan's Day, August 31, the parish church walks these bounds and a bishop blesses the island from the heugh. The bounds are: from the present church along the road by the shore (Fiddlers Green) right down Marygate, and right again along what was the original harbor shore (now the slope in Sanctuary Field), up to the heugh and back to the church.

Irish Christians shared with continental Christians the belief that God's invisible nature can be discerned in things that are visible (Rom 1: 20). The Columban monasteries used imagery to draw attention to Scripture and embellish it, but not to allure people through grandiosity. This simplicity was lost to Boniface, the English missionary to the Germans, who in 735 commissioned from the abbess Eadburgha a copy of the epistles of Peter written in gold so that, as he said, he might impress honour and reverence for the scripture before the eyes of the carnal in his preaching (Monumenta Germaniae Historia, Epistolae 111 (1892) page 60). That approach was alien to Aidan.

Chapter 16: Bega and the Britons

The story of Britannicum is imaginary. We do know, however, that Britons lived in Aidan's large Diocese. Wales as it is today only began in 1536. The Cymric (Welsh) speaking peoples covered a wider area in Aidan's time. Cumbria derives from Cymru.

Scholars debate the extent to which the Anglo-Saxon invaders replaced the indigenous population of Britons (who were known to the Romans as Celts) or merely replaced the ruling class. Simon Young points out in his *The Celtic Revolution: in search of 2000 Forgotten Years that Changed the World* (Gibson Square 2009) that the Saxons arrived in a small number of boats—there was never a mass invasion. The implication of this is that the Celtic population remained, albeit as the underdog, even in the

Anglo-Saxon areas. Recent research that reveals that over ten percent of the DNA in English residents is Celtic tends to confirm this view.

Northumbria included Cymric speaking Britons, who were more populous in the west. Cumbria presumably means the Celts north of the Humber. The Celtic languages fall into two groups: the Brythonic (or British), including Breton, Cornish, and Welsh; and the Goidelic (or Gaelic), including Irish, Scottish Gaelic, and Manx. The Brythonic branch is referred to as P-Celtic (like Gaulish) because the Brythonic reflex of the Proto-Indo-European phoneme k is p as opposed to the Goidelic c.

So Bishop Aidan had Cymric speakers in his large Diocese, and his Irish brothers would have understood this language more readily than they understood English.

Adomnan records Columba taking earth from Clonmacnoise. Bede records the healings from splinters of wood taken from the cross at Heavenfield. Bede records that "lands and property of other kinds were given by royal bounty to establish monasteries. . ." (Bede, Ecclesiastical History of the English People Book 3, chapter 3), and later he records that Oswald's successor, King Oswy, was persuaded by his wife to give land for monasteries as a penance for his cruel acts in battle. In Book 3 chapter 23 Bede records that shortly after Aidan's death Oswald's son Oethelwald, King of Deira, gave land to Bishop Cedd, "where he himself might frequently come to pray and hear the Word and where he might be buried. . . Cedd chose himself a site for the monastery amid some steep and remote hills which seemed better fitted for the haunts of robbers and the dens of wilds beasts than for human habitation; so that as Isaiah says, "In the habitations where once dragons lay, shall be grass with reeds and rushes," that is, the fruit of good works shall spring up where once beasts dwelt or where men lived after the manner of beasts . . .. The man of God was anxious first of all to cleanse the site which he had received for the monastery from the stain of former crimes by prayer and fasting, before laying the foundations. So he asked the king to grant him permission and opportunity to spend the whole of the approaching season of Lent there in prayer. He explained that this was a custom of those from whom he had learned the discipline of a Rule."

Material on Bega is drawn from the legendary '13th c Life' Vita et Miracula S Bege Virginis in Privincia Northanhimboru (British library, Cott. MS. Faustina, B IV. Translated G C Tomlinson, printed S Jefferson, Carlisle 1842). Melvyn Bragg's historical novel Credo draws on this material. According to this Life King Oswald arranged for this Irish princess, who was fleeing from a rapist prince, to find sanctuary in Northumbria, in which case Aidan must have received her vows. St. Bees Head, in Cumbria is named after the hermitage she is thought to have established there. Some commentators have assumed that the Begu recorded by Bede as one of Saint Hilda's nuns at Whitby's daughter monastery of Hackness is the same person. The fact that Begu "saw" Hilda's passage to heaven before the Whitby brothers had informed the sisters of her death might suggest that she was close to Hilda. On the basis of these assumptions I portray Aidan introducing Bega to Hilda.

I have heard it suggested that J.R.R. Tolkien took his story of the ring in his Lord of the Rings from the Life of Bega.

Chapter 17: Oswald, Oh Oswald!

The report in the Annals of Ulster for 638, "the battle of Glenn Muiresan and the besieging of Eten" (Din Eidyn, later Edinburgh), has been taken to represent the capture of Din Eidyn by Oswald. We have no details of Aidan's oversight of this part of his Diocese. We do know that churches were established at the places mentioned at some time during the period of the Irish Mission.

Bede records Oswald's links with Cynegils of Wessex, including the baptism and marriage, his dealings with Fursey and the East Angles, Heui's foundation at Hartlepool, the appointment of Eata and Boisil to Melrose. Boisil is the Irish name for Basil. According to Bede, Oswald completed the stone church begun by Edwin in York (Bede 2.14). Alcuin credits Oswald with lavish decorations of this church (Godman, Peter, Editor. (1982) Alcuin: The Bishops, Kings, and Saints of York Oxford: Clarendon Press pages 27–29). Those described by Alcuin are not typical of Irish Christianity. Considering that Bede credits Aidan's successor Finan with building the first church on Lindisfarne worthy of an episcopal seat, it is possible that Aidan's public cathedral was at York while Lindisfarne was a monastery for the private use of the clergy. Oswald would then have had an elaborate cathedral to show his power and wealth to the people, including Edwin's Romanist clergy and converts. Such displays of wealth and symbols of power, often in Roman fashion, were important to all prominent Anglo-Saxon kings including Oswald. The more southern location of the cathedral at York would also suit Oswald's ambitions south of the Humber. Had Oswald lived longer and finally tamed Mercia and its allies, York could have served as a missionary base to at least include the church of Lindsey which had been incorporated into the see of York under Bishop Paulinus. The burial of Edwin's head in the church at York may have been part of the process of incorporating Edwin's Christian mission into Oswald's administration. The compromise of having the cathedral in York but Aidan's base at Lindisfarne would have allowed

Aidan a foundation suitable for the simple life that the Irish clergy preferred and for teaching in the Irish style but with ready access to the royal court while still providing Oswald with an extravagant public cult center. Bede claims that the King was recognized as Bretwalda by all of Saxon England.

The river Tees empties north-east of Middlesbrough, once a halfway stop for monks going between Durham and Whitby Abbey in the seventh century. Billingham is beside the Tees. Kildale is on the edge of the North Yorkshire Moors where the Monk's Trod joins it to Guisborough. Marske is a stopping place on a sea journey south from Hartlepool (Hart's Pool) to Whitby (where Saint Hilda is later abbess), and has the remains of a Saxon cell. The story about Hilda's marriage is fiction.

Bede records the death and dying words of Oswald, his replacement by Oswy and Oswin, Hereswith becoming a nun at Chelles, and Oswin asking Aidan to remain bishop in the new Deira. The rest is my own summary or surmise.

Bede records how Aidan left the royal table promptly and how Oswy gave land for monasteries. He tells about Alchfrith, the recovery of Oswald's relics from Maserfield, the marriage to Eanfled. Leicester University archeologists have recorded what their excavations of the royal centre at Yeavering discovered.

Chapter 18: Troubled Waters

Bede records Oswy's retrieval of Oswald's relics, marriage to the Kent princess, Utta's escort, and Aidan's gift of oil to pour on troubled waters. This action of Aidan's is the origin of the British saying "pouring oil on troubled waters." Bede records actions of Oswy after Aidan's death which suggest that Oswy used religion for worldly purposes.

Chapter 19: Spiritual Foster Mothers for the English

We do not know when and where Hilda first met Aidan. The suggestion that she returned from exile because of Oswald's inclusive approach is in keeping with what we know of his alliance-building with other kingdoms. We do not know that Hilda visited Lindisfarne, but it would be surprising if she did not. The history of Hilda's forebears and the English rulers in the story reflects that recorded in sources such as Bede and the Anglo-Saxon Chronicle. This information is collated in Northanhymbre Saga: The History of the Anglo-Saxon Kings of Northumbria by John Marsden (Llanerch Facsimile 1992). Bede records the vision of Hilda's pregnant mother and the death of her father. The suggestion that Hilda's mother might have been a Briton, although she had taken a Saxon name, is based on the fact that her husband fled for safe keeping to the Britons' small kingdom of Elmet, and that she herself felt it was safe to search for him there.

We do not know whether or not Hilda married. If Bede knew she was not married he would have called her a "virgin of Christ." The fact that he refers to her as "a servant of Christ" suggests either that he knew she had married or that he did not know whether or not she had. It was unlikely that a princess who was not a nun would not have married. Hilda was not a nun in the first half of her life.

Although the conversations between Aidan and Hilda are imaginary, it is clear from Bede that Hilda was drawn to the approach of the Irish Mission.

The Anonymous Life of Cuthbert written by a Lindisfarne monk refers to Ebbe as a widow (Colgrave 1940:81). Ebchester is a small parish, separated from Northumberland by the river Derwent. It lies about 12 miles to the south-west of Newcastle and stands on a Roman fort which was known as Vindomora. Although the fort went out of use by the end of the fourth century, it is probable that the site was re-used again in the seventh century. It is thought that the church of St Ebbe was originally a monastery founded about this time by Ebbe. There are no remains and the present church was mainly built in the early eleventh century, using stone re-used from the Roman fort. The story's assumption that she had a monastery here is based on the fact that the church and place are named after her. According to the Breviary of Aberdeen, she took the veil from Bishop Finan of Lindisfarne, after Aidan's death, so I have surmised that she started the community at Ebchester as a novice, before taking full vows.

By then she must have been at least 35 years old, supporting the notion that she was a widow. It is possible that she waited from Domnall's death in 642 until at least 651 not only because her brother Oswiu appears to have had a poor relationship with Bishop Aidan but also because she had very young children in Dalriada that she was unwilling to leave until they were older. Eventually, she became the Abbess of Coldingham, the northernmost known Bernician double monastery.

Chapter 20: Deira's Bright Sun and the Eclipse

Bede records most of the content of this chapter including Aidan's prophetic foreboding and tears for Oswin.

Wilfred and Queen Eanfled

We learn of Queen Eanfled's following of the Roman ways and dates of Easter, her sponsorship of Wilfred and the nobleman, her later support of Wilfred, Wilfred's long stays in Rome, bishoprics and disputes, and his insistence that he be carried to his consecration ceremony as a bishop on a throne supported by nine bishops, from Bede and from Eddius Stephanus' Life of Bishop Wilfred.

Wilfred stayed at Lindisfarne for the last three years of Aidan's life. Before long after that he asked permission to explore other Christian centres such as Canterbury and Rome. Permission was readily given to such requests at the Lindisfarne monastery. Boys at the school were not required to become monks, they could feel free to do whatever they felt called to. Wilfred was to fall in love with Rome and all things Roman: its large buildings, its artifacts, libraries, and canonical regulations, the splendour and power of bishops and clergy. For the rest of his life he expended his powers to make the church in England like that. He founded monasteries, evangelised Sussex, and had outriders such as only Saxon kings employed. He had power struggles with Kings, one of whom imprisoned him. He took his causes to Rome who supported him. He led the delegation at the Synod of Whitby which successfully argued for the Roman to replace the Irish framework in the Northumbrian church.

Holy Communion and Baked and Blessed Bread

No complete Eucharistic texts from early Columban or from any British or Irish monasteries exist. By Aidan's time the western part of the universal church had developed more standardized liturgies—the Roman, Gallic, Mozarabic, and Celtic rites. Written records of Celtic rites were more like common place books—lots of eclectic and local prayers to choose from—which echo the eastern approach. The Stowe Missal, a sacramentary written mainly in Latin with some Gaelic in about 750 is now available online at www.celticchristianity.org/stowe.html. The wording used in the story echoes a Coptic rite.

As for the nature of the bread used, we have but a few clues. The Book of Kells, which comes from the Columban tradition, depicts the Communion bread as a cooked loaf. We know that the custom of distributing blessed bread was practiced in Britain and therefore presumably in Ireland. This is referred to in The Life of Saint Samson of Dol.

Waymarks

Bede records that there were none in Bernicia at the start of Oswald's rule. We know from numerous archeological remains and other records that High Crosses and other waymarks became widespread in Northumbria over the following two centuries, and we may assume that this process began under Aidan.

The main source for the story of the teenage Cuthbert on the shore is Bede's The Life and Miracles of St. Cuthbert.

Chapter 21: Fire from Heaven

Bede records Oswin's betrayal and assassination in his The Ecclesiastical History of the English People, Book 3, chapter 14, and Aidan's death in chapter 17. It is believed that today's St. Aidan's church Bamburgh is on the site of the little church where Aidan died. The traditional place of his death is marked in the church.

We know nothing certain about Aidan's dying other than that he died twelve days after his friend King Oswin was assassinated, shortly after a visit from Aidan, and on the orders of the king to whose garrison at Bamburgh Aidan had returned and in whose church he was suddenly taken so ill that he could not be moved. It is not unlikely that the shock upon receiving this news caused him to have a heart attack or stroke. He would certainly have been filled with grief for his friend and with foreboding for the future.

The suggestion that he had a near death experience is imaginary. The apostle Paul refers to a man (probably himself) who was caught up into the third heaven (2 Cor 12:2-4): "I know a man in Christ who fourteen years ago was caught up to the third heaven. Whether it was in the body or out of the body I do not know—God knows. And I know that this man—whether in the body or apart from the body I do not know, but God knows— was caught up to paradise. He heard inexpressible things, things that man is not permitted to tell." Bede records a near (or after) death experience of Drythelm, a wealthy Northumbrian Christian and family man about 700. Drythelm was so changed by the experience that he gave his possessions to his family and became a monk at Melrose. He established a reputation for being able to endure bodily torment, reciting psalms standing up in the river Tweed even when the river was icy.

While temporarily dead, Dryhthelm was apparently given a tour of the afterlife by a celestial guide. In the vision he was shown hell, purgatory, and heaven, along with some of the souls therein, but was denied entry to paradise. Purgatory was a place of extreme heat and cold, hell a place where souls burned, heaven a place of intense light, and paradise a place of even greater light. Some modern historians have called him a precursor of Dante's Divine Comedy, an epic allegory of heaven and hell. I have drawn from this material in my description of Aidan's out of the body vision.

Bede says that Dryhthelm related the tale to Aldfrith king of Northumbria, Æthelwold, bishop of Lindisfarne, and an Irish monk called Haemgisl. Two centuries after Drythelm's out of body visions Ælfric of Eynsham celebrated the vision and believed it had been given to instruct others. Prior to Bede, The Life of Fursey, now lost, records similar visions, quoted in parts by Bede.

In Aidan's imagined vision there is an echo, in relation to Lindisfarne, of Columba's prophecy that Iona would become a place with only the lowing of cows but that before the end of the world it would be as it once was.

Aidan's Bones

Bede records that Aidan was buried in the cemetery of Lindisfarne's original church, on the site of the present St. Mary's church. Later, when St. Cuthbert's relics were enshrined, Aidan's relics were buried with his in the shrine in the larger St. Peter's Church, which was on the site of the present priory ruins. It is thought that a relic might have been kept at Bamburgh, and that when the monks departed for Ireland, via Iona, in 664 following the Synod of Whitby, they might have left a relic at Iona, Innisboffin (where the Irish monks settled) and Mayo (where the Saxon monks settled). When the Vikings invaded Lindisfarne in 793 it is thought likely that brothers would have placed a relic of Aidan in St. Cuthbert's coffin. Glastonbury, which remained a major Christian centre safe from Viking invaders, claimed that a relic of Aidan was taken there—they made such claims for most popular saints!

Oswald's niece Osthryth had his relics taken to the monastery at Bardney in Lincolnshire. Bede tells of a miracle of light and another of healing attributed to him by its monks.

Epilogue

The Life of Cuthbert by an anonymous monk of Lindisfarne, and Bede's Life both describe Cuthbert's vision of Aidan being escorted to heaven by angels while Cuthbert was guarding sheep on the Lammermuir hills. The detail and wording in my story echo the vision of Aidan's mother's at the moment of Columba's death with which the book starts.

Later Legacy

Theodore, Archbishop of Canterbury visited Lindisfarne around 715 for the dedication of the Lindisfarne Gospels which the Sunday Times described as 'the book that made Britain'. Oswald developed a cult following in Europe, see Oswald: Northumbrian King to European Saint edited by Clare Stancliffe and Eric Cambridge (Paul Watkins, Stamford 1995).

In the light of the evolving nature of the family of countries that make up the United Kingdom and Ireland, and the establishment of a Council of the Isles, there are calls for a patron saint, for all of the UK, at least. Several national British newspapers have given prominence to Aidan as a candidate, for example:

Home-grown Holy Man:
Cry God for Harry, Britain and . . . St Aidan

From Downing Street to church spires the length of Albion, the flag of St George will fly today as part of what the present incumbent of No. 10 insists is a celebration of Britishness that does not – and should not – preclude taking pride in 'Englishness, Scottishness, Welshness, or Northern Irishness'

. . . Ian Bradley . . . a respected commentator on religious issues, argues that the early medieval bishop, who was born in Ireland, educated in Scotland, and lived for much of his life in Northumbria has the potential to represent Britishness in a way that none of the existing patron saints do.

. . . It's like Billy Bragg says in his song, 'Take Down the Union Jack', about Britain: It's not a proper country, it doesn't have a patron saint. Aidan was the sort of hybrid Briton that sums up the overlapping identites of Britain.'

. . . Supporters of St Aidan's candidacy argue that his great success was in marrying three emerging national identities (Ireland, Scotland and England) into what would become the sense of inclusiveness and diverse belief that define a key strand of Britishness.

The Independent newspaper April 23 2008

The international Community of Aidan and Hilda was launched in UK and USA in 1994 www.aidanandhilda.org and www.aidanandhilda.us/ It now has branches in four continents. On Saint Aidan's Day, August 31, those who commit to its Way of Life undertake a Double A: A for Aidan and an Act of justice.

A SELECTION OF BOOKS
BY RAY SIMPSON

A Holy Island Prayer Book (Morehouse/Canterbury Press)

Celtic Blessings—Prayers for Everyday Life (Loyola Press)

The Lindisfarne Gospels—the English Church and Our Multi-cultural World (MayhewBrodt/Mayhew)

Liturgies from Lindisfarne—Prayers and Services for the Pilgrimage of Life (MayhewBrodt/Mayhew)

Daily Light from the Celtic Saints: Ancient Wisdom for Modern Life (Anamchara Books)—Published as *Celtic Daily Light* in UK by Mayhew.

Soul Friendship—Celtic and Desert Insights (Anamchara Books)

Waymarks for the Journey—Daily Prayer to Change Your World (MayhewBrodt/Mayhew)

Hilda of Whitby: A Spirituality for Now (BRF)

Lightning Source UK Ltd.
Milton Keynes UK
UKOW05f1201190814

237165UK00002B/13/P